EYEWITNESS TRAVEL

NEW ORLEANS

EYEWITNESS TRAVEL
NEW
ORLEANS

MAIN CONTRIBUTOR: MARILYN WOOD

LONDON, NEW YORK,
MELBOURNE, MUNICH AND DELHI
www.dk.com

PROJECT EDITOR Alejandro Lajud
ART EDITOR Victor Hugo Garnica
EDITOR Karla Sánchez
DESIGNERS Carlos Muñoz, Alejandro Lajud, Victor Hugo Garnica

Dorling Kindersley Limited
SENIOR PUBLISHING MANAGER Louise Bostock Lang
PUBLISHING MANAGER Kate Poole
DIRECTOR OF PUBLISHING Gillian Allan
EDITORS Stephanie Driver, Mary Sutherland, Andrew Szudek
MAP CO-ORDINATORS David Pugh, Casper Morris
DTP CO-ORDINATORS Jason Little, Conrad van Dyk
PRODUCTION CONTROLLER Joanna Bull

MAIN CONTRIBUTOR
Marilyn Wood

MAPS
Ben Bowles, Rob Clynes and James Macdonald at Mapping Ideas Ltd.

PHOTOGRAPHERS
Julio Rochon, Jaime Baldovinos

ILLUSTRATORS
Ricardo Almazan, Ricardo Almazan Jr.

Reproduced by Colourscan, Singapore
Printed and bound by South China Printing Co. Ltd., China

First American Edition, 2002
10 11 12 13 10 9 8 7 6 5 4 3 2 1

Published in the United States by DK Publishing,
375 Hudson Street, New York, New York 10014

Reprinted with revisions 2004, 2005, 2008, 2010

Copyright 2002, 2010 © Dorling Kindersley Limited, London

PUBLISHED IN GREAT BRITAIN BY DORLING KINDERSLEY LIMITED.

A CATALOG RECORD OF THIS BOOK IS AVAILABLE
FROM THE LIBRARY OF CONGRESS.

ISSN 1542-1554
ISBN 978-0-7566-6191-5

Front cover main image:
Wrought-iron balcony in the French Quarter

MIX
Paper from
responsible sources
FSC
www.fsc.org   FSC™ C018179

**The information in this
DK Eyewitness Travel Guide is checked regularly.**
Every effort has been made to ensure that this book is as up-to-
date as possible at the time of going to press. Some details,
however, such as telephone numbers, opening hours, prices,
gallery hanging arrangements, and travel information are liable to
change. The publishers cannot accept responsibility for any
consequences arising from the use of this book. We value the
views and suggestions of our readers very highly. Please write to:
Publisher, DK Eyewitness Travel Guides, Dorling Kindersley,
80 Strand, London WC2R 0RL, Great Britain.

◁ View of the Central Business District from the Mississippi River

CONTENTS

**New Orleans ironwork,
Lower French Quarter**

INTRODUCING
NEW ORLEANS

**The bustling Central
Business District**

Mansion on St. Charles Avenue

Preservation Hall, one of New Orleans' best jazz venues

Vegetables and fruit for sale in the French Market

St. Charles Avenue streetcar

HOW TO USE THIS GUIDE

This DK Eyewitness Travel Guide helps you to get the most from your visit to New Orleans. It provides detailed information and expert recommendations.

The chapter titled *Introducing New Orleans* maps the city and the region, and sets it in its historical and cultural context; it also describes the most salient events of the year. *New Orleans at a Glance* is an overview of the city's main attractions. *New Orleans Area by Area* starts on page 44. This is the main

sightseeing section, and it covers all of the important sights, with photographs, maps and illustrations. *Beyond New Orleans* covers nearby Cajun Country, as well as the historic plantations.

Information about hotels, restaurants, shops and markets, entertainment, and sports is found in *Travelers' Needs*. The *Survival Guide* section has advice on everything from using New Orleans' medical services, telephones, banking, and post offices to the public transportation system.

FINDING YOUR WAY AROUND NEW ORLEANS

The city has been divided into five sightseeing areas, each with its own section in the guide. Each section opens with a portrait of the area, summing up its character and history, and listing all the sights to be covered. The sights

are numbered and clearly located on an *Area Map*. After this comes a *Street-by-Street Map* focusing on the most interesting part of the area. Finding your way about the area section is made easy by a numbering system.

1 Introduction to the area
For easy reference, the sights in each area are numbered and plotted on an area map. To help the visitor, this map also shows the main streetcar and bus stops, and parking areas. The area's key sights are listed by category, such as Museums and Historic Places.

A locator map shows where you are in relation to other areas in the city center.

Each area has color-coded thumb tabs.

A suggested route takes in some of the most interesting and attractive streets in the area.

2 Street-by-Street map
This gives a bird's-eye view of interesting and important parts of each sightseeing area. The numbering of the entries ties in with the area map and the fuller description of the sights on the pages that follow.

The list of star sights recommends the places that no visitor should miss.

NEW ORLEANS AREA MAP

The colored areas shown on this map *(see inside front cover)* are the five main sightseeing areas used in this guide. Each is covered in a full chapter in *New Orleans Area by Area (see pp44–135)*. They are highlighted on other maps throughout the book. In *New Orleans at a Glance*, for example, they help you locate the top sights *(see pp30–31)*.

Numbers refer to each sight's position on the area map and its place in the chapter.

Practical information provides everything you need to know to visit each sight. Map references pinpoint the sight's location on the *Street Finder* map *(see pp222–9)*.

3 Detailed information
All the important sights in New Orleans are described individually. They are listed in order, following the numbering on the area map at the start of the section. Practical information includes a map reference, opening hours, and telephone numbers. The key to the symbols is on the back flap.

The visitors' checklist gives all the practical information needed to plan your visit.

Façades of important buildings are often shown to help you recognize them quickly.

4 New Orleans' major sights
Historic buildings are dissected to reveal their interiors; museums and galleries have color-coded floor plans to help you find the most important exhibits.

Stars indicate the features that no visitor should miss.

B. la paroisse.

place Royalle.

dance. Vielle Intendance.   F.

INTRODUCING NEW ORLEANS

fleuve S. lovis
400 pieds de profondeur

FOUR GREAT DAYS IN NEW ORLEANS

New Orleans has always been a city where many cultures mingle. Today, that heritage is reflected in a great diversity of things to do and see. Here are four great days out, each showing different slices of life in this exuberant city. One reveals the French Quarter with its Gallic ambience; another explores

Music, New Orleans-style

elegant Uptown by streetcar; a third taps into the exciting visual and performing arts scene, and the fourth is aimed at entertaining families with children. Important sights have page references so you can check for more details. The price guides include cost of travel, food, and admission charges.

FRENCH QUARTER AND MISSISSIPPI CRUISE

- *Beignets* for breakfast
- Mardi Gras exhibit
- Lunch at Napoleon House
- Cruise on the *Natchez* and go for a Bourbon stroll

TWO ADULTS allow at least $125

Morning
Start the day with a classic coffee and *beignets* (donuts) breakfast at the **Café du Monde** (*see p76 and p176*). Cross Decatur Street to **Jackson Square** (*see p54*), where street performers entertain. Visit the Mardi Gras exhibit at the **Presbytère** (*see pp56–7*), a landmark state museum. Then, amble down Chartres Street to **Napoleon House** (*see p59 and p178*) for lunch. This mansion, built for the French

emperor, is now a charming café and bar that oozes French Quarter ambience.

Afternoon
Head to the riverfront and the Steamboat *Natchez* (*see pp64–5*) for a 2-hour cruise (departs at 2:30pm), with calliope music, fascinating narratives on the city, and views of the busy waterway. Back on land, a short walk from the dock, the **French Market** (*see p70*) is ideal for a spot of browsing in the shops, crafts booths, and flea market stalls. Return to Jackson Square and hire a carriage for a ride through the Quarter; you will be intrigued by the local architecture. Finally, stroll along **Bourbon Street** (*see pp46–7*), and relish its neon-lit, bawdy glory before heading to the **Acme Oyster House** (*see p176*) for oysters or gumbo (stew).

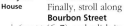

Oysters, at the Acme Oyster House

Stunning architecture at the Contemporary Arts Center

STYLE, ART, AND CREOLE CULTURE

- Explore the Arts District
- Creole history, art and antiques on Royal Street
- An evening at the theater

TWO ADULTS allow at least $120

Morning
Breakfast at the world-famous **Brennan's** restaurant (*see p176*) starts the day in laidback but elegant style. Catch the **St. Charles Avenue streetcar** (*see pp104–5*) or take a cab to **Lee Circle** (*see p96*) where, within a three-block radius, you can happily overdose on art at the **Ogden Museum of Southern Art** (*see p96*), the **Contemporary Arts Center** (*see p97*), and Julia Street galleries, which are clustered together in the district.

A few blocks away, built into an old river warehouse on S. Peters and Fulton

Garlic, and plenty of it, at the French market

◁ *Plan de la Ville/La Nouvelle Orléans/Capitale de la Province de la Louisiane*, by Thierry, 1755 streets, you'll find restaurants offering a variety of lunch options, including tapas, sushi, and Mexican food.

Afternoon

Head back to the French Quarter and visit the **Historic New Orleans Collection** (see pp60–61), where exhibits illustrate Creole life in the 19th century. Take a stroll along **Royal Street** (see pp48–9), with its galleries and antiques stores, where for six blocks performers and musicians are found on nearly every corner. If you want to experience Creole fine dining, stop at **Galatoire's** (see p177), an upscale bistro on Bourbon Street. Culture fans will love a modern play at the Southern Repertory Theatre in **Canal Place** (see p94), or a classic at **Le Petit Théâtre** (see p55).

A group of jazz players on Jackson Square

THE HISTORIC CHARM OF THE STREETCAR

- Go up and down town on stately streetcars
- Admire mansions and tombs in the Garden District
- Lunch in the Riverbend
- Cocktails at sunset

TWO ADULTS allow at least $75

Morning

Get your $1.25 fares ready and head to the first stop of the historic **St. Charles Avenue streetcar** (see pp104–5) at the corner of Canal and Carondelet streets. Passengers travel at a steady pace past the mansions and towering oaks. Disembark at Washington Avenue and head into the **Garden District** (see pp100–1), where you'll see opulent homes and splendid gardens that bear witness to the wealth of the antebellum South. Drop into the lobby of the renowned **Commander's Palace** (see p182) restaurant to pick up a free guide to historic homes.

A streetcar named St. Charles

Explore the maze of tombs at **Lafayette Cemetery** (see p100). Return to the streetcar route and board the next Uptown-bound car. At **Audubon Park** (see p111), walk through lush grounds, or cross the street to visit the campuses of **Tulane and Loyola universities** (see p110). Walk, or jump onto another Uptown-bound streetcar, to the **Riverbend** (see p111), an outdoor recreation area. If hungry, grab a counter seat at **Camellia Grill** (see p180), a charmingly retro diner.

Afternoon

After crossing Carrollton Avenue, window shop along bustling Maple Street, with its fine book stores and upscale boutiques. Return to St. Charles Avenue to board a downtown-bound streetcar to the **Columns Hotel** (see p166), and reward yourself with a cocktail at the Victorian Bar, either on its regal porch or inside at the ornate bar.

A predatory jaguar in the lush jungle at Audubon Zoo

A FUN DAY OUT FOR THE FAMILY

- Clowns and caricatures
- A riverboat ride to the zoo
- Swamps and rare alligators
- History and horror in wax

FAMILY OF 4 allow at least $150

Morning

Start at **Jackson Square** (see p54) where clowns, artists, and performers put on a show for all. A caricature drawn here makes for a unique souvenir. Head across Decatur Street to check out the dance troupes and other acts in the performance area next to the Jax Brewery. Behind the brewery follow the river past the statues of **Woldenberg Riverfront Park** (see p88) to the **John James Audubon** riverboat (see p217). A package deal offers an informative 45-minute cruise to the acclaimed **Audubon Zoo** (see pp112–13). If hungry, grab a bite at one of the zoo's cafés (you'll find the swamp section's popular eaterie is heaving). While there, check out the Louisiana swamp exhibit of local wildlife, especially the rare white alligator.

Afternoon

Jump aboard the riverboat for the return trip. Back in the French Quarter, enjoy scary dungeon settings, scenes from New Orleans' history, and famous figures in wax at the **Musée Conti Wax Museum** (see p58). Grab a *muffuletta* at the popular **Central Grocery** (see p177) – you've earned it.

Putting New Orleans on the Map

New Orleans is located in southeast Louisiana, between Lake Pontchartrain and the Mississippi River. The airport handles international and domestic flights, and there are good road and rail links to the rest of the country. Prior to Hurricane Katrina, in August 2005, the population of central New Orleans was approximately 485,000. Many New Orleanians lost their homes as a result of the terrible floods and had to move away. By 2008 the population had rebounded to around 300,000.

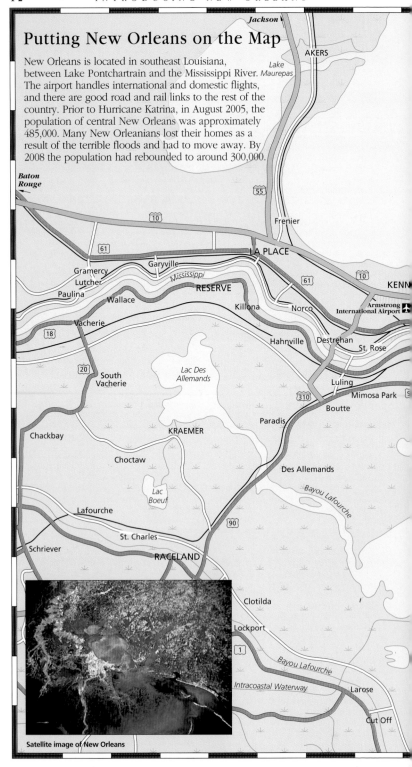

Jackson

Lake Maurepas

AKERS

Baton Rouge

55

Frenier

10

LA PLACE

61

Garyville

Gramercy
Lutcher

Mississippi

RESERVE

61

10

KENN

Paulina

Wallace

Killona

Norco

Armstrong
International Airport

Vacherie

18

Hahnville

Destrehan

St. Rose

20

South
Vacherie

Lac Des
Allemands

Luling

310

Mimosa Park

Boutte

Paradis

Chackbay

KRAEMER

Choctaw

Des Allemands

Bayou Lafourche

Lac
Boeuf

Lafourche

Schriever

St. Charles

90

RACELAND

Clotilda

Lockport

1

Bayou Lafourche

Intracoastal Waterway

Larose

Cut Off

Satellite image of New Orleans

GREATER NEW ORLEANS

Covington

Wiggins

Zachary
Baker
Port
Allen
Baton
Rouge

Bogalusa
Amite
Hammond

Poplarville
Picayune

Covington

Gulfport   Biloxi
Bay
St Louis

Plaquemine

See next page

Armstrong
International
Airport

Lake
Borgne

Gulf of
Mexico

Morgan
City

Grand
Isle

Venice

Port
Fourchon

Gulf of Mexico

0 kilometers   50

0 miles   50

*Lake
Pontchartrain*

Pontchartrain Causeway

Lakefront
Airport

METAIRIE

Lake
Borgne

NEW
ORLEANS

CHALMETTE

Algiers   *Mississippi*   Meraux

Avondale

Gretna

Terrytown

Poydras   St. Bernard

Marrero

Harvey

Westwego

Belle
Chasse

Estelle

Reggio

Dalcour   *Lake   Lery*

*Couba
Island*

Bertrandville

Willis
Point

Delacroix

Crown
Point

Jesuit
Bend

Belair

*Lake
Petit*

Barataria

Naomi

Lafitte

Carlisle

Ironton

Phoenix

Davant

Myrtle
Grove

*Lake
Laurier*

Magnolia

Bohemia

Diamond

KEY

Central New Orleans

Urban area

Bayou

International airport

Domestic airport

Freeway

Major road

Minor road

Amtrak station

Railroad

0 kilometers   10

0 miles   10

THE HISTORY OF NEW ORLEANS

I n 1541, Spanish explorer Hernando de Soto discovered the Mississippi River, but it was the Frenchman Robert de La Salle who sailed down the river for the first time in 1682 and erected a cross somewhere near the location of modern New Orleans, claiming it and the whole of Louisiana for his king, Louis XIV.

FRENCH COLONY

The first French settlements were established on the Gulf Coast at Biloxi. It took another 19 years before Jean Baptiste Le Moyne, Sieur de Bienville, established a settlement on the Lower Mississippi at New Orleans in 1718. In 1721, the engineer Adrien de Pauger laid out the French Quarter behind the levees that had been constructed. Two years later the capital of the colony was moved from Biloxi to New Orleans.

Jean Baptiste Le Moyne, founder of New Orleans

However, the colony did not prosper, and the French Regent, Philippe d'Orléans, turned over control to a private financier and speculator, Scotsman John Law, who floated stock in his Company of the West and promoted Louisiana as a utopia, which it was not. The natives were hostile, the land was a swamp, and the climate pestilential, but, lured by Law's advertisements, thousands of Germans and Swiss left for Louisiana and, if they survived the perilous ocean crossing, settled along the Mississippi. Whenever immigration to the new colony diminished, criminals and prostitutes were deported from France to New Orleans, the first 88 women arriving from La Salpêtrière, a Paris house of correction, in 1721. The first slaves had arrived a year earlier, and in 1727 the Ursuline Sisters arrived and founded their convent. The Company of the West speculative bubble eventually burst and Law's company collapsed. In 1731 the king resumed control and sent Bienville back to govern and to deal with the troublesome Chickasaw and Natchez Indians. Commerce began to grow, despite the restrictions that the French had imposed on trade with England, Spain, Mexico, Florida, and the West Indies. Much of it was illegal. By 1763 river traffic had grown so prodigiously that exports (indigo, sugar, rum, skins, and fur) totaled $304,000.

By that time, the contest for the control of North America had begun in earnest; in 1755 the Seven Years' War had broken out between Britain and France, Spain, and other European powers.

TIMELINE

1682 La Salle explores the Mississippi and claims Louisiana for Louis XIV

1720 The first shipment of slaves arrives on July 7

1727 The Ursuline Sisters arrive in New Orleans

1763 Exports top $300,000

1550   1650   1750

1541 Spanish explorer Hernando de Soto discovers the Mississippi River

1718 Jean Baptiste Le Moyne, Sieur de Bienville, establishes a settlement

1721 88 women arrive from a house of correction. Adrien de Pauger lays out the Vieux Carré

C. de la Motte, an aristocrat of the French colony

◁ **Americans take control of the city after the Louisiana Purchase**

St. Louis Cathedral, flanked by the Cabildo (left) and Presbytère, built during Spanish rule

SPANISH CITY

The Seven Years' War ended in 1763, and Louis XV signed the Treaty of Paris, which ended French ambitions in North America. Before signing, however, he had secretly ceded Louisiana to his cousin the Spanish king, Charles III. The French settlers in Louisiana were outraged at the news, and when the Spanish governor Don Antonio de Ulloa arrived in 1766 to take control, they rebelled, driving him back to Havana. Alexander O'Reilly, an Irish-born Spanish general, arrived with 24 warships, 2,000 soldiers, and 50 artillery pieces. He executed six ringleaders of the rebellion at the site of the Old US Mint, on October 25, 1769, and firmly established Spanish power.

During the American Revolution (1775–83), Governor Bernardo de Galvez supported the American colonists and skillfully defended Baton Rouge, Natchez, Mobile, and Pensacola. He also relaxed trade restrictions, allowing citizens to trade with countries other than Spain. In 1788 a fire on Good Friday, March 21, destroyed 856 buildings. The destruction was so extensive that most of the French-style buildings were lost. After the fire, the Spanish decreed that all buildings of two stories or more were to be constructed of brick, thus giving the rebuilt city a definite Mediterranean look.

In the 1790s, under Baron Carondelet (1792–7), New Orleans thrived. He granted free trade to the Americans on the Mississippi and made New Orleans the port of deposit for three years. The city's first theater and its first newspaper were soon established, gas lamps lit the streets, and a basic police force was recruited. Drainage ditches were dug too, to protect the city against flooding by the Mississippi. Prosperity increased, and the sugar industry was created in 1796, when Jean Etienne de Boré first granulated sugar on a commercial scale. The city was home to important

Spanish Governor Bernardo de Galvez (1776–85)

TIMELINE

1765 First Acadians arrive from Nova Scotia	**1769** Governor O'Reilly suppresses the 1766 rebellion		**1788** Fire on March 21 (Good Friday) destroys 856 buildings
1760	**1770**	**1780**	**1790**
	1763 Treaty of Paris signed; Louisiana and New Orleans ceded to Spain	**1775–83** Revolutionary War	**1791** Toussaint L'Ouverture leads slave revolt in Saint Domingue (Haiti)

Bernard de Marigny, an early plantation owner

plantations like the one owned by Bernard de Marigny in the Lower French Quarter. New Orleans also received an infusion of talented men from the French colony of Saint Domingue (now Haiti), who had fled the slave uprising there in 1791. By 1804, refugee planters and slaves were pouring into New Orleans. They added a distinct Caribbean cast to the colony, erecting West Indian-style houses. The planters' slaves and free people of color expanded the practice of voodoo in the colony.

Andrew Jackson leading the Battle of New Orleans

THE LOUISIANA PURCHASE AND THE BATTLE OF NEW ORLEANS

Although Spain ceded Louisiana to France in 1800, Napoleon, who was preoccupied in Europe, soon sold it to the United States for $15 million to help pay for his wars. General James

Representation of the Battle of New Orleans at Chalmette

Wilkinson and William C.C. Claiborne officially ratified the transfer on December 20, 1803, at the Cabildo. On April 30, 1812, Louisiana was admitted to the Union, six weeks before the United States declared war on Great Britain because of restraint of trade and the impressment of Americans into the British navy. In January 1815, despite the Treaty of Ghent, which had theoretically ended the war the month before, British forces launched a fresh attack on New Orleans. Under General Andrew Jackson, a ragtag army of pirates, American frontiersmen, French gentlemen, and free men of color beat back the British, validating the peace treaty and finally ending hostilities.

In 1812 the first steamboat had arrived in New Orleans, and soon after the victory at the Battle of New Orleans waves of newcomers, attracted by rapid commercial growth, drove the population to more than 40,000. Nevertheless, friction between the French Creoles and the Americans gave rise to the creation of two separate districts; the French Quarter and an uptown American section. Canal Street separated the two, and the space between was known as the neutral ground.

1796 Sugar industry established

Spanish treaty of 1794

1803 Louisiana Purchase ratified on December 20

1812 The steamer *New Orleans* arrives in the city in January

1815 Andrew Jackson triumphs at the Battle of New Orleans on January 8

1800   **1810**   **1820**

1795 United States and Spain sign a treaty opening the Mississippi to American trade

1800 Louisiana ceded from Spain to France

1812 Louisiana admitted to the Union on April 30

1814 Treaty of Ghent, signed on December 24, ends the War of 1812

STEAMBOATS, COTTON, AND SUGAR

The arrival of the first steamboat, in 1812, opened the city's trade to the interior and the upcountry plantations. Before the steamboat, cargo was carried on flatboats, which floated down the Ohio and Mississippi from Louisville, Kentucky, on a journey that took several weeks.

The *Robert E. Lee* steamboat on the Mississippi

The new steamboats cut the journey to a fraction of that time. Between 1803 and 1833, about 1,000 boats a year docked at the port of New Orleans. By the mid-1830s, the port was shipping half a million bales of cotton, becoming the cotton capital of the world. By 1840 it was the second most important port in the nation, after New York, and the population had passed 80,000. Other commodities that enriched the city were sugar, indigo, coffee, and bananas. As many as 35,000 steamboats docked at the wharves in 1860, clearing $324 million worth of trade.

By this time, New Orleans was the largest city in the South, and, with a population of 168,000, it was the sixth largest city in the nation. The immense wealth that was being generated led to the city's further expansion and cultural development. The city of Lafayette (now the Garden District) was annexed in 1852; the French Opera House was built in 1858; the Mardi Gras festival became more widely celebrated when the first parading krewe, Comus, was found-ed in 1857; it also developed a repu-tation for its courtly life, riverboat gambling, and easy living. The only blights were the frequent epidemics of cholera and yellow fever. Between 1817 and 1860 there were 23 yellow fever epidemics, killing more than 28,000 people. The worst, in 1853, killed 10,300 people.

1845 portrait of a family

CIVIL WAR AND RECONSTRUCTION

The Civil War brought pros-perity to an end. In 1861 Louisiana seceded from the Union. In 1862, Union Navy Captain Farragut captured New Orleans, and General Benjamin "Beast" Butler occupied the city on May 1, 1862. Butler hanged William Mumford for tearing the United States flag down from the Mint, confiscated the prop-erty of those who refused to sign an oath of allegiance, and passed an ordinance declaring that any woman who insulted a Union soldier would be regarded as a pros-titute and locked up. The citizens chafed under his rule and that of his successor, General Nathaniel Banks. After the war, the city struggled to

TIMELINE

Civil War gun

1831–5 New Orleans becomes the world's largest cotton market	**1845** New Orleans is the second biggest port in the country	**1853** Yellow fever kills 10,300 between July and November	
1830	**1840**	**1850**	**1860**
1820–30 The development of the steamboats allows the city to open trade to the interior of the country	**1852** The city of Lafayette is annexed, becoming the Garden District	**1861** Louisiana secedes from the Union **1862** Union General Benjamin Butler occupies the city on May 1	**1865** Civil War ends

recover, but the source of so much of the city's wealth – the upriver plantations – had been destroyed. The "Old South" never recovered; the steamboat era was over, and the economic shift toward the northeast left New Orleans languishing.

Poor race relations troubled the city after the Civil War. In 1865, at the end of the Civil War, slaves were freed but lived in legal limbo. In 1866, a race riot broke out near Mechanics Hall in downtown New Orleans, where a group of white and black men were drafting a new state constitution to extend full rights to black men (women would not vote until the 20th century). During the attack, 37 delegates were killed and 136 wounded; the violence of the Mechanics Hall riot was a key element in Congress's decision to organize Reconstruction as a military occupation of the old Confederacy by federal troops.

In 1877 federal troops withdrew, but the legal and social gains made by African Americans during Reconstruction soon began to erode as old Confederates resumed full political,

Slave cabin in a cotton plantation, circa 1860

civil, and economic power. Segregation became entrenched in 1896 when in Plessy v. Ferguson the US Supreme Court established the so-called "separate but equal" mandates. Segregation was not successfully challenged again for more than 50 years. Racial tensions only worsened as waves of Italians and Irish immigrants arrived in the late 19th century.

Although the 1884 Cotton Centennial Exposition boosted the city's profile as a major commercial center, crime, prostitution, and corruption remained rampant. In 1897, in an attempt to control the lawlessness that was troubling the city, Alderman Sidney Story sponsored a bill that legalized prostitution in a 38-block area bounded by Iberville, Basin, Robertson, and St. Louis streets. This area, which became known as "Storyville", fostered the beginnings of a new style of improvisational music, called jazz (see pp20–21). It was later demolished to make way for low-income housing.

Painting of a fleet of Civil War frigates

General Robert E. Lee

1866 Mechanics Hall Riot		1877 Reconstruction ends; federal troops leave		1890 Racial tensions reach their peak in New Orleans	1897 Sidney Story proposes official red light district
1870		1880		1890	1900
			1884 Cotton Centennial Exposition		1896 Supreme Court decision in Plessy v. Ferguson permits racial segregation

History of New Orleans Jazz

Blue Lu Barker

Jazz is America's original contribution to world culture. It evolved slowly and almost imperceptibly from a number of sources – from the music played at balls, parades, dances, and funerals, and New Orleans' unique blend of cultures. Its musical inspirations included classical music (the original jazz musicians were classically trained), spirituals, marches, and American folk influences – the entire mélange of music that was played in 19th-century New Orleans.

Trumpeter Oscar "Papa" Celestin
The founder of the Tuxedo Brass Band in 1911 also composed "Down by the Riverside."

Congo Square
On Sundays, slaves gathered here to celebrate their one day off, playing music and dancing.

Papa Jack's Dixieland Jazz Band
This all-white band, led by Nick LaRocca, made the first jazz recording in 1917.

Louis Armstrong
This world-famous jazz trumpeter began singing on the streets of New Orleans. He played with Kid Ory before leaving the city in 1923 to join King Oliver's band in Chicago.

Bordellos, or "sporting houses," were where jazz gained its popularity.

TIMELINE

Buddy Bolden (1877–1931), a barber born in New Orleans, played cornet and formed one of the first jazz bands in the 1890s

Joe "King" Oliver (1885–1938) started playing cornet in New Orleans in 1904, but moved to Chicago with his Creole Jazz Band

"King" Oliver

1880	1900	1920

Jelly Roll Morton (1890–1941) began his piano career in the brothels of Storyville. He was the first great jazz composer and pianist

Sidney Bechet (1897–1959) played clarinet and soprano saxophone with early leaders like Freddie Keppard

Riverboat Jazz Bands

After Storyville was closed down in 1917, New Orleans' best musicians moved onto the boats or migrated to northern cities. Pianist Fate Marable's band included Louis Armstrong, who played the cornet.

Kid Ory's Trombone
Edward "Kid" Ory played with King Oliver and Louis Armstrong's famous Hot Five band.

The Boswell Sisters
Connie, Martha, and Vet Boswell sang and recorded in the early 1930s. This was the most popular female jazz group of its time.

Musicians were screened off so that they could not see the patrons.

STORYVILLE JAZZ SALON

Many early jazz artists entertained in Storyville at the bordellos, playing behind screens – Buddy Bolden, King Oliver, Jelly Roll Morton, Sidney Bechet, Kid Ory, Freddy Keppard, and Manuel Perez among them.

Jelly Roll Morton
Ferdinand "Jelly Roll" Morton, who formed the band The Red Hot Peppers, claimed to have invented jazz in 1902.

1940		1960		1980		2000

Louis Armstrong (1901–1971) was the greatest of all jazz musicians. From 1940 to 1960 he played with his All Star Band

Louis Armstrong

Terence Blanchard (1962–), a trumpeter, played with Lionel Hampton and Art Blakey before forming his own quintet. He is famous for composing and playing the music for Spike Lee's films

Danny Barker (1909–1994) played guitar and banjo with the big bands in the 1930s and 1940s before returning to New Orleans

Pete Fountain (1930–) is considered one of the best clarinetists in the world

Harry Connick, Jr. (1967–) played in New Orleans clubs as a teenager, later becoming a major jazz-pop music star and arranging the score for *When Harry Met Sally*

A World War II Higgins boat

20TH-CENTURY NEW ORLEANS – FROM STORYVILLE TO 2000

Until it was abolished on October 2, 1917, Storyville was the most extraordinary spectacle of legalized vice in the United States. Patrons could pick up a copy of the "Blue Book" in a bar or hotel and find the names and addresses of 700 prostitutes listed with their prices and their color. Storyville also gave jazz a boost, because many early jazz artists began their musical lives in the brothels *(see pp20–21)*.

The Department of the Navy closed Storyville down in 1917, because it feared that it was too tempting to sailors shipping out from New Orleans to World War I battlefronts. Although the war briefly boosted business in the shipyards, the economy languished during the early 1930s. The effects of the Depression were evident by 1933, when five New Orleans banks failed and 11 percent of the citizenry was on welfare. Under the New Deal, Mayor Robert Maestri used federal dollars to build roads, bridges, parks, and public buildings. During World War II,

business picked up again in the shipyards, and New Orleans produced thousands of the famous Higgins boats that were used in Allied amphibious landings on all war fronts.

In 1946 Mayor de Lesseps Story "Chep" Morrison was elected as a reformer and served until 1961. During his administration the city began to take on its current appearance. He constructed the Pontchartrain Expressway, a new airport, and, in 1958, the $65-million Mississippi River Bridge (later renamed the Crescent City Connection), which opened the West Bank area to suburban development. In 1954, the Supreme Court ruling Brown v. the Board of Education ordered the desegregation of public education. Schools were integrated by federal marshals in 1960.

During the 1960s there was some economic regeneration when NASA took over an old aviation plant to build the Saturn rocket booster, and a ship channel was opened, enabling very large ships to enter the port. In 1969 the port was still the second in the

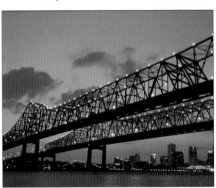

The Crescent City Connection Bridge, reconstructed in the 1990s

TIMELINE

1910	1920	1930	1940	1950

1933 Five New Orleans banks fail; 11 percent of the citizens are on relief

1941–45 Higgins boats produced at the shipyards

1954 Brown v. Board of Education orders desegregation

1917 Storyville abolished on October 2

1936 Vieux Carré Commission established

1936–46 Mayor Robert Maestri uses federal funds to repair the city's infrastructure

Storyville brothel sign

nation. During the boom, new buildings like the World Trade Center, Rivergate, and One Shell Square were erected, and several hotels rose up along Canal Street. In 1967 the city was granted an NFL (National Football League) franchise.

The 1965 Voting Rights Act changed the political picture in the city. In 1969, Mayor Moon Landrieu was elected primarily because he had the support of black voters, and he appointed the first black to a senior position in his administration, paving the way for the election of Ernest N. "Dutch" Morial, the first black mayor, in 1978.

NASA Saturn rocket, built in the 1960s at the Michoud plant

At the beginning of his administration Morial benefited greatly from the oil boom, but by 1986 the bubble had burst, due to the drop in international oil prices; as a result, the city's economy was devastated. Meanwhile, the white and middle class flight to the suburbs, which began in the 1950s, continued, leaving parts of the inner city to the poor. Morial sought to salvage city fortunes by advancing construction on the Convention Center, farther developing the waterfront, and encouraging tourism investment, but racial tensions increased, finally spilling over into Mardi Gras. In 1991 the City Council passed a stringent anti-discrimination law, refusing to grant parade permits to all; the Comus, Proteus, and Momus krewes refused to comply, and canceled their parades. The ordinance was later toned down. Proteus resumed its parade in 2000. In 1994, Dutch's son, Marc Morial, age 34, was elected mayor. He served two terms, building a powerful political machine. Some economic diversification and the boom in the late 1990s helped restore prosperity, but the city still suffers from a dependence on tourism and oil, and from the persistent problems of corruption. C. Ray Nagin was elected mayor in 2002 on a reform platform. In August 2005, a disastrous flood caused by Hurricane Katrina *(see pp24–7)* hit the city, killing more than 1,400 people, but sparing most historic neighborhoods. Several years later, much remains to be done, but the city is steadily recovering, doing what it does best; delivering the pleasures of food, drink, music, and art to the many visitors that flock here.

Millennium celebrations on the Mississippi River

	1975 Superdome opens	1980s Oil boom and bust	1987 Pope John Paul II visits the city	1994 Marc Morial elected Mayor, age 34	2000 New Orleans celebrates the millennium	
1960 N. O. schools re desegregated by federal marshals						
1960	**1970**	**1980**	**1990**	**2000**	**2010**
1961 NASA acquires the old Michoud aviation plant to assemble Saturn booster rockets	1984 Louisiana World Exposition helps riverfront development		1995 A flood in May causes $760 million worth of damage	2005 Hurricane Katrina hits the city	
		Pope John Paul II		2002 C. Ray Nagin elected Mayor	

Hurricane Katrina

Hurricane Katrina – and the subsequent levee failures – which hit New Orleans in August 2005 have been called the most expensive disaster in US history. More than 850,000 homes were damaged and entire communities along the Gulf Coast of Louisiana, Mississippi, and Alabama were destroyed overnight. The official death toll in Louisiana alone exceeded 1,400 people, and many more were forced to relocate across the country. Much of the destruction in the city was caused by floodwaters. The recovery effort has been a monumental undertaking: billions of dollars in insurance proceeds and government funds have been committed so far.

A satellite image of Hurricane Katrina

17th Street Canal and London Avenue Canal
Katrina's storm surge over-whelmed these canals and flooded much of the city.

Tulane and Loyola Universities
These institutions had to contend with damage to the facilities and the displacement of most employees and students. They managed to reopen in 2006.

The St. Charles Avenue streetcar was severely damaged by the winds, which tore down the overhead power lines. The rolling stock, however, survived the storm, and service was resumed in 2007.

The massive Mississippi River levees that help contain the river weathered Katrina without a problem, ensuring that the French Quarter, Central Business District, Uptown, and parts of the Garden District remained dry.

TIMELINE

Aug 26, 2005 State of emergency declared in Louisiana

Aug 28 Mayor Ray Nagin orders the mandatory evacuation of New Orleans

Aug 31 Attempts to plug levee breaches fail; flooding continues until waters reach the level of Lake Pontchartrain

Sep 24 Hurricane Rita makes landfall; parts of New Orleans are flooded again

Mayor Nagin

Feb 28, 2006 First post-Katrina Mardi Gras

2005

2006

Aug 29 Katrina makes landfall; storm surge inundates some communities; levees fail around New Orleans and massive flooding reported

Sep 6 Evacuation of Superdome is completed

Sep 15 President Bush pledges to rebuild the city

Sep 12 Federal Emergency Management Agency (FEMA) director Michael Brown resigns

Nov 28 City's first public school reopens

Oct 6 Drinking water declared safe in most of the city

THE CITY UNDERWATER

The historic neighborhoods built on higher ground did not flood, while the newer communities, built on reclaimed swamp land, were devastated as lake water surged through the levee breaches.

The New Orleans Fair Grounds racetrack flooded, but the venue was still able to host the New Orleans Jazz & Heritage Festival in 2006. Horse racing resumed in November 2007.

St. Louis Cathedral and other landmarks in the historic French Quarter were built on high ground and therefore avoided flooding.

WHY THE LEVEES FAILED

New Orleans relies on a network of man-made canals supported by concrete walls and earthen levees to drain water from the low-lying city into Lake Pontchartrain. The storm surge from Hurricane Katrina forced a massive amount of water from the lake back into the canals, and eventually this water overflowed the walls meant to contain it.

Water cascaded *over the canal walls with such force that it eroded the supporting earthen banks. This eventually weakened the levees so much that the walls collapsed and floodwater poured into the city.*

The Mississippi River-Gulf Outlet, a man-made shipping channel outside of New Orleans, helped funnel the storm surge into the city via the Industrial Canal.

Roof Damage at the Superdome

Storm winds tore off the roof of the city's largest sports arena, a refuge for several thousand residents. It took days for the people trapped there to be evacuated.

Lower Ninth Ward

In this area, water blasted through the failed levees with such force that homes were ripped from the ground, leaving little to salvage in the flood's wake.

May 6 All New Orleans neighborhoods declared officially open for return

Jun 29 Convention Center reopens

Sep 25 Louisiana Superdome reopens for first football game

Nov 23 New Orleans Fair Grounds racecourse reopens

Dec 23 St. Charles Avenue streetcar service fully restored

2007

Aug 24 Port of New Orleans operates at 100 percent of pre-Katrina cargo levels

Dec 24 City population officially estimated at 300,000

May 27 Audubon Aquarium of the Americas reopens

Jun 12, 2007 New Orleans appoints its first inspector general to root out city corruption

New Orleans streetcar

The Impact of Hurricane Katrina

Scrawled messages on a house in New Orleans

Hurricane Katrina was a disaster of unprecedented magnitude for New Orleans, combining the destructive force of a powerful hurricane with levee failures that left much of the city inundated by floodwaters for weeks. It was clear from the start that the city's recovery would take years, and early results materialized very slowly as bureaucratic issues mounted. However, the spirit and improvisation that have long made New Orleans such a captivating place for visitors have also fueled the city's recovery. As the rebuilding work continues, New Orleans has emerged as a showcase and proving ground for new ideas, while the warm atmosphere and unique charms of the historic city have survived to greet visitors once again.

Destruction in the wake of Hurricane Camille (1969)

A HISTORY OF HURRICANES

Like many other communities on the Gulf of Mexico, New Orleans has had to contend with powerful, devastating hurricanes throughout its history. In particular, Hurricane Betsy in September 1965, and Hurricane Camille in August 1969, caused much destruction in the metro area.

Each hurricane season, local residents would follow the storm forecasts, but while there had been several close calls, the city had managed to escape major damage for many years. However, rapidly accelerating coastal erosion was stripping away the massive wetlands that stand between New Orleans and the open waters of the Gulf. These wetlands would prove crucial as they provide a natural buffer against tropical storms.

LEVEE FAILURES AND A FITFUL RESPONSE

Hurricane Katrina formed over the Atlantic in late August 2005. As storm-track forecasts zeroed in on the New Orleans area, government officials and residents began making preparations. On August 26, the Louisiana governor declared a state of emergency, and on August 28, Mayor Ray Nagin ordered a mandatory evacuation of New Orleans. Several thousand residents took to the highways, but many others stayed put; the Louisiana Superdome was opened as a refuge to shelter them.

Katrina made landfall on August 29: winds knocked down trees, shattered windows, and tore roofs across the area. But much worse damage came from the wall of seawater the hurricane had driven towards the Gulf Coast. This storm surge inundated entire communities outside of the region's protection levees. In New Orleans itself, the levee walls collapsed, allowing water from Lake Pontchartrain to pour into the city.

The paralyzed city descended into chaos, with thousands of desperate citizens pleading for help from their rooftops. The Federal Emergency Management Agency (FEMA) was criticized for its disorganized, slow response, but eventually the military arrived in force to oversee a massive evacuation.

A MODERN DIASPORA

Amid the turmoil were moments of great courage and generosity. The US Coast Guard rescued an estimated 33,500 people from the area, and countless individuals stepped up to help those displaced and in dire need. When the evacuation was complete, the flooded city and its suburbs sat virtually empty as residents spread out across the US in search of temporary shelter.

On September 15, President George W. Bush delivered a televised speech from Jackson Square to pledge that the nation would do "whatever it takes" to rebuild New Orleans. Recovery efforts began by plugging levee breaks and draining the flooded neighborhoods, leaving behind endless vistas of washed-out destruction and a body count that would exceed 1,400 in Louisiana alone.

Aerial image of the city revealing the extent of the devastation

The grand reopening of the Louisiana Superdome

THE NEW ORLEANS SAINTS

With their hometown devastated and their stadium, the Superdome, in ruins, the New Orleans Saints football team ended the 2005 season with one of the National Football League's worst records. However, the team came roaring back the following year. The restored Superdome reopened in September 2006, just in time for the Saints' first home game since Katrina. The team won that game and went on to end the season with a trip to the conference championship. Along the way, the Saints' success provided an uplifting cause for New Orleanians, who embraced the team as a symbol of their city's recovery.

PICKING UP THE PIECES

Neighborhoods built on high ground, such as the French Quarter and the Garden District, did not flood and were open for re-entry just weeks after Katrina. For other areas, a slow planning process for rebuilding began as the government debated how to fund the immense recovery effort. Residents slowly trickled back and were provided with thousands of trailers for temporary lodging.

Debris amassed in front of a house in the aftermath of Katrina

OPEN FOR BUSINESS

Despite the devastation and lack of urban infrastructure, the recovery of New Orleans began to spread from the relatively intact historic core to the surrounding neighborhoods. Restaurants and businesses slowly reopened, sometimes in makeshift conditions, and the first schools resumed lessons before the end of 2005. The New Orleans port, the city's long-standing economic powerhouse, also got back to business, and volunteers from around the world flocked to the area to help with the recovery effort. Though the tourism and convention industries were severely reduced, and staffing shortages were rampant, New Orleans managed to host its traditional Mardi Gras celebration in February 2006.

REBUILDING BETTER

As residents continued to return to New Orleans, the Army Corps of Engineers began building a stronger, more advanced flood-control system. This project will take years to complete, but it is said to have already increased the city's level of protection. The federal government eventually approved billions of dollars in aid to repair local infrastructure and help residents rebuild their homes and businesses. After several central planning processes fell apart, frustrated neighborhood groups began crafting their own redevelopment plans. Private programs have also proliferated to encourage environmentally sensitive designs in rebuilding the city.

A NEW NEW ORLEANS

Today it is possible to visit New Orleans without seeing a trace of the disaster, though outside the historic areas the devastation often remains raw. Recovery continues on a block-by-block basis, even as large-scale reconstruction projects begin to take shape.

The city's population is still significantly smaller than before Katrina. However, many of the residents who have returned, and newcomers drawn to New Orleans since the disaster, have embraced the city's cultural heritage and are reinvigorating its many unique traditions. The population has also taken a renewed interest in politics and wide-ranging political reforms have been created to hold officials more accountable, and improve civic institutions.

Homes being built in the New Orleans Musicians' Village

History of Mardi Gras

Culminating on Mardi Gras – the day before Ash Wednesday – the Carnival celebrations in New Orleans attract visitors from across the United States and around the world. Since the 1700s the period between Twelfth Night (January 6) and Ash Wednesday, the start of Lent, has been celebrated with lavish balls, presented by private citizen groups known as "krewes." Although most balls are private, many krewes also put on parades, with ornate costumes and floats. These take place for 10 days before Mardi Gras, with the oldest and most famous parades on Tuesday itself.

Mardi Gras costume

Bacchus Kings
The Krewe of Bacchus has invited Bob Hope, Kirk Douglas, and Charlton Heston to be their king.

Rex
This krewe was founded in 1872 to organize a spectacle for Grand Duke Alexis, a younger son of Czar Alexander II.

King Cake
The traditional food of Carnival, each king cake contains a small plastic figure of a baby, representing the baby Jesus.

Parade Floats
Each krewe has 14 or more colorful floats, some still made of traditional papier-mâché, that are pulled through the city in the parades.

TIMELINE

1750	1775	1800	1825	1850	1875

1762 The Spanish pass a law forbidding slaves to wear masks

1805 Balls and masking banned

Old Mardi Gras costume

1827 Masquerade balls re-authorized

1870 The Twelfth Night Revelers Krewe formed; the first to choose and crown a queen

1872 Krewe of Rex formed

1857 Krewe of Comus founded at the Gem Saloon in the 100-block of Royal Street

1882 Krewe of Proteus formed by men from the Cotton Exchange

French Quarter Celebrations
Crowds jam the French Quarter to watch the costumed crowds and impromptu parades.

WHERE TO SEE MARDI GRAS

The history of Mardi Gras is displayed at a permanent exhibition in the Presbytère *(see pp56–7)*. Many floats are constructed at Blaine Kern's Mardi Gras World *(see p106)* and can be seen there all year long.

The Presbytère *presents a colorful display of Mardi Gras history.*

Throws
Souvenir doubloons (coins), beads, and dolls are thrown from the floats to the crowds. This tradition began with Rex in 1881.

Blaine Kern's Mardi Gras World *is the place where many of the floats are made.*

MARDI GRAS COLORS

The purple, green, and gold masks, banners, and other decorations that adorn buildings everywhere during the Carnival season are derived from the original costume worn by Rex in the 1872 parade. He used a theatrical costume made for *Richard III*, consisting of a purple velvet cloak with green rhinestones and a golden scepter and crown. Today, these colors are still used: purple symbolizing justice, green for faith, and gold for power.

Rex's Scepter
The King of Mardi Gras, a prominent New Orleans citizen, is chosen by the Rex organization every year.

Rex knight

1900	1925	1950	1975	2000	2025

1909 Zulu, the first black krewe, organized as a parody

1968 Krewe of Bacchus breaks traditions. It opens its ranks to all and invites celebrities to become its king

1991 A city ordinance requires parading Krewes to open their membership to all. Comus, Momus, and Proteus cancel their parades

1889 The first marching krewe, Jefferson City Buzzards, founded

1935 The Elks organize the first truck krewe

2000 Proteus resumes parading after a nine-year absence

2008 The city returns to its pre-Katrina Mardi Gras parade schedule, with 11 days of festivities

NEW ORLEANS AT A GLANCE

There are more than 100 places of interest described in this book. They range from the legendary Bourbon Street to the quiet and beautiful live oaks in City Park, and from Jackson Square, with its spontaneous jazz street-musicians, to the scientific exhibits in the Audubon Aquarium of the Americas. The following eight pages are a time-saving guide to the best New Orleans has to offer. Architecture, wrought and cast iron, and culture have their own sections. There is also a guide to the diverse cultures that have given this city its unique character and feeling. Below is a selection of sights that no visitor should miss.

NEW ORLEANS TOP TEN SIGHTS

Old US Mint
See pp74–5

Garden District and Uptown
See pp98–113

Royal Street
See pp48–9

St. Charles Avenue
Streetcar *See pp104–5*

Bourbon Street
See pp46–7

Audubon Aquarium of the
Americas *See pp90–91*

Audubon Zoo
See pp112–13

Jackson Square
See p54

City Park
See pp116–17

Steamboat *Natchez*
See pp64–5

◁ **Chartres Street, near Jackson Square**

Exploring New Orleans' Many Cultures

New Orleans' unique flavor derives from the incredible mix of peoples and cultures assembled on the banks of the Mississippi River; Native American, French, Spanish, African, Anglo-American, Jewish, Italian, German, and Irish. They have all contributed to the "gumbo" that is New Orleans.

African mask

French colonists signing a treaty with Native Americans

THE NATIVE AMERICANS

Numerous Native American tribes lived in the Delta: Attakpas, Bayougoula, Okelousa, Choctaw, Houma, Tunica, and Chitimacha. They were either wiped out like the Natchez, who were destroyed in the war of 1730, or removed, like the Choctaw, to Oklahoma. Only scattered traces of these tribes remain, mostly outside the city.

THE FRENCH

The French came down the Mississippi from Canada and explored and settled the region in the late 17th and early 18th centuries. Refugees from the French colony of Saint Domingue added a distinct West Indian flavor to the culture at the beginning of the 19th century. There was a continuous flow of immigration from France throughout the rest of the century. This influence is most clearly seen in the cuisine as well as in architecture and decorative arts, such as the furniture created by Prudence Mallard.

THE AFRICAN CULTURES

The first slaves arrived in 1720, and by 1724 there were enough to justify the *Code Noir* for their control. New Orleans became known for its large number of free people of color, many of whom came from Haiti during the 1791–1808 Haitian Revolution. On the eve of the Civil War, the city of 168,000 people had 13,000 slaves and free people of color. From Africa and the West Indies came music that influenced the birth of jazz *(see pp20–21)*. During Mardi Gras and on St. Joseph's Day (March 19), the Mardi Gras Indians pay homage to native Americans who hid runaway slaves.

THE SPANISH

The Spanish took over from the French as administrators of Louisiana from 1763 to 1800 *(see pp16–17)*, but few immigrants from Spain actually settled in New Orleans. Spanish is still spoken by descendants of the "Isleños" – people who came at the request of the Spanish from the Canary Islands in the 1770s. In the 1950s, Latin American refugees from Cuba, Nicaragua, and Honduras flooded into the city. The most obvious Hispanic influence can be seen throughout the French Quarter in the design of the buildings.

THE GERMANS

The first Germans arrived in 1722, lured by John Law's promotion of the colony as an earthly paradise *(see p15)*. About 10,000 had left their homes in the Rhineland between 1719 and 1720 after the Thirty Years' War. Nearly 2,000 arrived in the region, settling as small farmers about 25 miles (40 km) upstream from New Orleans, in an area known as the "German Coast." A second wave followed between 1820 and 1850, bringing thousands more, who were fleeing political turmoil in Europe. Another wave followed just before the

The French Market, where the city's diverse cultures mix

Mardi Gras Indian, unique to New Orleans

Civil War, and then another from 1865 to the 1890s. By 1870 there were more than 15,000 living in New Orleans itself. For a time they were the largest immigrant group in Louisiana.

THE CAJUNS

When the British gained control of French Canada, they insisted that the Acadians swear an oath to the British crown. When they refused, they were exiled. Many returned to France, but others traveled south to Catholic Spanish Louisiana. The first 650 people arrived in the region in 1765 and settled as farmers along the bayous west of New Orleans. Today, Cajun culture is undergoing a renaissance, assisted by Cajun and zydeco artists and chefs such as Paul Prudhomme, of K-Paul's Louisiana Kitchen *(see p177)*. While Cajun culture is separate from New Orleans' Creole-influenced culture, Cajun food, and music can be sampled here.

Cajun craftsman sitting at a traditional workbench

THE ANGLO-AMERICANS

The rough-and-ready men who piloted the riverboats down the Mississippi were the first Americans to arrive in New Orleans and give it its reputation as a City of Sin. They came in search of "dixies," or 10-dollar bills, and their carousing became notorious. After the Louisiana Purchase in 1803 *(see p17)*, government workers and land speculators migrated from the east coast, all seeking fortunes in the new territory.

A jazz band marching in the French Quarter

Many of them were of Scots-Irish or English descent. They settled in what became the American Sector on the upriver side of Canal Street, and brought another new architectural style to the city.

THE JEWS

The Jewish community made a big impact on New Orleans from the 19th century, when many Jews emigrated from Germany and Eastern Europe, and in 1828 the first synagogue was organized. In the 19th century, Samuel Zemurray, for one, started a fruit-importing company, which eventually became the United Fruit Company. He was a great philanthropist, and donated enormous sums of money to Tulane University *(see p110)*.

THE IRISH

The Irish arrived in the mid-19th century, fleeing the 1840 potato famine in Ireland. By 1860 there were 24,000 Irish in New Orleans, crowded into a narrow area dubbed the "Irish Channel" between the river and Magazine Street, east of Louisiana Avenue. The majority of them worked as laborers (building the New Basin Canal), and as stevedores. The later generations became very successful in politics.

THE ITALIANS

Although some Italians arrived before the Civil War, many more arrived later and replaced slaves as agricultural laborers. By 1890 there were more than 25,000 living in New Orleans, and more arrived at the turn of the century. Most came from Sicily and settled in the poor French Quarter, where they started out as laborers, peddlers, and market vendors, bringing interesting new flavors to the French Market. Their influence can be seen mainly in the cuisine, including the popular *muffaletta* sandwich *(see p172)*.

A New Orleans canal, built by Irish laborers

The Architecture of New Orleans

French dormer

New Orleans is one of the few American cities that has managed to retain much of its historic architecture. The French Quarter has many buildings dating back 150 years or more, while the Garden District has splendid mansions designed in a variety of styles. Beautiful houses line Esplanade Avenue, historically the residential nucleus of the Creole elite, and the city also possesses a good stock of 19th-century public buildings built in Greek Revival style. It is not always easy to categorize buildings by style, for many of them are hybrids, like the Gallier House, which incorporated both Creole and American features.

Eastlake-style townhouse on Esplanade Avenue

FRENCH COLONIAL

Only a few buildings, such as the Old Ursuline Convent *(see p68)* and Lafitte's Blacksmith Shop *(see p78)*, remain from this period, which combines various French styles of the 18th century. Most were destroyed by a series of fires: in 1788, 856 wooden buildings were destroyed; in 1794, 212 buildings. However, the city's many Creole cottages are reflective of this era.

The roof was made of wood tiles.

The brick chimney rose through the center of the house.

Brick, stucco, and timber walls

Lafitte's Blacksmith Shop *is a fine example of brick between posts, in which soft local bricks are supported by cypress timbers and protected by plaster.*

Water channels protected the wood from water damage.

Gas lamps were added in the 19th century.

SPANISH COLONIAL

After the 1788 and 1794 fires, the Spanish decreed that any building of more than one story must be constructed of brick. The houses that were subsequently built can still be seen in the French Quarter. They often combine residence and store, and feature arcaded walls, heavy doors and windows, and a flagstone alleyway leading to a loggia and fountain-graced courtyard.

The second floor was the family home.

The attic was used as a warehouse.

Walls were built of brick instead of wood.

19th-century cast-iron balconies

Napoleon House, *in the French Quarter, is a typical three-storied Spanish house. Only the crowning tower is unique.*

FEDERAL TOWNHOUSE

Americans from the Atlantic states brought their own architectural preferences with them, and the successful among them erected Federal-style homes that stand out from the French or Spanish cottages surrounding them in the Quarter.

Greek Revival elements, like the columns, were used in these houses.

Doorway with fanlight transoms

Galleries were supported by columns and window architraves.

Cast-iron details were used as decoration.

The Beauregard-Keyes House *was built in 1826 and restored in the 1940s by novelist Frances Parkinson Keyes.*

RAISED AMERICAN COTTAGE

Most of these raised cottages feature extensive eaves and an alleyway leading to a rear garden or courtyard. The interior usually contains four rooms arranged symmetrically and separated by a center hall. The kitchen and servants' quarters are away from the house at the rear.

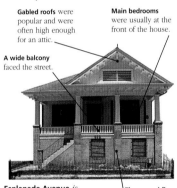

Gabled roofs were popular and were often high enough for an attic.

Main bedrooms were usually at the front of the house.

A wide balcony faced the street.

Esplanade Avenue *is lined with several kinds of these raised cottages.*

The ground floor was used as a storage area.

SHOTGUN HOUSE

These cottages were so called because a bullet fired from a shotgun through the front door would go straight through the house and out the back as all the doors were aligned. They come in single and double versions, and usually have a set of box steps in front.

The main doorway leads directly into the first room.

Simple balconies overlook the porch.

The Marigny *has several examples of traditional shotgun houses.*

Box steps

THE CREOLE PLANTATION HOUSE

The refugees from Saint Domingue (Haiti) brought this Caribbean-style dwelling to New Orleans. This one-story residence is usually raised on brick pillars (to catch the breezes and to cope with flooding) and incorporates a wraparound veranda. The space below the house and the flagstone piazza below the veranda are used as service or storage areas.

French doors gave access to the veranda.

Wide verandas were built at the front entrance.

Brick pillars raised the house.

Plantation houses *were the most popular style of residences built along the Bayou St. John.*

Famous New Orleanians

Because of its cultural roots, geographic importance, and easy-going ways, New Orleans has been a magnet for creative people since the 18th century. A great many writers and artists came here to live, and, like Tennessee Williams, called New Orleans their spiritual home. Others, like Louis Armstrong, were born here. Nurtured by its culture, they carried their musical, literary, and artistic creations to the rest of the world.

Marie Laveau
The most famous voodoo queen in New Orleans (see pp82–3), Laveau celebrated her rituals on the banks of Bayou St. John.

Louis Armstrong
Born in a shack at 723 Jane Alley, Louis Armstrong strongly influenced the development of solo jazz performances (see pp20–21). Armstrong Park (see p79), near the French Quarter, and the city's airport are named after him.

Mahalia Jackson
This gospel singer (see p80) was born on Water Street and grew up at an aunt's house at 7467 Esther (now Pitt) Street.

Truman Capote
This famous author was born in Touro Infirmary in the Garden District. He wrote his first work, Other Voices, Other Rooms, *in a rented room at 711 Royal St.*

GARDEN DISTRICT
AND UPTOWN

NEW ORLEANS AT A GLANCE

Edgar Degas
The French painter visited the city in 1872–3 (see p126). During this period he painted many well-known pictures and portraits.

William Faulkner
His first novel, Soldier's Pay, *was written at 624 Pirate's Alley (see p55), when he was living in the city in 1925.*

MID-CITY

TREME

MARIGNY

LOWER FRENCH QUARTER

UPPER FRENCH QUARTER

WAREHOUSE AND CENTRAL BUSINESS DISTRICTS

Esplanade Avenue

Canal Street

Tulane Avenue

Jackson Avenue

M I S S I S S I P P I

Andrew Jackson
This general won the Battle of New Orleans in 1815 (see p17) at Chalmette Battlefield downriver.

John James Audubon
Throughout his career the noted naturalist and painter lived on the edge of poverty, first at 706 Barracks Street, then at Oakley House plantation, where he stayed in 1821 (see p151).

Anne Rice
Born in New Orleans, author Anne Rice attended Redemptorist School and once lived at 1239 First Street in the Garden District. The city stars in her Vampire Chronicles (see p107).

0 kilometers 1

0 miles 1

New Orleans Ironwork

Cast-iron detail

The shadows cast by New Orleans ironwork add a romantic touch to the city. Wrought iron, which came first, was fashioned by hand into beautiful shapes by German, Irish, and black artisans. Cast iron, on the other hand, was poured into wooden molds and allowed to set. As a result, the latter has a somewhat solid, fixed appearance, unlike wrought iron, which is handmade and has a more fluid aspect. Examples of both kinds of work can be seen throughout the city, particularly in the French Quarter and the Garden District.

Colonial-style house, Royal Street

Decorative iron balconies *with unique designs and patterns are seen on many galleries. They are admired as much today as they were in antebellum times.*

The Pontalba Buildings, *commissioned by Baroness Pontalba (see p55), spurred on the craze for ironwork. Completed in 1850, they transformed the profile of Jackson Square (see p54). Some of the patterns were designed by the Baroness's son.*

Royal Street's famous corn-stalk fence

The signature of New Orleans *is Creole ironwork, which appears in many forms, including fences, gates, window grilles, balconies, hinges, doorknobs, and lanterns.*

Wrought ironing *contains a purer iron. Handmade and stronger than cast iron, it is very common in the French Quarter.*

Ironwork details *were added to many buildings in the 1850s. Lacy balconies depicting oak leaf and acorn can be seen on the LaBranche House at 700 Royal Street.*

Cast iron *shaped in elaborate designs was often used in homes in the Garden District. It was superior to wood because it withstood humidity.*

CORNSTALK FENCES

There are three "cornstalk" fences in New Orleans, so-called because of their decorative motifs. One is at 915 Royal Street *(see p77)*, another at Colonel Short's Villa in the Garden District *(see p107)*, and a third is at the Dufour-Plassan house on the corner of White and Bell streets in Faubourg St. John.

IRONWORK MOTIFS

In the 1850s, Philadelphia iron-mongers Wood & Perot opened a branch office in New Orleans. Offering hundreds of patterns specially designed for the city, the company quickly grew, its motifs including abstracts, acorns, fruits, cherubs, bacchants, vines, and animals. These were soon seen in railings throughout the city.

Cast-iron railing detail

Popular balcony motifs

NEW ORLEANS THROUGH THE YEAR

The spring and fall, enjoying the most temperate weather, are the best times to visit. Although the pace slows with the heat of the summer, the city is still alive with indoor and outdoor events. Some festivities celebrate themes specific to New Orleans, such as the French Quarter Festival in April. The city also throws parties for the major holidays,

Jazz Fest musician

especially 4th of July, Bastille Day, and New Year's Eve. At Christmas time, local restaurants celebrate with traditional French "Reveillon" dinners. The high points of the year, however, are Mardi Gras with all the Carnival festivities, beginning in January and running through early March, and the New Orleans Jazz and Heritage Festival (Jazz Fest) in late April and early May.

SPRING

During the spring the weather is at its best in New Orleans, neither too hot nor too humid. There are two main events in the city, both of which are internationally renowned: Mardi Gras, with its parades, street celebrations, and masked balls all over the city, and the Jazz Fest, which is held over two long weekends. It is very important to have confirmed reservations for transportation and lodging during this peak season.

MARCH

Mardi Gras *(Feb, dates vary)*. The lively Carnival festivities *(see pp28–9)* begin two or three weeks before Mardi Gras and end with the last

A family dressed in colorful Mardi Gras costumes

parade on Mardi Gras ("Fat Tuesday", or the Tuesday before Lent). There are day and night parades, and masked balls (few of which are open to the public). The whole city is on party time, so it's advisable to book hotels well in advance (for parade dates and times see www.mardigras.com).
St. Patrick's Day Parade *(weekend before and on Mar 17)*. The city commemorates Ireland's famous patron saint with parades through the French Quarter, Irish Channel, and Old Metairie Road, where cabbages are thrown to the public. An all-day street party around Parasol's Bar in the Irish Channel takes place on St. Patrick's Day itself.
St. Joseph's Day *(on and around Mar 19)*. The city's Italian population honors the patron saint of Sicily with elaborate altars of food. Angelo Brocato's ice-cream parlor *(see p183)* is one of the best places to see an altar.
Crescent City Classic *(last Saturday)*. Since 1979 world-class runners have gathered in New Orleans for this 10,000-meter race from the French Quarter to City Park. Thousands of amateur runners join in (www.ccff.org).
Tennessee Williams New Orleans Literary Festival and Writers' Conference *(late Mar)*. This five-day cultural festival takes place in various

locations to honor the celebrated writer, with theatrical productions, lectures, readings, literary walking tours, and panel discussions on New Orleans-based authors and books. Don't miss the "Stella and Stanley" screamfest held in Jackson Square (www. tennesseewilliams.net).

A huge jazz brunch at the French Quarter Festival

APRIL

French Quarter Festival *(second weekend)*. To celebrate the food and music of New Orleans, this festival is held in the French Quarter, with free musical entertainment, "the world's largest jazz brunch," fireworks over the Mississippi River, and children's activities (www. frenchquarterfestivals.org).
Spring Fiesta *(begins Fri night after Easter, lasting five days)*. With the French Quarter's historic homes as the main attraction, this celebration also has a parade

AVERAGE DAILY HOURS OF SUNSHINE

Hours

Jan Feb Mar Apr May Jun Jul Aug Sep Oct Nov Dec

Sunshine Chart
From May through September the weather is hot and humid, and the sun shines for 6 to 8 hours a day. From October through March the temperature is colder, and there are often heavy fogs.

Crowds enjoying the music at the Jazz Fest

that ends with the coronation of a local queen.
New Orleans Jazz and Heritage Festival (Jazz Fest) *(last weekend in Apr and first weekend in May)*. In this seven-day festival, held at the Fair Grounds, more than 4,000 jazz musicians entertain, with a large selection of traditional food, crafts, and evening concerts (www.nojazzfest.com).

MAY

Zoo-to-Do *(first Fri in May)*. The largest one-night fundraising event in the country takes place at Audubon Zoo *(see pp112–13)*, with unforgettable dances among the animals, under the stars.
Greek Festival *(weekend before Memorial Day weekend)*. The Hellenic Cultural Center, near Lake Pontchartrain, hosts two days of cuisine, music, and arts and crafts.
New Orleans Wine & Food Experience *(Memorial Day weekend)*. US and European wineries come to town for parties, talks, and tastings (www.nowfe.com).

SUMMER

Hot and extremely humid weather along with daily thunderstorms make summertime in New Orleans the off-season period. Since the late summer is also the time when hurricanes and tropical storms are frequent, it is wise to be prepared for weather alerts. The biggest celebration in the city is 4th of July (Independence Day).

JUNE

Great French Market Creole Tomato Festival *(first weekend)*. Held in and around the French Market, this unique festival offers cooking demonstrations and local cuisine (www.frenchmarket.org).

JULY

Go 4th on the River *(Jul 4)*. The riverfront hosts the Independence Day celebrations. There is music, food, and entertainment for the whole family, plus a spectacular fireworks display (www.go4thontheriver.com). This coincides with Essence, which draws top acts in black entertainment (www. essencemusicfestival.com).

AUGUST

White Linen Night *(first Sat)*. An open-air event in which a number of art galleries take their exhibits outdoors to the Warehouse Art District.
Satchmo SummerFest *(first weekend)*. This annual festival is usually scheduled to coincide with the great jazz icon's birthday. Held in the French Quarter, with jazz, food, kids' events, and special programs (www.satchmo summerfest.com).
Southern Decadence *(last week of Aug to Labor Day)*. Southern Decadence is a gay street party that has over-the-top costumes, parades, rowdy behavior, and a great time for adults. Centered in the French Quarter, it culminates on Labor Day, the first Monday of September (www. southerndecadence.com).

Go 4th on the River celebration at Woldenberg Park

AVERAGE MONTHLY RAINFALL

MM		Inches
300		12
240		9
180		6
120		
60		3
0		0

Jan Feb Mar Apr May Jun Jul Aug Sep Oct Nov Dec

Rainfall Chart
New Orleans is one of the rainiest cities in the United States, and July and August are its rainiest months, with daily showers. Tropical storms can cause widespread power failures. The hurricane season lasts from June to November, peaking in August and September.

Alligator close-up at the Louisiana Swamp Festival

FALL

Although there may still be rainy days in September, the driest months of the year are October and November, when both humidity and heat decrease. Halloween is the most important celebration of this season, and it launches the biggest selling period of the year. The New Orleans' Saints football team starts the NFL season which lasts through December.

SEPTEMBER

Madisonville Wooden Boat Festival *(last weekend Sep).* The largest gathering of wooden water craft in the the New Orleans area, at picturesque Madisonville on the Tchefuncte River. A Kids Dingy Workshop, Quick and Dirty Boat Building Contest, and live entertainment (www. woodenboatfest.org).
Saints Football *(Sep–Dec, Louisiana Superdome).* The NFL football season starts in September with games at the Louisiana Superdome *(see p95)* through December or January *(see pp196–7).*

Louisiana Swamp Festival *(late Sep, early Oct).* For two weekends, at the Audubon Zoo *(see pp112–13),* live Louisiana swamp animals are the center of attention. Those brave enough to touch them are allowed to do so, under close supervision. There is also Cajun food, music, and crafts.

OCTOBER

Oktoberfest *(every weekend).* The German community celebrates its cultural roots at the Deutsches Haus (200 Galvez St, (504) 522-8014) with music, food, and beer.
New Orleans Film and Video Festival *(early to mid-Oct).* This week-long event at the Canal Place Landmark Theater presents the works of filmmakers from all over the world. Visiting celebrities, authors, and film stars always attend the event.
Jazz Awareness Month *(all month).* Celebrating jazz at its birthplace, daily concerts are held throughout the city.

Halloween in New Orleans *(on and around 31 Oct).* A mini-Mardi Gras with masking, costumes, and impromptu street parties on Decatur Street. Kids get a big party at Audubon Zoo – the Boo-at-the-Zoo.

NOVEMBER

Turkey Day Race *(fourth Thu in Nov).* This 5-mile (8-km) run has celebrated Thanksgiving for a century.
New Orleans Fair Grounds Horse Racing Season *(opens Thanksgiving Day).* The thoroughbred racing season lasts from late November through March, at the country's third-oldest racetrack *(see p126).*
Celebration in the Oaks *(late Nov through early Jan).* City Park *(see pp116–17)* is transformed by countless sparkling Christmas lights.
Bayou Classic *(late Nov).* Football fans swarm downtown for the annual showdown between Louisiana's historically black colleges.

The Fair Grounds, home to thoroughbred racing in the Deep South

AVERAGE MONTHLY TEMPERATURE

Temperature Chart
New Orleans is a semi-tropical city, and during the summer the temperature may rise above 90°F (33°C). Winters are relatively mild, as are spring and fall, which are the most comfortable times of year to visit.

WINTER

The winter months are enlivened by the holiday spirit of Christmas and New Year. As soon as Christmas festivities end on Twelfth Night (Jan 6), the excitement of Mardi Gras begins to build with events and preparations for the main celebrations before Lent.

DECEMBER

Christmas *(all month)*. Candlelight caroling in Jackson Square *(see p54)*, Reveillon dinners, and historic homes decorated for Christmas in the French Quarter and Garden District.
Festival of Bonfires *(early to mid-Dec and on Christmas Eve)*. Both riverboats *(see pp64–5)* and paddlewheelers ply the Mississippi River in this blazing festival in which local people build bonfires to guide Santa Claus to their hometown for Christmas.
Countdown *(Dec 31)*. On New Year's Eve, people gather at Jackson Square *(see p54)* to await and celebrate the arrival of the New Year with live music, food, and fireworks.

JANUARY

Sugar Bowl *(first week)*. Thousands of college football fans gather in the Louisiana Superdome *(see p95)* for this important postseason game.
Battle of New Orleans Anniversary *(weekend closest to Jan 8)*.

Mardi Gras Parade at Lafayette Square

A live reenactment of this 1815 battle *(see p17)* is performed at Chalmette Battlefield in St. Bernard Parish, featuring colorful period costumes and artillery demonstrations.

FEBRUARY

New Orleans Boat & Sportfishing Show *(second week)*. A display at the Louisiana Superdome *(see p95)*, with all the latest fishing accessories.

Mardi Gras *(early Feb to early Mar)*. Carnival begins on Jan 6 with masked balls and other celebrations. However, the majority of the parades do not begin until the second weekend before Mardi Gras itself (the Tuesday before Lent).

PUBLIC HOLIDAYS

New Year's Day (Jan 1)
Martin Luther King Day (3rd Mon, Jan)
Mardi Gras Day (varies, Feb 3–Mar 9)
Presidents Day (3rd Mon, Feb)
Memorial Day (end May)
Independence Day (Jul 4)
Labor Day (1st Mon, Sep)
Columbus Day (2nd Mon, Oct)
Veterans Day (Nov 11)
Thanksgiving (4th Thu, Nov)
Christmas Day (Dec 25)

Fireworks at the traditional Countdown on New Year's Eve

NEW ORLEANS AREA BY AREA

A View of Bourbon Street

**Tile street sign on
Bourbon Street**

Today Bourbon Street, rather than Basin Street, is synonymous with sin. The name has nothing to do with bourbon, despite the string of bars that line this legendary street; it is named after the French royal family of Bourbon. One bar after another proffers vats of such lethal concoctions as Nuclear Kamikaze, Brain Freeze, and Sex on the Bayou, most often to the accompaniment of blasting rock or blues. Other emporiums offer everything from peep shows and topless and go-go dancers, to drag shows and gay action. During Mardi Gras, the lacy balconies above the sidewalks sag from the weight of drinking revelers.

The Famous Door
This nightclub lives with the beat of live 1970s and 1980s rock music.

IBERVILLE ST   BIENVILLE ST   CONTI ST

Arnaud's
Count Arnaud Cazenave opened the original Arnaud's in 1918. There are 17 dining rooms with mosaic tiles, mirrored walls, and paddle fans (see p176).

Galatoire's
Run by the Galatoire family since 1905, this restaurant has the ambience of a perpetual cocktail party.

Old Absinthe House
This building is notable for its entresol, the half-story between the first and second floors.

The World Jeweler
Lafcadio Hearn, the famous American journalist, once rented a room here.

◁ **The bustling Central Business District**

Chris Owen's Club
The legendary Owens has been on Bourbon Street for decades. Dynamic shows include Las Vegas-style cabaret.

Preservation Hall
An aptly named music venue, Preservation Hall has helped preserve traditional New Orleans jazz. It opened in 1961, and still provides top-quality jazz.

The French Opera House
Until it burned down in 1919, the French Opera House was the social and artistic hub of New Orleans. Nowadays there is a hotel on the spot.

Cats Meow
A young crowd frequents this lively bar and its balcony.

Pat O'Brien's
The birthplace of the internationally renowned "Hurricane" cocktail, O'Brien's has a spectacular fire fountain in the main courtyard.

Fritzel's
Fritzel's is the only traditional European live jazz club in the city.

A View of Royal Street

Tile street sign on Royal

This is the most fetching street in the French Quarter. It is lined with antique shops that are filled with beautiful, often French, treasures associated with an opulent Southern lifestyle; crystal chandeliers, massive inlaid armoires, ormolu furnishings, and more. In the early colony this was the city's financial center and its main and most fashionable street. Today, many stores occupy handsome landmarks.

Street musicians provide open-air entertainment on Royal Street

CONTI ST

Louisiana State Bank (# 403)

Built in 1821, this building was designed by Benjamin Latrobe (right), who also designed the US Capitol's south wing.

Brennan's (# 417)

Built around 1802 for a Spanish merchant, this building later became a bank and the property of Judge Alonzo Morphy. Brennan's restaurant moved here in 1954 (see p176). Its balcony seal is made of cast iron.

0 meters 10

0 yards 10

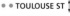

ST. LOUIS ST — TOULOUSE ST

Rumors

This gift shop sells Mardi Gras paraphernalia all year long. Masks, beads, krewe costumes, and posters are all for sale (see p192).

The Historic New Orleans Collection (# 533)

Occupying a complex of houses built in 1792 for Jean-François Merieult and his wife, this museum boasts a magnificent collection of art and artifacts (see pp60–61).

A Street of Living Tradition

Royal Street is the pride of the French Quarter. Its beautiful buildings have been carefully maintained and are today occupied by fine stores and restaurants.

LOCATOR MAP

0 meters 10

0 yards 10

● ST. LOUIS ST ↕

Moss Antiques offers a fine range of French antiques.

0 meters 10

0 yards 10

Antoine Peychaud's Pharmacy (# 437)

The cocktail was born here when pharmacist Antoine Peychaud mixed brandy with his bitters and served the potion in a coquetier *(see p174). Today it is an antique shop.*

↕ ST. PETER ST ● ORLEANS ST ↕

St. Anthony's Garden

This beautiful garden (see p55) stands at the back of St. Louis Cathedral. Its serenity hides the fact that it was a staging ground for duels in the 18th century.

The La Branche Buildings (# 700)
Embellished with fine oak-leaf ironwork, these buildings were constructed in 1835 for sugar planter Jean Baptiste LaBranche.

UPPER FRENCH QUARTER

The French Quarter is synonymous with New Orleans. The original 20 blocks were laid out around present-day Jackson Square in 1721. The Upper French Quarter runs from Iberville Street to St. Ann and includes the busiest blocks of Decatur, Chartres, Royal, and Bourbon streets. The last of these is particularly lively, offering several bars that promise rollicking good times. Architecturally,

Cupid statue in Le Petit Théâtre

the Vieux Carré (meaning Old Square) is quintessential New Orleans. The colorful Creole-style cottages featuring jalousie-shuttered windows stand flush along the sidewalks. There are also several Spanish-style buildings decorated with lacy iron galleries. This iconic neighborhood escaped with very little wind damage from Hurricane Katrina and experienced no flooding in the days that followed.

SIGHTS AT A GLANCE

Historic Buildings
Louisiana Supreme Court Building ⑪
Napoleon House ⑫
Père Antoine Alley and St. Anthony's Garden ⑦
Pirate's Alley ⑥
Pontalba Buildings ④
St. Louis Cathedral, Cabildo, and Presbytère pp56–7 ②

Museums and Galleries
The 1850 House ③
Hermann-Grima Historic House ⑨
Historic New Orleans Collection pp60–61 ⑩
Jean Lafitte National Historical Park Visitor Center ⑭
Musée Conti Wax Museum ⑧
New Orleans Pharmacy Museum ⑬

Theaters
Le Petit Théâtre du Vieux Carré ⑤

Parks and Gardens
Jackson Square ①

Boat Trips
Steamboat *Natchez* ⑮

KEY

▦ Street-by-Street map
See pp52–3

🚏 Streetcar stop

0 meters 200
0 yards 200

GETTING THERE

The No.3 Vieux Carré bus circles the Quarter on Chartres and Dauphine streets. The Canal streetcar runs from the Mississippi River to Mid-City. The St. Charles Streetcar on Canal has stops at Carondelet and St. Charles. The Riverfront streetcar covers the riverside of the Quarter to Elysian Fields.

◁ **St. Louis Cathedral in Jackson Square**

Street-by-Street: Upper French Quarter

This is the heart of the French Quarter, containing a striking and harmonious collection of buildings. The lively Jackson Square initially served as a military parade ground, or *place d'armes*, where troops were trained and drilled, executions carried out, and public meetings held. The Cathedral, Cabildo, and Presbytère face the square. It was redesigned in 1848, when Baroness Pontalba built the two elegant apartment buildings on the upriver and downriver sides of the square. An impressive statue of General Jackson was also unveiled in the center of the square, where artists now display their work.

Leech jar, Pharmacy Museum

Père Antoine Alley and St. Anthony's Garden
This garden was a favorite local dueling place in the 19th century ❼

Tennesee Williams wrote *A Streetcar Named Desire* in an apartment at 632 St. Peter Street.

Le Petit Théâtre du Vieux Carré
This theater, established in 1916, moved to its current location in 1919. The building is a replica of the original ❺

The **Omni Royal Orleans** hotel *(see p162)* is constructed on the site of the 1836 St. Louis Hotel.

TOULOUSE ST

CHARTRES STREET

DECATUR STREET

KEY

- - - - Suggested route

Napoleon House
The most beloved bar in the French Quarter is devoted to Napoleon's memory. His portraits and other memorabilia adorn the walls ❶❷

STAR SIGHTS

★ The 1850 House

★ Jackson Square

★ St. Louis Cathedral, Cabildo, and Presbytère

For hotels and restaurants in this region see pp162–3 and pp176–7

★ **St. Louis Cathedral, Cabildo, and Presbytère**
These were the most important religious and administrative buildings in the French and Spanish periods ❷

LOCATOR MAP
See Street Finder maps 4 and 5

Street musicians
play in front of the cathedral.

★ **The 1850 House**
This small museum displays opulent furniture and decorations that convey the middle-class lifestyles of the antebellum era ❸

ST. ANN STREET

ST. PETER ST

★ **Jackson Square**
A magnificent statue of General Jackson takes center stage in the square, where artists hang their works "on the fence" ❶

Pontalba Buildings
The handsome Pontalba apartments, built in 1848 for $302,000, are located on the upriver and downriver sides of the square ❹

| 0 meters | 30 |
| 0 yards | 30 |

Jackson Square ❶

Map 5 D2. �È *Riverfront.* 🚌 *3, 5, 55.*

Today an attractive and lively meeting place, this square was named the *Place d'Armes* in the early French colony, when it was little more than a muddy field. Here the troops were drilled, criminals were placed in the stocks, and executions were carried out. In 1850, it was renamed for the hero of the Battle of New Orleans *(see p17)*, after the Baroness Pontalba paid for its beautification and laid out the gardens and pathways of the square as they exist today. Under her auspices, the Pelanne brothers designed the handsome wrought-iron fence that encloses the square. At the center stands a statue of General Andrew Jackson astride a rearing horse, which was sculpted by Clark Mills for $30,000. The inscription, "The Union must and shall be preserved," on the plinth was added by Union General Benjamin "Beast" Butler, when he occupied the city during the American Civil War *(see p18)*.

Jazz band playing in Jackson Square

The park is landscaped in a radial pattern, with walkways stemming out from the center and there are plenty of benches to sit and enjoy the charm of the historical houses.

Outside the park, diverse artists rent space and hang their works on the enclosing fence, and there are plenty of artists waiting to draw your portrait or caricature. On the flagstones around the square, tarot-card readers, jazz musicians, and clowns entertain visitors throughout the week. There are also shops on the ground level of the Pontalba Apartments, selling gifts, clothing, candy, and ice cream.

Water vessel in The 1850 House

St. Louis Cathedral, Cabildo, and Presbytère ❷

See pp56–7.

The 1850 House ❸

523 St. Ann St. **Map** 5 D2. *Tel 568-6968.* 🚌 *3, 5, 55.* ⏱ *10am–4:30pm Tue–Sun.* ⊙ *public hols.* 🎫 🛈

In the Lower Pontalba Building, this museum recreates an antebellum apartment. The three-story residence above the ground-floor space is accessed by a dramatic circular staircase. The bedrooms contain all the innovations of their day, including walk-in closets and private bathrooms.

The Pontalba Buildings, the upriver side of Jackson Square

For hotels and restaurants in this region see pp162–3 and pp176–7

Also displayed are decorative arts and everyday artifacts of the period. A gift shop occupies the ground floor.

Pontalba Buildings ❹

St. Peter and St. Ann Sts. **Map** 5 D2. 🚋 *Riverfront.* 🚌 *3, 5, 55.* 🖵 🛗

In 1848, Baroness Micaela Pontalba supervised the building of these block-long apartments flanking the up-town and downtown sides of Jackson Square. They were erected for over $300,000, and at the time they were considered the best and the largest apartments of their kind.

At the age of 15, Micaela married the foppish aristocrat Celestin Pontalba, a distant cousin, and moved to Paris. There, her father-in-law tried to force her to sign over her entire estate. When she refused, he attempted to kill her, but succeeded only in shooting off two of her fingers.

She courageously separated from her husband in 1848 and returned to New Orleans. The baroness, like her father the philanthropist Don Andrés Almonester y Rojas, was a developer. With plans brought back from Paris, she proceeded to build apartments like the ones she had seen in Paris. Architects James Gallier and Henry Howard drew up the plans. The design of the initials A and P (for Almonester and Pontalba) in the cast-iron railings of the galleries and balconies is attributed to one of the baroness's sons, an artist.

Le Petit Théâtre du Vieux Carré ❺

616 St. Peter St. **Map** 5 D2. *Tel* 522-2081. 🚌 *3, 5, 55.* **Box Office** ◯ *10:30am–5:30pm Tue–Sat.* ⬤ *Sun, public hols.* 🌐

This small theater was the brainchild of a group of actors called the Drawing Room Players, who came together in 1916 under the management of Mrs. Oscar Nixon. Their

Interior of Le Petit Théâtre du Vieux Carré

first theater was located in the Lower Pontalba Building, but in 1922 the current site was bought and was used for the first American productions of Eugene O'Neill's *Beyond the Horizon* and Oscar Wilde's *Lady Windermere's Fan*. It is a pretty building with a beguiling courtyard and fountain.

The structure is actually a 1962 reconstruction of a house that was built here in 1796. Some of the original grillwork, by the brilliant ironworker Marcellino Hernandez, was reused, but little else, in an effort to create a modern theater space.

Today, the theater presents an annual season of performances between September and June, and functions as a headquarters during the Tennessee Williams New Orleans Literary Festival and Writers' Conference.

Pirate's Alley ❻

Map 5 D2. 🚌 *3, 5, 55.*

Although it is named after the famous pirate brothers, Jean and Pierre Lafitte *(see p17)*, there is no evidence here that this was once a pirates' haunt or a slave market. Today, the alley's classic bohemian atmosphere and open-air cafés are what make it worth seeking out.

The Faulkner House, a bookstore where the shelves are lined with William Faulkner first editions as well as works by other major

Southern authors, is located in the building where Faulkner wrote his first novel, *Soldier's Pay*, in 1925.

Père Antoine Alley and St. Anthony's Garden ❼

Map 5 D2. 🚋 *Riverfront.* 🚌 *3, 5, 55.*

This alley is named for one of the city's most beloved clergymen, Father Antonio de Sedella (Père Antoine), who served as pastor of St. Louis Cathedral for 40 years. He was loved for his compassionate ministry to the poor, whom he assiduously fed and clothed.

The fenced garden, once a popular dueling ground, features a great sculpture of the Sacred Heart. In the early morning and evening the scent of sweet olive lingers in the air.

Faulkner House, a bookstore in Pirate's Alley

St. Louis Cathedral, Cabildo, and Presbytère ❷

This complex of buildings was the most important ensemble in the early colony. The Cabildo, designed by Guilberto Guillemard, was built and financed in 1795 by Don Andrés Almonester y Rojas. It served as a capitol for the legislative assembly of the Spanish colonial government, and subsequently as the City Hall. From 1853 to 1911 it housed the state Supreme Court. The Casa Curial, or Presbytère, was built between 1794 and 1813, and served as a courthouse until 1911. Today, both buildings are flagship properties of the Louisiana State Museum. Two earlier churches on the site of the St. Louis Cathedral were destroyed, the first by a hurricane in 1722, the second by a fire in 1788. The current building was begun in 1789 and dedicated as a cathedral in 1794. It has been substantially modified since then.

★ Main Altar
The carved-wood Baroque altars were constructed in Ghent, Belgium, and brought to the cathedral in pieces.

Cathedral Dome
A great mural of St. Louis announcing the Seventh Crusade was painted above the altar.

Old Press
Printing presses were widely used from colonial times. This one is displayed on the third floor of the Cabildo.

Cabildo

★ Sala Capitular
The Louisiana Purchase (see p17) was signed in this room; this desk set was in place at the time.

Ceiling Murals
Painted by Alsatian artist Erasme Humbrecht in 1872, the murals portray different biblical stories.

VISITORS' CHECKLIST

Jackson Square. **Map** 5 D2. *Tel* *525-9585 (St. Louis Cathedral); 568-6968 (Cabildo and Presby- tère).* St. Charles Ave and Canal streetcars. *3, 5, 55, 81.* 10am–4:30pm daily (St. Louis Cathedral); 9am–5pm Tue–Sun (Cabildo and Presbytère). *all major holidays (Cabildo and Pres- bytère).* Cabildo and Pres- bytère. St. Louis Cathedral, regular services daily. **www**.saintlouiscathedral.org **www**.lsm.crt.state.la.us

Stained-glass windows with figures of Catholic saints adorn the cathedral's interior.

A permanent exhibition on Hurricane Katrina will open here in fall 2010.

Presbytère

Mardi Gras Exhibits
Various Mardi Gras objects and memorabilia are displayed throughout the building.

St. Louis Cathedral

The clock bell, given the name "Victoire" by Père Antoine, was cast in Paris. It has tolled hourly since 1819.

The steeples, the portico, and the pilasters were added in 1851.

STAR FEATURES

★ Main Altar

★ Mardi Gras Museum

★ Sala Capitular

★ **Mardi Gras Museum**
Audio-visual and other exhibits about Mardi Gras fill the rooms of the Presbytère today.

Master bedroom, the Hermann-Grima Historic House

Musée Conti Wax Museum ⑧

917 Conti St. **Map** 4 C2. **Tel** 525-2605. 🚋 3. ◐ 10am–4pm Mon, Fri, Sat. ● Sun, Thanksgiving, Dec 25, Mardi Gras. ◪ ◪ ◪ ◪ **www**. neworleanswaxmuseum.com

The major part of this museum's space is taken up with a series of 25 vivid tableaus featuring lifelike historical figures. The museum presents the tempestuous story of New Orleans' development, from its founding in the 18th century to the lynching of 11 Italians accused of gunning down the police chief in 1891. One of the most imaginatively conceived scenes depicts Napoleon in his bathtub gesticulating madly as he informs onlookers of his decision to sell Louisiana

to America *(see p17)*. The museum also features wax representations of political figures such as the legendary governor of Louisiana, Huey Long (1893–1935). Also present is four-time Governor Edwin Edwards, who was found guilty of racketeering.

The tour ends with a series of tableaus featuring stock horror figures such as Dracula and Frankenstein in dungeon-like surroundings. Statues of Andrew Jackson, the pirate Jean Lafitte, and Marie Laveau also compete for your attention.

Hermann-Grima Historic House ⑨

820 St. Louis St. **Map** 4 C2. **Tel** 525-5661. 🚋 3. ◐ 10am–3:30pm Mon–Tue, Thu–Sat. ● public hols. ◪ ◪ ◪ **www**.hgghh.org

This gabled brick house stands out from those around it because it is one of the few examples of American Federal-style architecture in the French Quarter. William Brand built it in 1831 for Samuel Hermann, a German-Jewish merchant. Unfortunately, he lost his fortune in 1837 and had to sell the house to Judge Felix Grima. The house features a central doorway with a fanlight and marble steps; another window with a fanlight graces the second floor.

Inside, the floors and doors are made of cypress, and the rooms feature elegant marble fireplaces. The three-story service quarters, located in a separate building off the parterre behind the house, are also striking. They feature slave quarters and a kitchen containing a rare four-burner wood-fired stove with a beehive oven.

Historic New Orleans Collection ⑩

See pp60–61.

Louisiana Supreme Court Building ⑪

400 Royal St. **Map** 4 C2. **Tel** 310-2300. 🚋 3. 🚊 Riverfront. ◐ 8:30am–5pm Mon–Fri. ● public hols. **www**.lasc.org

When this massive granite and marble structure was built in 1908–10, the French Quarter was on the downside. Erecting this splendid Beaux Arts court building was an early exercise in urban renewal. Despite a few protests, an entire block of historic 18th- and early 19th-century buildings was razed to make way for it. The Louisiana Supreme Court occupied it from 1910 to 1958. Thereafter, the

Recreation of America's purchase of Louisiana, Musée Conti

Façade of the Louisiana Supreme Court Building

Napoleon House, surmounted by its landmark cupola

courthouse began to decline and massive trees were planted on the site to hide the dazzling white marble exterior. It was home to a string of state agencies, none of which took on the maintenance necessary for such an architecturally intricate structure. In the 1990s the state finally launched a renovation program and since 2004 the building has once again served as the home of the Louisiana Supreme Court, the Louisiana Law Library, and various other state legal offices. There are plans to add a legal museum, but visitors may view some public rooms and the Law Library.

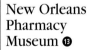

Marble detail from the Supreme Court Building

Together, they were the home of Mayor Nicholas Girod, who planned to free Napoleon from imprisonment on St. Helena Island. With the help of Dominique You and a pirate band *(see p17)*, Girod intended to bring Napoleon to this refuge, but Napoleon died before the mission could be undertaken. Today, the walls of the house are adorned with all kinds of Napoleonic decor and memorabilia. Both buildings are attributed to Hyacinthe Laclotte, and the balcony railings were crafted by William Malus. The cupola on the roof is a New Orleans landmark.

Napoleon House ⑫

500 Chartres St. **Map** 5 D2.
Tel 524-9752. 🚌 3, 5, 55, 81.
⏰ 11am–5:30pm Mon, 11am–10pm Tue–Thu, 11am–11pm Fri–Sat. ♿ 🍴
📷 🍸 www.napoleonhouse.com

One of the city's most atmospheric bars, Napoleon House is famous for its Pimm's Cup and for a warm version of the *muffaletta (see p172)*, a traditional New Orleans deli sandwich. It occupies two buildings, one of which is a two-story structure, built in 1798, facing St. Louis Street; the second, built in 1814, is a three-story building with a mezzanine.

New Orleans Pharmacy Museum ⑬

514 Chartres St. **Map** 5 D2.
Tel 565-8027. 🚌 3, 5, 55, 81.
⏰ 10am–5pm Tue–Sat (to 2pm Tue, Thu). ● public hols. 📷 📹 ♿
www.pharmacymuseum.org

This museum is located on the site of the first licensed pharmacy in the United States, operated by Louis Joseph Dufilho from 1823 to 1855. The original display cases and mahogany cabinets contain some gruesome-looking early surgical tools – saws, knives, and bloodletting instruments – as well as early herbal remedies, many of which were forerunners of today's drugs. These include a bottle of salicin, an early form of aspirin produced by Bayer & Co. from black willow bark. The museum also features a splendid 1855 marble soda fountain at which appealing sodas were first concocted to help the medicine go down. The second floor features a 19th-century sick room, a fine collection of eye glasses, plus homeopathic remedies and an impressive collection of 19th-century dental instruments. The walled courtyard garden is filled with medicinal herbs.

Jean Lafitte National Historical Park Visitor Center ⑭

419 Decatur St. **Map** 4 C3. *Tel* 589-2636. 🚌 3, 5, 55, 81. ⏰ 9am–5pm daily. ● Dec 25, Mardi Gras. 📷 📹 ♿ 🎵 www.nps.gov/jela

This visitor center has some excellent displays on the geography, history, and culture of the Mississippi River Delta region. It also offers slide shows and ranger-led walking tours of the French Quarter at 9:30 every morning.

The Jean Lafitte National Historical Park comprises six sites in all, including three in Cajun Country *(see p152 and p157)* and the Chalmette Battlefield *(see p88)*.

A 19th-century soda fountain at the Pharmacy Museum

Historic New Orleans Collection ⑩

Spanish coat of arms

This massive collection, born of one couple's interest in the Battle of New Orleans, is housed in several 18th- and 19th-century structures. The Merieult House (1792) features 10 galleries displaying historical artifacts, ranging from maps and paintings to furnishings and decorative objects. Free changing exhibitions are held in a gallery on the first floor. The Williams residence, at the rear of the courtyard, was the home of the collectors, General and Mrs. L. Kemper Williams, who lived here from the 1940s to the 1960s. The Williams Research Center at 410 Chartres Street offers changing exhibits in its newly opened annex.

Williams Research Center
This facility houses the largest collection of historical documents in the city.

Old courtyard

Williams Residence

20th-Century Gallery
On display here are books and artworks depicting the city in the 1900s, such as this Brulator Courtyard *by C. Bennette Moore.*

The Counting House, once used for banking activities, is now a lecture hall

Plantation Gallery
Plantation life was often captured in art. This collage portrays the hauling of cotton.

STAR EXHIBITS

★ Antebellum Gallery

★ Spanish Colonial Gallery

★ Victorian Gallery

★ **Victorian Gallery**
This gallery features elaborate furniture, and smaller objects, such as this teapot.

Slave Funeral
One of a series of paintings by John Antrobus evokes life on a Louisiana plantation in the Plantation Gallery.

VISITORS' CHECKLIST

533 Royal St. **Map** 4 C2. *Tel* 523-4662. St. Charles Ave. 3, 55, 81, 82. 9:30am– 4:30pm Tue–Sat. major hols. www.hnoc.org

★ Spanish Colonial Gallery
Portraits of residents during the Spanish colonial era are shown here.

French Colonial Gallery
French period items such as this refectory table, used in the Old Ursuline Convent, are displayed here.

A dining room in 1792, this area is now closed to the public

Louisiana Purchase Gallery
With its message of prosperity, this image presents a rare welcome to the Americans after the Purchase (see p17).

★ Antebellum Gallery
On display in this gallery are items related to the city prior to the Civil War, including this painting of a fleet of frigates off the Louisiana coast.

The shop at the collection

Main entrance

Visitor welcome center

The French Quarter, open for business at dusk ▷

Steamboat *Natchez* ⓯

Upper deck light

For a reminder of the old days of river travel, visitors can take a two-hour cruise on the Steamboat *Natchez*. In the 19th century, steamboats traveled the length of the Mississippi, taking between three and five days to get from Louisville, Kentucky, to New Orleans. The boatmen were notorious brawlers who went looking for women and liquor at the end of a trip and established New Orleans' reputation as the "City of Sin." In their heyday, from 1830 to 1860, some 30 steamboats lined up at the levee. The steamboat era ended by the close of the 19th century as railroads and highways replaced them.

Steam Whistle
The genuine copper-and-steel steam whistle is a treasured antique.

Pilot House
A telegraph is used for communication between the Pilot House and the Chief Engineer in the engine room.

Bridge

The copper bell is inlaid with 250 silver dollars to produce a purer tone.

Capstan

Bowthruster

Magnolia Suite i the lower deck, f private events

Stage
Gigantic ramps were used to board, load, and off-load the steamboat.

STAR FEATURES

★ Dining Room

★ Engine Room

★ Steam Calliope

★ **Dining Room**
A casual buffet dinner is served on the second deck, featuring live jazz music by the Dukes of Dixieland.

Lifesavers
are distributed around the ship.

Gift shop

★ **Steam Calliope**
This 32-note steam calliope was custom-crafted and modeled after the "Gilded Age" craft of the 1800s.

The Hurricane Deck features live jazz music.

NATCHEZ.

★ **Engine Room**
These powerful steam engines were built for the US Steel Corporation's sternwheeler Clairton in 1925.

Paddlewheel
Twenty-five tons of white oak propel the steamboat along the river.

LOWER FRENCH QUARTER, MARIGNY, AND TREME

Extending from beyond St. Ann Street to Esplanade Avenue is the more residential part of the French Quarter. Within this area the busiest sidewalks are those around the French Market, where stalls display hot sauces, strings of garlic and peppers, and other Creole and Cajun specialties. The surrounding streets are lined with handsome Creole-style cottages. Esplanade Avenue divides the French Quarter and the Faubourg Marigny. Soon after the

Louis Armstrong statue

Louisiana Purchase (see p17), the Marigny Plantation was subdivided, and the area was settled. Today, the Marigny is a lively place with restaurants and clubs. The area just west of the French Quarter is the Faubourg Treme, which was settled largely by free people of color. This area was moderately affected by Hurricane Katrina: the Old US Mint's roof was torn off by high winds, and the Mahalia Jackson Theater of the Performing Arts suffered flood damage.

SIGHTS AT A GLANCE

Museums and Galleries
Beauregard-Keyes House **6**
Gallier House Museum **8**
Madame John's Legacy **15**
New Orleans Jazz National
 Historical Park **4**
Old US Mint pp74–5 **1**

Parks and Gardens
American Aquatic Gardens **20**
Armstrong Park **21**
Congo Square **22**
Washington Artillery Park &
 Moon Walk **17**
Washington Square **19**

Cemeteries
St. Louis Cemetery #1 **25**
St. Louis Cemetery #2 **26**

Historic Buildings
Cornstalk Fence **16**
Gauche Villa **11**

Lafitte's Blacksmith Shop **18**
Lalaurie House **9**
Latrobe House **10**
Old Ursuline Convent **5**
Soniat House **7**

Landmarks
Café du Monde **14**
Central Grocery **13**
Esplanade
 Avenue **12**

Flea Market **2**
French Market **3**

Churches
Our Lady of Guadalupe **24**

Theaters
Mahalia Jackson Theater of
 the Performing Arts **23**

GETTING THERE
The 48 bus runs from Mid-
City to Esplanade; the
3 circles the Quarter on
Dauphine and Chartres.
The Riverfront Streetcar
has two stops here.

KEY

Street-by-Street map
See pp68–9

Streetcar stop

Tourist information

0 meters 300
0 yards 300

◁ Lacy, New Orleans ironwork, Royal Street

Street-by-Street: Lower French Quarter

The area surrounding the French Market is loaded with atmosphere. It has long been a place for meeting and mixing. In the city's early days, Native Americans came to this area to sell wild herbs, and today the district still offers a range of exotic goods. French Market Place, formerly Gallatin Street, was once the most notorious street in the Quarter, populated by prostitutes, rowdies, criminals (like the Black Hand Gang), and visiting sailors, who ventured here at their peril. It was lined with so many brothels and bars that it was dubbed "Louisiana's Barbary Coast." Today, it still has plenty of bars, and some of the oldest and most important buildings in the French Quarter.

Gallier House Museum
Set in a former residence, this is an informative showcase of 19th-century life ❽

Soniat House
This residence has been restored to its original splendor, and serves as a lovely small hotel (see p164) ❼

Beauregard-Keyes House, former home of Frances Parkinson Keyes, is now a museum ❻

★ **Old Ursuline Convent**
Designed in 1745, and built in 1752, this is the oldest building in the Mississippi Valley ❺

★ **Farmers' Market at the French Market**
Containing a farmers' market full of fresh produce, the French Market has been a New Orleans institution since 1791 ❸

KEY

– – – Suggested route

Gauche Villa
Built in 1856, this house is notable for its beautiful cast-iron balcony. Architect James Freret designed the house ⑪

LOCATOR MAP
See Street Finder maps 4 and 5

Esplanade Avenue
This beautiful avenue was the aristocratic residential street of the Creole community in the 19th century. It marks the division between the French Quarter and the Faubourg Marigny ⑫

★ Old US Mint
Coins were minted here until 1909. Today the building is home to the Jazz Museum ❶

Flea Market at the French Market
Handcrafts, souvenirs, and curiosities can be found at this popular flea market ❷

STAR FEATURES

★ French Market

★ Old Ursuline Convent

★ Old US Mint

Old US Mint ❶

See pp74–5.

Flea Market ❷

French Market, North Peters St, between Gov. Nicholls and Barracks Sts. **Map** 5 E1. 🚋 *Riverfront.* 🚌 *3, 55.* ⭘ *9am–6pm daily.* ♿ ▯ ▯
ℹ️ www.frenchmarket.org

At stalls and tables inside and outside the French Market buildings, all kinds of items can be bought, from jewelry and pottery to African arts and crafts. The flea market stands on the site of the notorious neighborhood once called the "port of missing men," because so many men who visited the local bars and brothels were shanghaied or killed.

Colorful wares for sale at New Orleans' Flea Market

French Market ❸

North Peters St to Barracks St. **Map** 5 E1. 🚋 *Riverfront.* 🚌 *3, 5, 48.* ⭘ *9am–7pm daily (some parts are open later).* ▯ ▯ ▮ ▮

Despite its name, this spot has been a gathering place for many different ethnic groups. Originally, Native Americans came here to sell their baskets, beads, and filé (ground sassafras leaves used in gumbo). Later, African-American women sold various wares including calas (hot rice cakes). German farmers from upriver sold agricultural produce, and Italians operated most of the stalls in the late 1800s. Today, the French Market officially covers the five blocks between St. Ann and Barracks streets, but in

Typical French Market stand displaying fresh garlic and vegetables

daily use, it usually denotes the open-air markets starting at St. Philips Street. At the Farmers' Market (starting at Ursulines St) you can still find fresh produce, but most of the space is now given over to the Flea Market, selling a diverse range of clothing, antiques, and art.

New Orleans Jazz National Historical Park ❹

916 N Peters St. **Map** 5 D1. *Tel* 589-4841. 🚋 *Riverfront.* 🚌 *3, 5, 82.* ⭘ *9am–5pm Tue–Sat.* ⬤ *Jan 1, Thanksgiving, Dec 25.* ▯ www.nps.gov/jazz

A new, large complex in Armstrong Park, devoted to the history and development of jazz, is due to open by 2010. Until then, the temporary visitors' center offers seminars, lectures, and free afternoon jazz concerts. There is also a permanent collection of photographs charting the history of jazz, as well as guided walks to nearby sites of interest.

Old Ursuline Convent ❺

1100 Chartres St. **Map** 5 D1. *Tel* 529-3040. 🚋 *Riverfront.* 🚌 *3, 55.* ⭘ *10am–4pm Tue–Fri, 11am–4pm Sat, Sun. (Guided tours only.)* ▯ ▯

Dating from 1752, this is the oldest building in the Mississippi Valley. With its steep-pitched roof punctuated by a row of dormers and tall chimneys, it is typically French Colonial.
In the 1820s, when the nuns departed to new quarters, the convent became the first official residence for the bishops and archbishops of New Orleans, and the home of the archdiocesan archives. Later, the convent became part of a parish complex and the old nuns' kitchen and laundry became (as it remains today) the rectory for Our Lady of Victory Church.
The current chapel, consecrated in 1845, was originally known as St. Mary's, but today it is called Our Lady of Victory.

Main façade, Old Ursuline Convent

Beautiful ironwork adorning the Soniat House

Inside, visitors can admire the splendid pine and cypress ceiling, two fine Bavarian stained-glass windows, and a window depicting the Battle of New Orleans (*see p17*) beneath an image of Our Lady of Prompt Succor.

A formal French garden containing a handsome iron gazebo lies in front of the building. It is accessed via the porter's lodge.

Beauregard-Keyes House ❻

1113 Chartres St. **Map** 5 D1. *Tel 523-7257.* 🚇 *Riverfront.* 🚌 *3, 55.* ⏰ *10am–3pm Mon–Sat.* 🎟️ 🎫 *hourly.*

Twin staircases lead up to this Federal-style townhouse, designed by François Corre-jolles in 1826. It is associated with several famous New Orleanians, including master

chess player Paul Morphy who was born here in 1837, when it was the residence of his grandfather, Joseph Le Carpentier. General P. G. T. Beauregard lived here briefly for 18 months in 1866–7, and because he was such a famous Civil War hero his name is still associated with the building.

Novelist Frances Parkinson Keyes, who wintered and wrote many of her 51 novels here, including *Dinner at Antoine's*, restored the property. Today, many of her personal possessions are on display, including all of her novels, plus a collection of dolls from all over the world. The rooms are arranged around an attractive court-yard, which contains a fountain that Mrs. Keyes brought from Vermont, her home state.

Soniat House ❼

1133 Chartres St. **Map** 5 D1. *Tel 522-0570.* 🚇 *Riverfront.* 🚌 *3, 55.* **www**.soniathouse.com *See Where to Stay, p164.*

This historic residence was built in 1829 as a townhouse for wealthy sugar planter Joseph Soniat Dufossat and his family. Joseph was the second son of Chevalier Guy Saunhac du Fossat, who had been sent to Louisiana by Louis XV of France in 1751 to help the fight against the Native Americans.

The house combines Creole style – the flagstone carriage-way, a courtyard, an external spiral staircase, and lacy iron galleries – with Greek Revival detail in the mantels and moldings. In the 1940s, the Nathaniel Felton family restored it completely. Today it is a small hotel, exquisitely furnished with authentic antiques and decoration.

Grand entrance to the Beauregard-Keyes House

Gallier House Museum ⑧

1132 Royal St. **Map** 5 D1. *Tel 525-5661.* 🚌 *3, 5, 55, 81.* ⬜ *10am–3:30pm Mon, Fri, Sat.* ⬛ *public hols.* 📷 📱 www.hgghh.org

In 1857, James Gallier, Jr. designed this attractive residence, which combines architectural elements of the Creole, with great height and verticality, and the American townhouse, with Federal-style windows and doorways *(see pp34–5)*. The interior incorporated many innovations of its time, including an ingenious hot-water and ventilation system. The kitchen was also inside the house, which was unusual for the period because of the danger of fire. On the exterior, the rosebud design of the railings is striking.

Inside, visitors can view the "isolation room," a sparsely furnished room designed for the sick. Many households had such a room, which was not surprising in a city that experienced 23 yellow fever epidemics between 1718 and 1860.

James Gallier, Jr. was the son of the city's renowned architect James Gallier, Sr., who designed Gallier Hall *(see p95).* Gallier Hall served as the City Hall until the 1950s. James Gallier, Jr. also designed the portico of the Louisiana State Bank building *(see p48).*

Gallier House, an innovative 19th-century residence

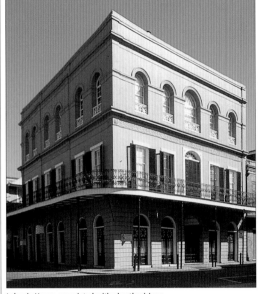

Lalaurie House, associated with ghostly visions

Lalaurie House ⑨

1140 Royal St. **Map** 5 D1. 🚌 *3, 5, 55.* ⬛ *to the public.*

Residents of the French Quarter still hurry past this otherwise lovely building because of its grim associations and reputation for ghosts. It was built in 1832 for a distinguished couple, Dr. Leonard Louis Nicolas Lalaurie and his wife, Delphine, who were well known for their fashionable and lavish parties.

At these social events, though, guests could not help but notice the condition of the servants, who were painfully thin and seemed to be terrified of their mistress. The gossip about how she treated her slaves was confirmed on April 10, 1834, when a fire broke out at the residence. When neighbors rushed in to extinguish the fire and save the contents, they found seven half-starved and manacled slaves. A story in the local press further fueled the outrage,

Front door at Lalaurie House

and a mob arrived intent on destroying the place. During the melee, Madame Lalaurie and her husband escaped unharmed. After she died in 1842, it is believed that her body was secretly returned from Paris and was buried in St. Louis Cemetery #1 *(see p82)* or #2 *(see p83).* During the Civil War *(see pp18–19)* the house served as a Union head-quarters; later it was used variously as a school, conservatory of music, and gaming house.

A private residence now, some locals still swear that the house is haunted, and that the clanking of chains can be heard.

Latrobe House ⑩

721 Governor Nicholls St. **Map** 5 D1. 🚌 *3, 5, 55.* ⬛ *to the public.*

When Benjamin Henry Latrobe designed this building in 1814, with its sturdy Doric columns, he helped launch the mania in New Orleans for Greek

Revival-style architecture. Known as the first professional architect in the US, Benjamin Henry Latrobe (1764–1820) was born in England, and after working as a professional architect for several years in Europe he came to the United States in 1796. Latrobe was highly influential, and built a variety of private residences and public buildings, the latter ranging from waterworks to cathedrals. He is largely responsible for the interior of the US Capitol Building, and for the East Portico of the White House. He died in New Orleans of yellow fever while supervising the building of a new waterworks.

Gauche Villa, with its superb original ironwork

Gauche Villa ⓫

704 Esplanade Ave at Royal.
Map 5 D1. 🚌 3. 🚋 *Riverfront.*
🚫 *to the public.*

The beautiful ironwork of this residence is uniquely integral to the villa's overall design, which accounts for the building's harmonious appearance. Little of the cast ironwork in New Orleans was constructed at the same time as the building – mostly it was added as an after-thought. Numerous patterns are used on the fence, the gate, the balconies, and the parapet, casting lovely shadows on the stucco exterior on sun-filled days. A bacchant surrounded by grapevines adorns the balcony, cast in Saarbrucken, Germany, and shipped to New Orleans. Rows of anthema and other Greek floral motifs decorate the edge of the roof and the fence posts. Architect James Freret designed the house for crockery merchant John Gauche in 1856.

Esplanade Avenue ⓬

Maps 2 B2/C2–3 and 3 D3/E4.
🚌 *3, 46, 48.*

Today, Esplanade Avenue acts as the dividing line between the French Quarter and Faubourg Marigny, and extends from the Mississippi to Bayou St. John. As early as the 1830s, this broad, tree-lined 3-mile (2-km)-long street cut through what was the most aristocratic Creole neighborhood of impressive villas and townhouses. The fashionable elite paraded in their carriages past the many elegant residences, some of which have survived to this day.

Many of these homes were designed by the city's fore-most architects, including Henry Howard, James Gallier, Sr., and William and James Freret. Their styles range from Greek Revival to Italianate and Queen Anne. Most are still private residences, but some have been converted into handsome bed-and-breakfasts. A stroll along this street will reveal over 190 homes that were built before 1900. Every block contains numerous architectural gems.

Elegant residences lining Esplanade Avenue

Old US Mint ❶

Fort St. Charles was the original occupant of this site; it was here that Andrew Jackson reviewed his troops before the Battle of New Orleans *(see p17)*. The Greek Revival building seen today, was built in 1835 by William Strickland, and functioned as a mint until 1909. In 1931, it was converted into a federal prison; later, it was used by the Coast Guard. Today the Mint houses a permanent exhibition on coins and coin-making as well as the Louisiana State Museum's world-famous jazz collection. Following severe damage from Hurricane Katrina, it is undergoing a major renovation to create a new Jazz Museum and performance space.

Trombone slide detail

★ History of the Old US Mint Exhibition
A selection of the gold and silver coins formerly minted here are displayed in this glittering exhibit.

Early Jazz
Vintage photographs depict the early bands with their jug and tin drums, washboards, kazoos, and other homemade instruments.

Ironwork
The balconies and railings display some of the city's beautiful wrought iron.

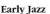

Ebony Clarinet
George Lewis, who was most popular during the 1950s and 1960s, played this clarinet.

★ New Orleans Jazz Collection
Original musical instruments, vintage photographs, and historic documents show the evolution from Dixieland to modern jazz music.

Cornet
Louis Armstrong learned to play jazz on this horn.

VISITORS' CHECKLIST

400 Esplanade Ave. **Map** 5 E1.
Tel (504) 568-6968. 🚇 Riverfront. 🚌 3, 55. ◯ 10am–4:30pm Tue–Sat, noon–4:30pm Sun.
⬤ public hols. 🚫 📷 📱 **http://** lsm.crt.state.la.us/mintex.htm

Conference room

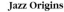

New Orleans-style Band
Murals such as this, showing the traditional jazz line-up, formed by cornet, clarinet, trombone, drums, string bass, and banjo, are part of the Jazz Museum at the Mint.

Louisiana State Museum Archive

Daniel Dana
fashioned this spear-pointed fence in the 1850s.

Jazz Origins
A selection of photographs of early jazz bands and musicians, as well as a steamboat scale model, are displayed at the Jazz Collection entrance.

Main Façade
Visitors enter the Old US Mint through a grand Neo-Classical portico, which has been carefully restored along with the rest of the building.

STAR EXHIBITS

★ History of the Old US Mint Exhibition

★ New Orleans Jazz Collection

Central Grocery ⑬

923 Decatur. **Map** 5 D2.
Tel 620-0174. 🚌 3, 5, 55.
🚋 Riverfront. ◯ 9am–5pm Tue–Sat.
◼ ⑪

This historic store, one of the
few Italian delis left in the
city, sells all kinds of Italian
food, from pasta, provolone,
and mozzarella, to sausages,
parmesan, and olive oil. In
the 1890s many Italians began
to move to the French
Quarter, and became major
stallholders at the nearby
French Market *(see p68)*.
Today, customers gather at the
counters at the back of the
store to order another specialty,
the *muffaletta (see p172)*,
which is a sizable sandwich
filled with deli meats and
cheeses. The most vital
ingredient, however, is the
olive salad – a blend of olives,
celery, carrots, cauliflower,
and capers, which can also be
purchased at the store.

**Olive salad and other deli
specialties at the Central Grocery**

Café du Monde ⑭

800 Decatur. **Map** 5 D2.
Tel 525-4544. 🚌 3, 5, 55.
🚋 Riverfront. ◯ 24 hours daily.
⬤ Dec 24 and 25. ♿ ▢ ▯
www.cafedumonde.com

Everyone who visits New
Orleans stops here for a plate
of sugar-dusted *beignets*
(square French donuts)
accompanied by *café au
lait* or the famous chicory-
flavored version, iced coffee
or a glass of milk. This 100-
year old coffeehouse is perfect
for relaxing at a table under
the arcade and listening to
the street musicians entertain,

Taking a break at Café du Monde, with *beignets* and coffee

or just people-watch. During
the mid-19th century there
were as many as 500 similar
coffeehouses in the French
Quarter. Coffee was one of
New Orleans' most important
commodities, and the coffee
trade helped the economy
recover after the Civil War,
when New Orleans vied with
New York City to control
coffee imports. During the
Civil War, locals drank coffee
flavored with peanuts and
pecan shells, to make
the coffee supply last.

Madame John's Legacy ⑮

632 Dumaine St. **Map** 5 D2.
Tel 568-6968. 🚌 3, 5, 55.
🚋 Riverfront. ◯ 10am–4:30pm
daily. ⬤ public hols. 📷 ▯
http://lsm.crt.state.la.us/madam

Dating from 1789, this is
one of the oldest surviving
residences in the Mississippi
Valley. It is a typical
Creole plantation-
style house,
supported on brick piers
which rise some 9 ft (3m) off
the ground. A veranda,
accessible via French windows
from all the rooms, extends
around the first floor.

The name Madame John's
Legacy refers to George
Washington Cable's famous
story *Tite Poulette* (1873), in
which the hero leaves a
residence as a legacy to his
quadroon mistress, who sells
the building, deposits the cash
in a bank, and loses it all when
the bank fails. Cable used this
residence as a model of the
home in his story. In the late
19th century, the house was
converted into rental apartments, which were occupied
by a mixture of immigrants.

Today, exhibits in the first-
floor galleries relate the history
of the house and its many
owner-residents. Among them
were Jean Pascal, a Provençal
sea captain who built the
original house on this site
before being killed by Natchez
Indians in 1729; pirate-admiral
René Beluche, who
was born here

Madame John's Legacy, the oldest residence in the Mississippi Valley

and later served in the Venezuelan Revolutionary Navy; and the Segher family, whose house-hold inventory featured four slaves, including a mulatto, valued at $2,500, and his daughter, who was valued at only $1,200, because she had been promised her freedom at age 30. The second-floor galleries are now used for contemporary art exhibitions.

Cornstalk Fence 🟏

915 Royal St. **Map** 5 D2. 🚌 *3, 5, 55.*

This handsome cast-iron landmark fence is one of three remaining in the city *(see p106)*. It was erected around 1850, when cast iron began replacing wrought iron *(see pp38–9)*. The cornstalks are entwined with morning glories, and each element is painted in its natural color – yellow for the ears of corn, green for the stalks, and blue for the morning glories. A butterfly decorates the central portion of the gate, and a spray of holly adorns the bottom. It was cast by the prestigious Philadelphia company, Wood & Perot.

View of Artillery Park and Moonwalk on the Mississippi River

Washington Artillery Park and Moon Walk 🟐

Decatur Street (between St. Ann and St. Peter sts). **Map** 5 D2. 🚌 *3, 5, 55.* 🚋 *Riverfront.*

Washington Artillery Park faces Jackson Square from across Decatur Street. Inside the park is an austere concrete amphitheater with a central staircase leading to the Moon Walk. This community boardwalk was named after former New Orleans Mayor Maurice "Moon"

Landrieu, who approved the construction of a boardwalk that made the riverfront area accessible to the public in the 1970s. For decades, it had been walled off by port authorities, so the public was able to re-establish its historic relationship with the riverfront.

Today Moon Walk is favored by street performers. Crowds often gather to witness impromptu performances by solo musicians, including guitarists, clarinetists, saxophonists, trombonists, and steel drummers, who play with an open music case at their feet to collect donations.

Standing on the Moon Walk, the audience can enjoy a welcome break from the city's humidity, as a constant breeze along the waterfront makes temperatures feel several degrees cooler than in the rest of the city. It also provides an excellent vantage point from which to view the river, Jackson Square, and the surrounding area.

Stone steps lead right down from the boardwalk to the Mississippi River where you can sit and dangle your feet in the whiskey-colored water, or watch the steamboats, ocean-going barges, and other river traffic float past. Do not attempt to stand in the river, however, as the current is deceptively rapid and powerful.

If you do want to get closer to the water, there are plenty of river cruises – from 1-hour sight-seeing trips to romantic night-time dinner cruises *(see p217).*

Cast-iron Cornstalk Fence and hotel

Tree-shaded passage in Washington Square

Lafitte's Blacksmith Shop ⑱

941 Bourbon St. **Map** 5 D1.
Tel 593-9761. 🚌 *3, 55, 89.*
◯ *10am–4am daily.* ♿ 🏠
🍴 🍸 🍽 🎵

This is the oldest bar in New Orleans. It is an example of the brick between posts *(see p34)* French-style building, and was constructed some-time before 1772, although the precise date is unknown. Inside, several small fireplaces warm the place on cool evenings, and there is also a small patio containing a sculpture of Adam and Eve embracing on a bed of ivy. The sculpture was created by an artist as payment for his bar bill.

Despite its name, there is no proof that the pirate brothers, Jean and Pierre Lafitte, oper-ated a smithy here as a front for their smuggling activities. Very little documentation of their lives exists, so that many myths have been woven around these two legendary figures. They operated as smugglers and were prominent slave traffickers, selling all manner of contraband, including seized slave ships, when the importation of slaves into the United States was forbidden in 1808. They earned local gratitude by warning the Americans of the planned British attack on

New Orleans, and with their band they fought bravely in the ensuing battle *(see p17)*. Regardless of whether this shop was indeed occupied by the Lafitte brothers, the building certainly existed to witness Jean Lafitte brazenly walking the streets when posters calling for his capture were plastered all over town.

Just up Bourbon Street from Lafitte's stands another bar, called Lafitte's in Exile. It is so called because, until the early 1950s, gays frequented the old Lafitte's; when the bar changed hands, its new owner refused to renew the lease, and in 1953 its gay patrons were driven into exile. They established their new quarters just up the street at Lafitte's in Exile, making it the oldest gay bar in the US.

Washington Square ⑲

Frenchman between Royal and Dauphine. **Map** 5 E1. ◯ *9am–6pm daily.* 🚌 *3, 5, 55.* ♿

Washington Square, one of the earliest parks to be laid out in New Orleans, was created in 1808. It lies at the center of the Faubourg Marigny, today the most "bohemian" part of the city and home to most of the city's gay community. The park is a good place to throw a frisbee and for ball games, or just to relax on the vast green areas it offers. There are also open-air concerts here in summer, a wine festival in September and caroling in December.

Water lily at the American Aquatic Gardens

American Aquatic Gardens ⑳

621 Elysian Fields. **Map** 5 E1.
Tel 944-0410. 🚌 *3, 5, 55.* ◯ *9am–4pm daily.* ◯ *major holidays.* 🏠
www.americanaquaticgardens.com

This delightful "store," which occupies half a city block, is the largest – and widely con-sidered the best – aquatic plant nursery and garden supply

The historic Lafitte's Blacksmith Shop

Main entrance to Armstrong Park

store in the United States. It is worth visiting for its glorious display of aquatic and exotic plants in the outdoor gardens, which include an Asian garden complete with decorative Buddhas and Oriental lanterns. The water gardens contain exquisite water lilies, and there are also spectacular sculpted fountains, handsome statuary, attractive pond designs, and ornamental wall planters. The gardens were quite badly damaged by Hurricane Katrina, but they have now been repaired.

Armstrong Park ㉑

Rampart St between St. Peter St and St. Ann St. **Map** 4 C1.
🚌 5, 48, 88, 89. 🎵

Named for the legendary trumpeter Louis "Satchmo" Armstrong *(see pp20–21)*, this spacious park stands on hallowed jazz ground. It is situated near what used to be Storyville *(see p81)*, the legal red-light district that nurtured so many of the early jazz artists.

Armstrong's statue stands in the park, and his name is emblazoned on the arch at St. Ann Street. He was born in New Orleans on August 4, 1901, and as a boy he spent his time singing on the streets

in a quartet until he was sent to the Colored Waifs' Home after firing a pistol in public. It was there that he learned to play the trumpet, and soon he was talented enough to challenge such leading players as Joe "King" Oliver and Freddie Keppard. He left New Orleans in 1922 to join King Oliver in Chicago, and went on to build an international career, entertaining audiences until his

death in 1971. The park features an artificial lake, the Municipal Auditorium, the Mahalia Jackson Theater of the Performing Arts *(see p80)*, and Congo Square *(see p80)*, and has a bust of Sidney Bechet, the great clarinetist and soprano saxophone player. Bechet was born in New Orleans in 1897, but spent most of his life performing in London, Paris, and New York.

WOMEN IN JAZZ

Jazz was not solely a male preserve; many noted female singers and musicians also made their names in New Orleans. Blanche Thomas declined the life of endless one-night stands and stayed in the city singing the blues with such artists as Al Hirt and Pete Fountain. She could be heard in the bars along Bourbon Street in the early 1970s, where her command of traditional jazz and big blues voice made her a particular favorite. Singer Louise "Blue Lu"

Blanche Thomas

Barker is said to have influenced both Billie Holiday and Eartha Kitt. Lizzie Miles dazzled the crowds in the 1920s, and Esther Bigeou was dubbed the "Creole songbird" in the 1930s. There were also some prominent female instrumentalists in the early jazz bands – pianists like Sweet Emma Barrett and Lil Hardin. The most famous female jazz musicians to emerge from New Orleans were the Boswell Sisters *(see p21)*, a trio of middle-class white girls who learned jazz from growing up in a mixed-race neighborhood. Their close harmonies and up-tempo tunes propelled them out of New Orleans and on to a national weekly radio program in the 1930s, and then into movies.

Congo Square ㉒

N Rampart St, between St. Peter St and St. Philip St. **Map** 4 C1.
🚌 5, 48, 88, 89. ♿

Under the *Code Noir* (an edict concerning the treatment of slaves), slaveholders were forbidden to work slaves on Sunday in order to encourage them to attend church and become good Roman Catholics. Such minimal amounts of freedom allowed the slaves of New Orleans to retain more of their African heritage than those in other parts of the South. On Sunday afternoons, during the 18th and early 19th century, slaves and free people of color would gather in Congo Square (also known as *Place des Nègres*), part of Armstrong Park *(see p79)*, to speak in their native African tongues. They would sing and dance, and perform the *calinda*, an African line dance, and the *bamboula*. These dances were one of the chief origins of jazz, and Congo Square is thus remembered as one of the birthplaces of jazz music. The infamous Marie Laveau *(see p83)* is said to have performed voodoo rituals here.

Sidney Bechet's statue

Congo Square, home of the calinda and bamboula dances

Mahalia Jackson Theater of the Performing Arts ㉓

Armstrong Park, Rampart St between St. Peter St and St. Ann St. **Map** 4 C1. **Tel** 525-1052. 🚌 48, 46, 52, 57. 📷 ♿ www.mahaliajackson theater.com

Named for the celebrated gospel singer Mahalia Jackson (1911–72), this theater is used by local and visiting dance, music, and theater companies.

A New Orleans native, Jackson began her career singing in the local church, where her father was a pastor. At the age of 16 she moved to Chicago and opened first a beauty shop, then a flower store. Despite her strict upbringing, she fell in love with the syncopated rhythms of blues but never sang the more bawdy songs in its repertoire. Jackson was discovered in the 1930s and made her first recording in 1934. Her career took her to Carnegie Hall, the Newport Jazz Festival, and other major music venues. Jackson was also active in the civil rights movement and was a supporter of Martin Luther King, Jr.

The theater suffered flood damage after Hurricane Katrina but has been restored.

The Mahalia Jackson Theater of the Performing Arts

For hotels and restaurants in this region see pp163–4 and pp177–9

**Stained-glass window,
Our Lady of Guadalupe**

Our Lady of
Guadalupe ㉔

411 N. Rampart St. **Map** 4 B2.
Tel *525-1551.* 48, 46, 52, 57.
9am–5pm daily.

Renamed Our Lady of Guadalupe in 1875, when it served
an Italian congregation,

St. Anthony's Chapel was built
on the outskirts of the French
Quarter in 1826, when funerals
were no longer being held
in St. Louis Cathedral, for fear
of spreading yellow fever
(see p18). It was originally
known as "Mortuary Chapel"
because all the bodies were
taken directly from the chapel
to St. Louis Cemetery #1
(see p82), via the back
entrance. It displays several
brilliantly colored stained-glass
windows, representing different
saints honored by devoted
New Orleanians.

The most visited altar is dedicated to St. Jude, the "patron
saint of hopeless causes," but
a more light-hearted one stands
to the left of the exit; this is
dedicated to New Orleans' very
own St. Expedite, whose name
is not in any official dictionary
of saints. According to apoc-
ryphal legend, a crate marked
with the word "Spedito!"
(meaning "rush") arrived in
the chapel one day. The statue
inside it was removed and
mounted on the wall, and its
name was confused with the
word on the box. To this day,

New Orleanians visit the altar
to pray for help when they
need something in a hurry.
St. Expedite is also associated
with voodoo *(see p83)*, which
is why the church is called
the "voodoo church." Guadalupe is the official place of
worship for the police and
fire departments, whose altar
stands to the right of the
main altar.

Our Lady of Guadalupe

STORYVILLE

From 1897 to 1917 the 38 blocks roughly
bounded by Iberville, Basin, Robertson, and
St. Louis streets were set aside as a legal red-
light district *(see p22)*. Saloons and high-class
brothels lined Basin Street, cheap bawdy
houses clustered along Dauphine, Burgundy,
St. Louis, Conti, and Bienville streets, while
the poorest huts, called cribs, were found
along Rampart and Iberville streets. Names
and addresses of 700 prostitutes were listed
in the Blue Book, which was available at
bars like the Annex, which was operated
by state legislator and political boss Tom

Anderson, the informal "Mayor" of Storyville.
Many of the brothels were quite luxurious,
furnished with velvet drapes, gilt-framed
paintings and leopard-skin fabrics. At No.
317 Basin Street, Countess Willie Piazza held
court. She regularly employed pianist Jelly
Roll Morton, who played behind a screen, as
did most musicians at these establishments,
so they were not able to observe the patrons.
The district was officially closed in 1917 by
the Navy Department *(see p22)*. In the 1940s,
the Federal government leveled Storyville to
make way for low-income housing.

Mahogany Hall in Basin Street, one of Storyville's notorious bordellos

Poignant statue atop an above-ground tomb at St. Louis Cemetery #1

St. Louis Cemetery #1 ㉕

Basin St between St. Louis and Conti. **Map** 4 B2. **Tel** 482-5065. 🚌 48, 46, 52, 57. 🕐 8:30am–4pm Mon– Sat, 8:30am–3pm Sun. 🚻 🎫

This cemetery opened in 1789 and is the oldest in the city. Because of its age, it is one of the most fascinating to visit. However, this cemetery and its neighbor, St. Louis Cemetery #2, should not be visited alone; both are ideal places for muggers and pickpockets to operate. By 1829 St. Louis #1 was already filled, mostly with victims of yellow fever. Today, the narrow alleyways are full of mausoleums, many in advanced stages of decay. Although Catholic, it at one time accepted Protestants (although these graves were later moved). There are numerous legendary local figures buried here: Homer Adolph Plessy (1862–1925), who challenged the segregation laws in the 1890s (see p19); Bernard de Marigny (1788–1871), who inherited $7 million at age 15 and squandered it playing craps (dice), the game he introduced to the United States (see p102). Daniel Clark (1766–1813), the wealthy Irish merchant who challenged Governor Claiborne (see p17) to a duel and wounded him in the leg, lies here, along with his daughter Myra Clark Gaines (1803–85). She fought for 65 years to secure her father's estate, in a case that generated 8,000 pages of court documents. Jean Etienne Boré (1741–1820), the plantation owner who

was the city's first post-colonial mayor, is buried in a low brick vault. Boré contributed much to the city's prosperity as he was the first to granulate sugar on a commercial scale in 1796. Boré's grandson, the historian Charles Gayarré, is also buried here, as is Paul Morphy (1837–84), the genius chess player who was a world champion at age 13 but who later went mad. Most famous of all is probably Marie Laveau (see box, opposite), known as the voodoo queen. Crowds visit her tomb (though some believe it is not the correct one) to leave unusual voodoo "gifts" or mark it with X's, which symbolizes a request that she grant a particular wish. A more recent figure is Ernest "Dutch" Morial (1929–1989), the first black mayor and the father of another former mayor, Marc Morial. The largest tomb belongs to the Société Française de Bienfaisance, which contains 70 vaults. The tallest monument, sculpted by Pietro Gualdi in 1857 for $40,000, belongs to the Italian Society. It was the background in the psychedelic scenes in the film Easy Rider. A plaque memorializes Benjamin Henry Latrobe (see p72), the architect who came to New Orleans to build a waterworks and died in 1820 of yellow fever (see p18). No one knows where his remains are. Many bodies were moved from the St. Louis Cemetery #1 in 1823 to Lafayette Cemetery (see p102) and from there to Metairie Cemetery (see p127) in the 1950s. Somehow, Latrobe's body was lost in the shuffle.

Recommended tours (see p198) are given by the Save our Cemeteries organization, and by New Orleans Tours, Inc. Both provide plenty of excellent local information.

A beseeching angel

Ornate family mausoleums in St. Louis Cemetery #1

VOODOO WORSHIP

Voodoo arrived in New Orleans from Africa, via the Caribbean, where it originated as a form of ancestor worship among the West African tribes who were brought to North America as slaves. With the revolution in Saint Domingue in 1793, slaves and free people of color arrived as refugees and increased the practice in the city. Voodoo enabled those slaves to preserve their African culture and roots alongside the Roman Catholic religion, for it mixed both traditions. The most famous of all 19th-century voodoo leaders was Marie Laveau (c.1794–1881), a mulatto and a great marketer. She used such Catholic elements as prayer, incense, and saints in her rituals, which she opened to the public for an admission fee. The high point of the voodoo calendar was the celebration she held along the Bayou St. John on St. John's Eve. She is believed to be buried at St. Louis Cemetery #1.

Portrait of Marie Laveau

The Barelli tomb

St. Louis Cemetery #2 **26**

Iberville to St Louis St, between N Claiborne Ave and N Robertson St. **Map** 4 B1. **Tel** 482-5065. ⊞ 48, 46, 52, 57. ☐ 8:30am–4pm Mon–Sat, 8:30am–3pm Sun. ☐ ☐

By the end of the colonial period, and mostly because of a devastating series of epidemics, this cemetery was established as the natural extension of St. Louis Cemetery #1 around 1823. The final resting place for much of New Orleans' 19th-century Creole aristocracy, it contains remarkably ornate mausoleums. Many of them were designed by Jacques Nicholas Bussière De Pouilly, who arrived in New Orleans from France in the 1830s. His plans were inspired by the tombs in Paris's Père Lachaise Cemetery. Grand in design and scale, and modeled on Greek, Egyptian, and other Classical styles, the patterns for these ambitious mausoleums became very popular in New Orleans.

Creole family mausoleum, fallen into disrepair

The tombs are like impressive residences, often enclosed within beautiful wrought-iron gates, featuring such motifs as lyres, winged hourglasses, hearts, inverted torches, and urns with arrows. The fences around the tombs are some of the finest wrought-iron work in the city. The intricate immortelles made of wire, beads, and glass are also unique and represent everlasting tributes to the dead.

Among the notables buried here are General Jean Baptiste Plauché, who fought with Andrew Jackson at the Battle of New Orleans (see p17). J. N. B. DePouilly himself is humbly buried in a modest wall vault with his brother, who was also an architect. Other famous New Orleans figures buried here include jazz musician Danny Barker, and the pirate Dominique You (see p17), who rests in the main aisle in a tomb marked with a Masonic emblem and the inscription: "This New Bayard could have witnessed the end of the world without fear or trembling." Near the cemetery office, the Barelli tomb recalls the tragedy that occurred on November 15, 1849, when the steamer *Louisiana* exploded, killing 86 people, including the young son of Joseph Barelli, who erected the memorial in 1856. Five sculpted angels hover around the tomb and a bas-relief depicts the explosion.

A common legend says that Napoleon Bonaparte's followers were waiting for his arrival in New Orleans from his exile in St. Helena, but since he died beforehand on December 20, 1821, a funeral service for him was held here.

Like St. Louis #1, the cemetery is in a secluded area where lone visitors have been robbed. Guided visits, available from several organizations (see p198), are advisable.

Tree-shaped statue

WAREHOUSE AND CENTRAL BUSINESS DISTRICTS

When the Americans arrived after the Louisiana Purchase *(see p17)* they developed a community of their own on the upriver side of Canal Street. It was called the Faubourg St. Mary and extended from Canal Street to Louisiana Avenue. Between 1820 and 1860 the waterfront was developed, and behind it grew a commercial and residential district that matched the Creole district downriver. Today the CBD incorporates narrow streets lined with Victorian warehouses, banks, and office buildings, as well as such broad thoroughfares as Poydras, which is lined with skyscrapers belonging to oil companies, hotels, and financial institutions.

Louisiana State Seal at the Spanish Plaza

SIGHTS AT A GLANCE

Museums and Galleries
Confederate Memorial Hall **16**
Custom House/Audubon
  Insectarium **9**
Gallier Hall **11**
Louisiana Children's Museum **18**
The National WWII Museum **19**
New Orleans Contemporary
  Arts Center **17**
Ogden Museum of
  Southern Art **15**

Shopping Areas
Canal Place **8**
Riverwalk
  Marketplace **4**

Entertainment
*Audubon Aquarium of the
  Americas pp90–91* **7**
Harrah's Casino **6**
Louisiana Superdome **12**
Orpheum Theater **13**

Landmarks
World Trade Center **5**

Churches
St. Patrick's Church **10**

Parks and Squares
Lee Circle **14**
Spanish Plaza **3**
Woldenberg Riverfront Park **1**

Boat Trips
Ferry to Algiers **2**

KEY

- ▨ Street-by-Street map *See pp86–7*
- 🚆 Railroad station
- 🚌 Bus station
- 🚊 Streetcar stop
- ⛴ Ferry boarding point
- ⊠ Post office

GETTING THERE
RTA routes 44, 41, and 34 run from the Lakefront, Mid-City, and Uptown to this area. The Canal Street, St. Charles Avenue and Riverfront streetcars have stops in the area.

◁ Canal Street at dusk

Street-by-Street: CBD

Spanish coat-of-arms

When the Americans arrived from the North in the early 1800s they developed the uptown side of Canal Street. It is still the city's commercial area, where the headquarters of oil, energy, and banking corporations and many public institutions are located. The median running through the middle of Canal Street was the neutral ground separating the English-speaking Americans from the French-speaking Creole community. Today, Canal Street is lined with hotels, restaurants, and stores. A casino and the ferry to Algiers are located at the riverfront end. During the last three decades the riverfront has been totally redeveloped with parks, walks, and such major attractions as the Aquarium and Riverwalk Marketplace.

Harrah's Casino
This enormous casino, with its garish over-the-top decor, is open 24 hours a day, 365 days a year ❻

World Trade Center
Built in the shape of a Greek cross, this 1960s skyscraper towers over the river, port, and Warehouse District ❺

Riverwalk Marketplace
Containing more than 120 stores, including a huge food court, this is one of the largest malls in the city ❹

TCHOPITOULA

MISSISSIPPI RIVER

Ferry to Algiers
A free ferry takes visitors across the Mississippi to Algiers ❷

Spanish Plaza
This plaza has a beautiful fountain at its center ❸

For hotels and restaurants in this region see pp164–5 and pp179–80

STAR SIGHTS

★ Audubon Aquarium of the Americas

★ River Cruises

Canal Place
The city's most upscale shopping mall features big names such as Saks, Gucci, and Williams-Sonoma. There is also a theater and a cinema on the third floor ❽

LOCATOR MAP
See Street Finder, maps 4, 5, and 8.

| 0 meters | 100 |
| 0 yards | 100 |

★ **Audubon Aquarium of the Americas**
Marine life sculptures by Ida Kohlmeyer are at the entrance ❼

★ **River Cruises**
The Cajun Queen *and* John James Audubon *offer cruises from the Audubon Aquarium of the Americas (see p217).*

Woldenberg Riverfront Park
Named for local businessman Malcolm Woldenberg, the park contains a charming statue of Woldenberg, but the most notable sculpture is the 16-ft (5-m) tall kinetic steel Ocean Song, by John Scott ❶

KEY

 Suggested route

Woldenberg Riverfront Park ●

2 Canal St. **Map** 5 D3.
Riverfront. 3, 55, 57.

The 16-acre Woldenberg Park extends all the way along the riverfront from St. Peter Street to the Riverwalk Marketplace, providing a pleasant garden setting studded with contemporary sculpture. From Jackson Square, visitors can access Woldenberg Riverfront Park via Washington Artillery Park and the Moon Walk. Here, many of the city's street performers can be found; the latter is named after Moon Landrieu, who is widely regarded as paving the way for the first black mayor, "Dutch" Morial, to be elected in 1978 *(see p23)*. The park is open from dawn till dusk daily.

Ferry to Algiers ●

The ferry is at the end of Canal St.
Map 5 D4. *Riverfront.* 55, 57.
www.oldalgiersmainstreet.com

From the foot of Canal Street, a free ferry crosses the Mississippi to the historic neighborhood of Algiers on the West Bank, offering spectacular views of the New Orleans skyline on the short journey.

Algiers was established in 1719 and is the second oldest part of the city. For over a century it was used as a depot for imported slaves,

River view from the Woldenberg Riverfront Park

who were held here before being sold on. It is possible that Algiers is the site of the origins of jazz, as single-line melodies were probably used by the slaves to communicate and to comfort themselves and their families.

The area was not connected directly to the rest of the city until a bridge was built in the late 1950s, so it has a separate, small-town feel. It has beautiful late-Victorian churches, homes, parks, and businesses, and at the heart is the Romanesque Revival-style Algiers Courthouse dating from 1896, which can be seen from the French Quarter across the river. It continues to serve the residents of the entire city as a courthouse, and is home to various municipal offices.

The courthouse is also the setting for much of the Old Algiers RiverFest, a weekend-long festival celebrating

the role of the area in the development of jazz. Visitors can enjoy great live music, various arts and crafts, and sample typical New Orleans cuisine. The festival takes place in April each year.

Spanish Plaza ●

2 Canal St. **Map** 5 D4. *Riverfront.*
3, 55, 57. 24 hrs daily.

This small plaza at the entrance to the Riverwalk Marketplace is a good place to take a rest and enjoy an uninterrupted view of the river. A fountain stands at its center, surrounded by a circular mosaic bench on which the coats of arms of Spain are depicted.

The *Creole Queen* paddle-wheeler departs from the Plaza and takes passengers downriver to the Chalmette Battlefield Park, the site of Andrew Jackson's victory at the Battle of New Orleans *(see p17)*. Rangers provide a 40-minute tour of the site. Adjacent to the battlefield is Chalmette National Cemetery, where thousands of Union soldiers are buried. An antebellum house, the Malus-Beauregard home stands on park property. This residence was built in 1833 and purchased in 1880 by the son of General P. G. T. Beauregard *(see p71)*.

Fountain at the center of the Spanish Plaza

For hotels and restaurants in this region see pp164–5 and pp179–80

Riverwalk Marketplace ❹

1 Poydras St. **Map** 5 D4. *Tel* 522-1555. 🚊 *Riverfront.* 🚌 *3, 55, 57, 65.* ◯ *10am–7pm Mon–Sat, noon–6pm Sun.* 🎫 🏛 📷 **www**.riverwalkmarketplace.com

This massive riverside shopping mall, designed by the same company that developed Boston's Faneuil Hall, contains more than 140 stores, including brand-name favorites like Eddie Bauer, Brookstone, Banana Republic, and the Museum Company. The entire top floor is the food court, while a highlight of the ground floor is the Creole Delicacies Gourmet Shop *(see p189)*, which offers a 2-hour course in cooking.

In addition to shopping opportunities, the mall has an outdoor walkway that runs along the Mississippi River, giving visitors one of the best views of the river and river traffic in the city. International and other cruise ships dock alongside the marketplace, the most notable being the one operated by the Delta Queen Steamboat Company, which was established in 1890. A number of information plaques attached to railings along the walkway describe everything from the types of boats plying their trade on the river to the seagulls that drift up from the Gulf of Mexico.

Entrance to the Riverwalk Marketplace

World Trade Center ❺

2 Canal St. **Map** 5 D4. *Tel* 529-1601. 🚊 *Riverfront.* 🚌 *57, 65.* **www**.wtcno.org

The World Trade Center building was designed by Edward Durrell Stone in the 1960s. Originally called the International Trade Mart Building, it housed the headquarters of various mercantile companies and consulates. Architecturally, it has little to recommend it; however, being built in the shape of a Greek cross, it serves as a useful landmark.

Riverside view of the WTC Building

Currently, the building is mostly vacant. The City of New Orleans, as its owner, is exploring ways to redevelop the building to take advantage of its prime location at the foot of Canal Street.

Harrah's Casino ❻

228 Poydras St. **Map** 5 D4. *Tel* 533-6000. 🚊 *Riverfront.* 🚌 *3, 57, 65.* ◯ *24 hrs daily.* 📷 🎫 🍸

This casino, which opened in October 1999, is close to the riverfront. Covering 100,000 sq ft (9,290 sq m) of floor space, Harrah's offers a vast ballroom in addition to a wide selection of games, including 2,900 slot machines and 117 table games featuring baccarat, blackjack, craps, and roulette.

Launched in July 2005, Masquerade is a state-of-the-art entertainment venue set at the heart of the casino. It features a four-storey tower surrounded by a stage for the free nightly shows. There is also an ice-topped bar and exclusive lounge area.

Audubon Aquarium of the Americas ❼

See pp90–91.

The modern and lively Harrah's, a popular New Orleans casino

Audubon Aquarium of the Americas ❼

Concentrating on the waters around New Orleans, from the Mississippi and the swamps to the Gulf of Mexico and the Caribbean, this aquarium complex features some 500 species of marine life. Highlights include a tank containing a Caribbean reef, and a replica of an oil rig. The aquarium lost much of its sea life due to generator failures in the aftermath of Hurricane Katrina. It reopened in May 2006.

Sea Horses
These are among the many creatures that can be seen being fed by divers in the Caribbean Reef tank.

The Amazon Rainforest
Piranhas lurk in the waters that flow under the forest canopy, which is inhabited by tropical birds and wild orchids.

Shark cove

Food Court
with several different kinds of restaurants.

Main entrance and information center

Gift shop

★ The Caribbean Reef
An acrylic tunnel underneath a 132,000-gallon tank provides a startling perspective to view the rays, parrot fish, and other denizens that float above.

Jellyfish
These transparent, fluid creatures sway and dance in an exhibit that is one of the largest of its kind anywhere in the United States.

★ The Gulf of Mexico
A 400,000-gallon tank holds a replica of an offshore oil rig, around which swim the species that share the waters – sharks, tarpon, sting rays, and sea turtles.

VISITORS' CHECKLIST

Canal St at Mississippi River. **Map** 5 D3. **Tel** 581-4629. Riverfront. 3, 5, 55, 57. 10am–4pm Tue–Sun (to 5pm Sat, Sun). Dec 24 and 25, Thanksgiving, Mardi Gras.

Adventure Island
This interactive play area gives kids the chance to learn what sharks and stingrays feel like and to explore a pirate ship.

Frogs! has poison dart frogs and other amphibians from around the world.

The Entergy IMAX Theater
This cinema adds a high-tech dimension to the complex. The screen is 5 ½ stories high.

Sea Otter Gallery
A lovable pair of sea otters frolic in this exhibit where a waterfall creates waves for their amusement.

★ The Mississippi River and Delta Habitat
Check out the blue-eyed, white alligator that hangs suspended in the water along with some other Mississippi regulars – catfish, gar, and turtles.

STAR FEATURES

★ The Caribbean Reef

★ The Gulf of Mexico

★ The Mississippi River and Delta Habitat

Main entrance to Canal Place and its many luxury stores

Canal Place ❽

Canal and N Peters Sts. **Map** 4 C3.
🚋 3. 🚋 Canal. ◯ 10am–7pm
Mon–Sat, noon–6pm Sun. 👤 🏠 💻
🍴 www.theshopsatcanalplace.com

Downtown's most upscale shopping mall is anchored by Saks Fifth Avenue, and contains fashionable stores such as Betsey Johnson, Kenneth Cole, Brooks Brothers, Williams-Sonoma, and Gucci. The third floor features the food court, plus the only cinema in the city that shows foreign, arthouse, and independent films.

The third floor also houses the Southern Repertory Theater, which stages cutting-edge productions and provides a showcase for local playwrights. There are spectacular views of the Mississippi River from the fourth floor.

Custom House/ Audubon Insectarium ❾

423 Canal St. **Map** 4 C3.
🚋 3. 🚋 Canal. **Audubon Insectarium Tel** 861-2537.
◯ call for opening hours.

This architectural landmark is home to the Audubon Insectarium, a state-of-the-art interactive museum with fascinating displays of termites, butterflies, and roaches.

Two of the highlights are the cooking show, which illustrates the art of cooking with insects, and Metamorphosis, a lab where visitors can observe insect courtship, mating, and life cycles.

Alexander Thompson Wood was the original architect of the Custom House, though he was succeeded by James Dakin, Confederate General Beauregard *(see p71)*, and Thomas K. Wharton. Construction began in 1847 and was completed in 1881.

Inside, the Marble Hall is a dramatic space under a ground-glass ceiling with a decorative stained-glass border and a skylight above. Juno and Mercury embellish the capitals of the marble columns that support the structure. Over the years the building has served as a post office, armory, and prison.

St. Patrick's Church ❿

724 Camp St. **Map** 4 C4. **Tel** 525-4413. 🚋 3, 41. 🚋 St. Charles.
◯ 11am–1pm Mon–Sat, 9am–1pm Sun. (Guided tours only.) 👤 📷
www.oldstpatricks.org

Old St Patrick's Church was completed in 1841 to minister to the Irish Catholic population at the urging of Father James Ignatius Mullon. The brothers Charles and James Dakin were the original architects, but James Gallier, Sr. replaced them. It is an impressive church with a 185-ft (60-m) high tower, a Gothic-inspired interior, and splendid stained-glass vaulting in the sanctuary.

Behind the altar are three paintings by the French artist Leon Pomarede. At the center is a copy of *Raphael's Transfiguration of Christ*, flanked by *St. Patrick Baptizing the Irish Princesses* and *Christ Walking on Water*. Each of these works dates to 1841. Although the Irish community has largely moved away from the neighborhood, the congregation still draws loyal followers from other districts. Father Mullon is still remembered as an ardent Confederate. He prayed publicly for a Confederate victory, and when General Benjamin "Beast" Butler *(see pp18–19)* accused him of refusing to bury a Union soldier, he volunteered that he would be "very happy to bury them all." At noon on St. Patrick's Day, a mass is attended by most Catholics as an important part of the festivities held all over the city.

The impressive tower of St. Patrick's Church

Greek Revival-style façade of Gallier Hall

Gallier Hall ⓫

543 St. Charles Ave. **Map** 4 B4.
Tel 658-3623. 🚋 St. Charles.
🕐 for tours only: 10am, 11am, noon, 2pm, 3pm. **www**.gallierhall.com

James Gallier, Sr.'s masterpiece was built between 1845 and 1853, at a cost of $342,000. Constructed of bricks that were plastered and scored to look like stone, the building is 215 ft (65.5 m) deep, extending behind a façade only 90 ft (27 m) wide. Six fluted Ionic columns support the tympanum on the façade, which is decorated with bas-reliefs of Justice and Commerce created by Robert A. Launitz.

Gallier Hall was built to serve as the headquarters of the Second Municipality when the city was briefly served by three separate governments. In 1852 it became City Hall, when the three "cities" (or districts) were reunited. Many great historical figures have lain in state here, including Jefferson Davis, president of the Confederacy, and General Beauregard.

The building faces Lafayette Square, which was laid out in 1788 as Place Gravier, and renamed in 1824. The square contains statues of statesman Benjamin Franklin by Hiram Powers, and famed Senator Henry Clay by Joel T. Hart. John McDonogh, the great benefactor of the New Orleans public schools, is remembered with

a statue by Atallio Piccirilli. Today, the building is a popular vantage point during the famous Mardi Gras parades (*see pp28–9*).

Louisiana Superdome ⓬

Sugar Bowl Drive. **Map** 4 A3.
Tel 587-3663. 🚌 16. 🚋 St.Charles.
🕐 for sporting events only. ♿ 📷
www.superdome.com
New Orleans Arena 1501 Girod St. **Map** 4 A3. *Tel* 587-3663.
www.neworleansarena.com

This flying saucer-shaped landmark is home to local football teams the Saints and Tulane University's Green Wave. It is also the venue for the annual Sugar Bowl, and other sports and entertainment events.

The Superdome has become synonymous with the suffering of those affected by Hurricane Katrina. It was here that many thousands sought refuge from the flood waters. The building was severely damaged by wind, flooding, and the frustrations of the desperate people it harbored. In September 2006, the Superdome reopened after a $193 million restoration.

As the world's largest steel-constructed stadium that is unobstructed by posts, it has hosted the Super Bowl more times than any other facility: Super Bowl XXXVI in 2002 was the sixth to be held here. The stadium will again

host the game in 2013. It was built between 1971 and 1975; it occupies 52 acres, and stands 27 stories high.

The New Orleans Arena, the "babydome", opened in 1999. In 2002 the Charlotte, North Carolina, Hornets professional basketball team moved to New Orleans and became the home team. The Arena is also home to the Tulane University basketball team.

Orpheum Theater ⓭

129 University Place. **Map** 4 B3.
🚌 3, 41. 📷 for restoration. ♿ 🎵

This Beaux-Arts terracotta building opened in 1918 as a vaudeville theater. It was designed by G. Albert Lansburgh and Samuel Stone, who lavished impressive detailing on the façade as well as an ornate vaulted ceiling and baroque-inspired interior decoration. The Orpheum has played host to a variety of music festivals, plays, and a range of public and private events but it has sat unused since being damaged by the flood of 2005. It also used to be the home of the Louisiana Philharmonic Orchestra (LPO).

Orpheum Theater detail

The LPO currently performs in the Mahalia Jackson Theater and other venues around town.

Louisiana Superdome, one of the world's largest indoor stadiums

Memorial to Robert E. Lee at Lee Circle

Lee Circle ⑭

St. Charles Ave & Howard Ave. **Map** 4 B5. 🚌 *3, 41.* 🚃 *St. Charles.* ♿

The towering 60-ft (18-m) column at the center of Lee Circle, topped by a 16-ft (5-m) statue of Confederate general Robert E. Lee, is one of the city's key landmarks. For many years the Lee Circle area was merely a grubby intersection favored by homeless people. More recently, however, it has become the anchor of an attractive new museum district. The brand new Ogden Museum of Southern Art opens on to the circle and the D-Day Museum is just a block away. Meanwhile, these additions have boosted the regeneration of existing museums nearby, such as the New Orleans Contemporary Arts Center and the Confederate Memorial Hall.

The statue of Robert E. Lee is one of three prominent tributes to Confederate leaders in New Orleans, the others being of Jefferson Davis and Gen. P.G.T. Beauregard, located in separate parts of Mid-City. However, the city was not an especially staunch rebel stronghold. It was evenly split over the secession

issue, and it fell early in the Civil War due to poor defenses and an unwillingness to see the city burned down.

Ogden Museum of Southern Art ⑮

Camp St at Howard Ave. **Map** 4 B5. **Tel** 539-9600. 🚌 *3, 11.* 🚃 *St. Charles.* ◻ *10am–5pm Wed–Sun.* 📷 🅿 ♿ **www**.ogdenmuseum.org

Opened in 1994, this museum is named for Roger H. Ogden, a philanthropist who donated the core collection of some 1,200 works by more than 400 Southern artists. The museum displays its artworks in a two-building complex connected by a corridor gallery. The Romanesque-style Howard Memorial Library was designed by native-born

Henry Hobson Richardson in 1888. This architectural masterpiece, with its splendid wood-paneled rotunda, is incorporated into the newly designed, modern Goldring Hall. These two structures are designed to wrap around the Confederate Memorial Hall, so that the complex fronts both Camp Street and Lee Circle.

The museum contains works from the 18th to the 21st century, and portrays the diversity of urban and rural life in the South from the Depression to the modern day. The collection includes works by William Henry Buck, Clarence Millet, John McCrady, George Dureau, Robert Gordy, Clementine Hunter, and Ida Kohlmeyer.

The museum is operating a reduced timetable as a result of Hurricane Katrina. On Thursdays, the Ogden After Hours features live music, refreshments, and special exhibits.

Confederate Memorial Hall ⑯

929 Camp St at Howard Ave. **Map** 4 B5. **Tel** 523-4522. 🚌 *3, 11, 41.* 🚃 *St. Charles.* ◻ *10am–4pm Wed–Sat.* 🔵 *major holidays.* **www**.confederatemuseum.com

One of the oldest museums in the city, Confederate Memorial Hall offers a moving experience. The memorabilia on display tell the often tragic, personal stories of the many young men who fought in the Civil War. Some were teenagers, like Landon Creek, who had fought in seven battles and was wounded three times by the age

The Howard Memorial Library, now part of the Ogden Museum

of 15. Several display cases contain objects relating to the occupation of the city by General "Beast" Butler *(see p18)*, including the document ordering that all women who insulted Union officers, wore Confederate colors, or sang Southern songs, were to be locked up as if they were common prostitutes.

The museum also possesses a large collection associated with the Confederate president Jefferson Davis, from his cradle to his military boots. Several interesting exhibits are devoted to the black regiments, which served on both sides during the Civil War. The cypress hall of the museum was originally constructed in 1891 as a meeting place for Confederate veterans to reflect on their Civil War experiences and to house and protect their relics.

Replica of one of the Higgins boats in The National WWII Museum

Modern art bench, at the Contemporary Arts Center

New Orleans Contemporary Arts Center ⑰

900 Camp St. **Map** 4 C5. *Tel* 528-3805. 🚋 11. 🚃 St. Charles. ◐ 11am–4pm Thu–Sun. ● public hols. 📷 📹 🔵 **www**.cacno.org

This warehouse-style center is the city's premier space for all of the contemporary arts, from dance, painting, film, and video, to performance art, theater, and music. The museum combines the original structure with modern designs to its full advantage, presenting a unique, modern space mostly illuminated with natural light that houses four galleries and two theaters. The rotating shows in the galleries usually remain for four to eight weeks. The café provides free Internet access.

Louisiana Children's Museum ⑱

420 Julia St. **Map** 4 C5. *Tel* 523-1357. 🚋 10, 11. 🚃 St. Charles. ◐ 9:30am–4:30pm Tue–Sat, noon–4:30pm Sun. ● public hols. 📷 📹 🔵 **www**.lcm.org

This activity-oriented museum allows children to entertain themselves with a variety of role-playing games, plus other interactive exhibits with a didactic focus. Kids can anchor their own news show in the TV studio, go shopping in the supermarket, or pilot their own tugboat, and there is an area designed specifically for one- to three-year-olds. One of the museum's newest exhibits is a child-sized replica of the Port of New Orleans.

The Louisiana Children's Museum, playground for children of all ages

The National WWII Museum ⑲

945 Magazine St and Howard Ave. **Map** 4 C5. *Tel* 527-6012. 🚋 3, 41. ◐ 9am–5pm Tue–Sun. ● Thanksgiving, Dec 24 and 25, Mardi Gras. 📷 📹 🔵 **www**.ddaymuseum.org

This museum honors the veterans of World War II and celebrates New Orleans shipbuilder Andrew Higgins, who played a major role in many events, including D-Day in June 1944 *(see p22)*. More than 20,000 of Higgins's crafts were deployed in US landings on all fronts during the war, from North Africa to the Pacific Islands. Among the most inspiring exhibits on display are nine oral history stations which feature real-life stories narrated by the participants. They are accompanied by all kinds of wartime memorabilia donated by veterans, including letters, uniforms, and weapons. Electronic maps, mini-theaters, and photomurals illustrate the role played by the US in World War II. The museum is currently undergoing a $300-million expansion that will quadruple its size by 2015. The new facility will cover all the theaters of World War II and include vintage vehicles, such as tanks and planes, and a 400-seat theater.

Loyola University

SIGHTS AT A GLANCE

Historic Buildings
Brevard-Wisdom-Rice House ⓭
Briggs-Staub House ❹
Carroll-Crawford House ❼
Claiborne Cottage ❸
Colonel Short's Villa ⓫
Louise S. McGehee School ❻
Musson-Bell House ⓬
Payne-Strachan House ⓮
Robinson House ❺
Toby's Corner ❾
Women's Guild Opera
   House ❿

Museums and Galleries
Amistad Collection ⓱
Mardi Gras World ❽
Newcomb Art Gallery ⓲

Cemeteries
Lafayette Cemetery ❷

Universities
Loyola University ⓯
Tulane University ⓰

Entertainment
Audubon Park ⓳
Audubon Zoo pp112–13 ⓴
Riverbend ㉑

Landmarks
*St. Charles Avenue Streetcar
   pp104–5* ❶

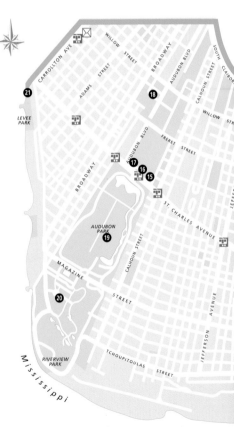

GARDEN DISTRICT AND UPTOWN

In 1832 a residential quarter was established uptown on the former Livaudais Plantation. The land was subdivided and developed to create the city of Lafayette, which was incorporated into New Orleans in 1852. Here, between Jackson and Louisiana avenues, and St. Charles Avenue and Magazine Street, wealthy merchants, planters, and bankers built mansions in a variety of styles, ranging from Greek Revival to Italianate and Queen Anne. The area became known as the Garden District because of the lush gardens that were laid out around the mansions. Settlement continued across Uptown as New Orleans annexed Jefferson City and Carrollton. Fears were high that these architecturally and historically significant neighborhoods would be damaged in the aftermath of Hurricane Katrina, but they were spared by the waters and remain as beautiful as ever.

Stone sculpture at Tulane University

KEY

- Street-by-Street map
  See pp100–1
- Streetcar stop
- Ferry boarding point
- Post office
- Hospital

0 meters 500
0 yards 500

GETTING THERE

The St. Charles Ave. streetcar runs through the entire area. RTA routes 90 and 24 run from Carrollton and Napoleon avenues to Mid-City. Route 10 runs along Tchoupitoulas St. and 11 goes along Magazine St.

Street-by-Street: Garden District

When the Americans arrived in New Orleans, they settled upriver from the French Quarter. The plantations that lined St. Charles Avenue in the 1820s were subdivided and the city of Lafayette established. It was incorporated into the city of New Orleans in 1852. Today, this area is referred to as the Garden District, a residential neighborhood filled with grand Victorian mansions built by wealthy city merchants and planters. The gardens, planted with magnolia, camellia, sweet olive, jasmine, and azalea, are as stunning as the residences themselves.

LOCATOR MAP
See Street Finder maps 6 and 7

★ **Lafayette Cemetery**
Confederate General Harry T. Hays and Samuel Jarvis Peters, a wealthy 19th-century developer of the Garden District, are buried in this cemetery, which often appears in Anne Rice's books ❷

Commander's Palace
Excellent Creole food is the specialty of this landmark restaurant, one of the best in the US (see p182).

KEY

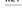

― ― ― Suggested route

★ **Colonel Short's Villa**
Built in 1859 for Colonel Robert Short of Kentucky and designed by Henry Howard, the house has an exquisite morning glory and cornstalk fence (see p39) ⓫

Claiborne Cottage
This cottage was built in 1857 for the daughter of the first American governor of Louisiana. It has served as a school and a convent ❸

Briggs-Staub House
This handsome Gothic Revival mansion was designed by James Gallier, Sr. in 1849 ❹

ST CHARLES AVENUE

STREET

| 0 meters | 40 |
| 0 yards | 40 |

Women's Guild Opera House
This Greek Revival mansion was designed in 1858 by William Freret ❿

3RD STREET

★ Robinson House
One of the grandest residences in the Garden District, Robinson House was built between 1859 and 1865 for Virginia tobacco merchant Walter Robinson ❺

Musson-Bell House
This was the home of Michel Musson, uncle of artist Edgar Degas; an iron merchant added the lacy galleries later ⓬

STAR SIGHTS

★ Colonel Short's Villa

★ Lafayette Cemetery

★ Robinson House

St. Charles Avenue Streetcar ❶

See pp104–5.

Lafayette Cemetery ❷

1400 block of Washington Ave.
Map 7 F3. 🚋 *St. Charles.* 🚌 *11, 14.* ◯ *7am–2:30pm Mon–Fri, 7am–noon Sat.* ◉ *public hols.* ☑ **www**.lafayettecemetery.org

This walled cemetery was laid out in 1833 by Benjamin Buisson to accommodate the residents of the adjacent Garden District. The second Protestant cemetery to open in New Orleans, it is the resting place of many German and British Protestants, as well as numerous Americans who had migrated here from the east coast. By 1840 it was full, mostly with yellow fever victims, and a new cemetery was needed.

Angel statue at Lafayette

Among the notables buried here are Confederate general Harry T. Hays and Samuel Jarvis Peters (1801–85), an influential city politician and land developer. A Canadian,

Peters arrived in New Orleans and ascended to a powerful position by the time he was 30. He was one of the movers and shakers who developed the area above Canal Street, fashioning it into a Second Municipality comparable to the downtown Creole community below Canal Street. It had its own fashionable hotel, the St. Charles, which was equal to the St. Louis and mirrored its Creole counterpart in other ways.

One of the most striking memorials in this cemetery is the one built in 1852 to commemorate the Jefferson Fire Company #22. It is embellished with a typical pumper. In her book *Interview with the Vampire* Anne Rice often gives Lestat and Claudia free rein to wander around this cemetery. The author herself staged a mock burial here in 1995 to promote her book, *Memnoch the Devil.*

The wall vaults were added to the cemetery in 1858.

Greek columns, Claiborne Cottage

Claiborne Cottage ❸

2524 St. Charles Ave. **Map** 7 F3.
🚋 *St. Charles.* 🚌 *11, 14.* ◉ *to the public.*

The history of this Greek Revival-style cottage is disputed, but the plaque in front states that it was built in 1857 for Louise Claiborne, the daughter of the first governor of Louisiana. She was married to Mandeville Marigny, the youngest son of Bernard de Marigny *(see p82)*, who introduced dice to the United States. His gambling friends thought he resembled a frog, and so he was nicknamed "Le Crapaud," after which the game "craps" takes its name.

Some experts date the house to 1860 and claim that it was built for a Virginian, James Dameron.

Briggs-Staub House ❹

2605 Prytania St. **Map** 7 F3.
🚋 *St. Charles.* 🚌 *11, 14.* ◉ *to the public.*

A rarity in New Orleans, this Gothic Revival home was built for gambler Cuthbert Bullitt in 1849. The Gothic style is uncommon in this part of the city, because

Above-ground vaults at Lafayette Cemetery

Gothic arched windows, Briggs-Staub House

many Protestant Americans claimed it reminded them of Roman Catholic France. After James Gallier, Sr. had designed the building, Bullitt refused to pay for it, perhaps because of a gambling loss, and the house subsequently became the property of Charles Briggs, an English insurance executive.

The second-floor galleries at Robinson House

Robinson House ❺

1415 3rd St. **Map** 8 A3. 🚋 St. Charles. 🚌 11, 14. 🚫 to the public.

One of the grandest and largest residences in the Garden District, this house was built for the Virginia tobacco merchant, Walter Robinson. Designed by Henry Howard, it was built between 1859 and 1865. The galleries of this Italian-style villa are supported with Doric columns on the first floor and Corinthian on the second. Domenico Canova, a famous European craftsman, was hired to decorate the interior, which boasts elaborate

painted ceilings. It was one of the first buildings in the city to have indoor plumbing. An unusual feature of this mansion is the curved portico.

Louise S. McGehee School ❻

2343 Prytania St. **Map** 8 A3. 🚋 St. Charles. 🚌 11, 14. 🚫 to the public.

James Freret designed this elaborate French Second Empire home in 1872 for sugar planter Bradish Johnson, for $100,000. Freret had recently returned from Paris and was enamored of the École des Beaux-Arts, which is evident in this mansion's Renaissance Revival style. When it was built, the house incorporated all of the fashionable interior design elements and conveniences

of the day: a conservatory, a marble pantry, a passenger elevator, and a magnificent circular staircase. It is one of the few houses in the city to have a basement.

Since 1929 it has served as a private school for girls. The cafeteria was once a stable, and the gym is a refurbished carriage house. Note the steep mansard roof with its wrought-iron parapet and the unique bull's-eye window on the façade. The gardens contain some magnificent magnolias and ginger trees.

Carroll-Crawford House ❼

1315 First St. **Map** 8 A3. 🚋 St. Charles. 🚌 11, 14. 🚫 to the public.

This broadly proportioned house was designed by Samuel Jamison in 1869 for Joseph Carroll, a cotton merchant from Virginia. The surrounding gardens include venerable live oaks and other lush plantings. A two-story home with octagonal wings, the house is Italianate in design with fine cast-iron galleries, made in New Orleans by Jacob Baumiller.

The original carriage house can still be seen around the corner on Chestnut Street. Jamison also constructed an identical building at 1331 First Street for cordage dealer Joseph C. Morris.

The ornate façade of the Carroll-Crawford House

St. Charles Avenue Streetcar ●

**Statue of
John McDonogh,
Lafayette Square**

For a slow-moving romance, take a ride on the St. Charles Avenue streetcar, which passes many of New Orleans' most famous landmarks. It was this type of streetcar that inspired Tennessee Williams's drama *A Streetcar Named Desire*. It travels 6.5 miles (10 km) from Canal Street through the Central Business District, along tree-shaded St. Charles Avenue to Carrollton Avenue. It began operating in 1835 under steam power; in 1867 mule power took over, then, in 1893, it was electrified. Due to electrical damage sustained during Hurricane Katrina, the St. Charles Avenue streetcar was out of commission for more than two years. The return of its familiar green cars was greeted with delight by New Orleanians during the holiday season of 2007.

Claiborne Cottage
This classic raised cottage was built in 1857 for the daughter of the first American Louisiana governor (see p102).

A metal pole conducts power from an overhead cable.

ST. CHARLES   06

922

Touro Synagogue
This building is named after Judah Touro, who came to New Orleans from Newport, Rhode Island, and donated the money for its construction.

Lee Circle
This 60-ft (18-m)- tall Doric column supports a statue of General Robert E. Lee, looking north (see p96).

Christ Church
This building is one of the few examples of Gothic Revival style in the city.

ST. CHARLES AVENUE SIGHTS

Christ Church ④
Claiborne Cottage ③
Lafayette Square ①
Lee Circle ②
St. Charles House ⑦
The Columns ⑤
The Latter Public Library ⑧
Touro Synagogue ⑥

KEY

🚋 Streetcar stops

– – Streetcar route

0 kilometers 2
0 miles 1

The seats are made of slatted polished wood with brass handles and can be reversed for the return trip.

Blinds protect against the sun.

Windows open wide for a fresh breeze.

St. Charles House
Dating from the 1850s, this house may be the oldest on the street.

The Columns
Built for a wealthy cigar manufacturer, this imposing building was used by director Louis Malle as one of the sets for his movie Pretty Baby *(1978).*

The Latter Public Library
One of the most elegant library buildings, the Latter Public Library started life in 1907 as a private mansion and was donated to the city in the 1940s.

One of the impressive floats at Mardi Gras World

Mardi Gras World ❽

1380 Port of New Orleans Place. **Map** 8 C3. 🚋 *Riverfront.* ⏲ *9:30am–4:30pm daily.* 📷 ✔ 🚻 www.mardigrasworld.com

Blaine Kern is often called "Mr. Mardi Gras" because so many of the massive floats that roll through the streets during Carnival *(see pp28–9)* are constructed here in the 20 warehouse-dens of his company.

A tour of Mardi Gras World begins with a short film showing the floats in the parades and the stages of their production, from the original drawings to the manufacture of the final pieces. Visitors are then free to don some of the costumes that krewe members have worn in past parades. Many of these are very heavy and ornate. Visitors can also wander through the warehouses and view gigantic decorative figures, made of either fiberglass or Styrofoam overlaid with papier-mâché. It is also possible to climb on to the floats to get an idea of what it is like to ride them. The cost of the floats is borne by the krewes themselves, with contributions from their members.

Toby's Corner ❾

2340 Prytania St. **Map** 8 A3. 🚋 *St. Charles.* 🚌 *11, 14, 27.* ⬤ *to the public.*

Built around 1838, this house was constructed for Thomas Toby and is believed to be the oldest residence in the Garden District. Toby was a native Philadelphian, who moved to New Orleans and became a very successful wheelwright. He amassed a huge fortune but lost it financing Sam Houston and the cause for Texas independence from Mexico. It was, in fact, his wife who paid for the construction of the house. Subsequently, Toby worked as a plantation manager until he died.

After the Civil War *(see pp18–19)* the house was foreclosed and sold at auction for $5,000. Nowadays, it is privately owned and closed to the public. However, its façade is an impressive example of the Greek Revival style.

Women's Guild Opera House ❿

2504 Prytania St. **Map** 8 A3. **Tel** 899-1945. 🚋 *St. Charles.* 🚌 *11, 14, 27.* ⏲ *for tours by appointment only.* 📷 ✔

William Freret designed the original Greek Revival section of this house in 1858 for a wealthy merchant. In 1996 the house was bequeathed to the Women's Guild of the New Orleans Opera Association, and it is now used for meetings and receptions. It also features some exhibits relating to the history of opera in the city; in the 19th century New Orleans was a major opera center, although the original opera house burned down in 1919.

It is open to the public for guided tours for 20 or more people with reservations.

Colonel Short's Villa ⓫

1448 Fourth St. **Map** 7 F3. 🚋 *St. Charles.* 🚌 *11, 14, 27.* ⬤ *to the public.*

Henry Howard designed this large Italian-style residence in 1859 for native Kentuckian Colonel Robert Short. The veranda, with fine iron railings, extends around three sides of the house. An exquisite

The Women's Guild Opera House, combining an octagonal tower and a Greek Revival main house

Colonel Short's Villa, with its remarkable cornstalk fence

born in New Orleans and grew up in the Irish Channel, has portrayed the city in many of her best selling *Vampire Chronicles*, which began with the *Interview with the Vampire*, published in 1976. She and her husband, poet-scholar Stan Rice, returned to New Orleans from San Francisco in 1988. Rice used this house as the setting for her book *The Witching Hour* (1990). Rice spent her teenage years at 2524 St. Charles Avenue, which inspired much of her novel *Violin*. The author has restored several historic buildings. After Stan died in 2003, Anne began to sell her New Orleans properties.

ironwork fence, incorporating a morning glory and cornstalk motif, encloses the gardens *(see pp38–9)*. The story goes that the Colonel had it installed to please his wife. Unlike a similar fence on Royal Street in the French Quarter *(see p77)*, famous for its detailed ironwork, this one has not been painted and shows its original colors. In September 1863, the Union troops seized the residence. It was returned to the family after the Civil War *(see pp18–19)*. Although closed to the public, the famous cornstalk fence is much visited.

Musson-Bell House ⑫

1331 Third St. **Map** 8 A4.
🚃 *St. Charles.* 🚌 *11, 14, 27.*
⬤ *to the public.*

When this handsome Italianate villa was built in 1853 for Michel Musson (1812–85), he was a successful cotton merchant and prominent Creole, and was also the New Orleans postmaster *(see p126)*. Musson had close ties with his extended family, including his sister Celestine Musson Degas, who lived in France. Celestine's son, Edgar Degas, was to become one of the world's great artists.

After the Civil War Degas came to visit Louisiana but it is unlikely he ever saw this house. The war had dealt Musson's fortunes a severe

blow and he sold the house in 1869, moving his family to a rented house on Esplanade Avenue *(see p126)*.

Brevard-Wisdom-Rice House ⑬

1239 First St. **Map** 8 A3.
🚃 *St. Charles.* 🚌 *11, 14, 27.*
⬤ *to the public.*

Fans of the Gothic author Anne Rice stop to gawk at the Brevard-Wisdom-Rice House, where she lived from 1989 to 2003. The house was designed by James Calrow for merchant Albert Hamilton Brevard in 1857 and cost $13,000, at the time a formidable sum. It is adorned with ornate ironwork, including a fence incorporating a charming rose motif, for which reason the house is referred to as "Rosegate." Ionic and Corinthian columns support the galleries. The second owners of the property, the Clapp family, added the hexagonal wing in 1869. The gardens are splendid and feature some stunning camellias.

Anne Rice, who was

Payne-Strachan House ⑭

1134 First St. **Map** 8 A4.
🚃 *St. Charles.* 🚌 *11, 14, 27.*
⬤ *to the public.*

This grand home was built in the 1850s by Judge Jacob U. Payne, who brought slaves from his plantation in Kentucky and had them construct it. The two-story Greek Revival residence features Ionic columns on the first gallery and Corinthian on the second. The house passed to Payne's son-in-law, Charles Erasmus Fenner, a close friend of Jefferson Davis, United States senator and president of the Confederacy *(see pp96–7)*. Davis died here on December 6, 1889, in the first-floor guest room.

Musson-Bell House, in the Italianate style

A stately Victorian home on St. Charles Avenue ▷

A side window of Loyola University's chapel

Loyola University **⑮**

6363 St. Charles Ave. **Tel** 865-3240. **Map** 6 B3. 🚋 St. Charles. 🚌 22, 15. ◯ 9am–7pm daily. ▨

The Jesuit Order established the College of the Immaculate Conception downtown in 1840. It merged with Loyola College in 1912, and together they became Loyola University. The Tudor-Gothic buildings house the largest Catholic university in the South. The three buildings facing St. Charles Avenue are Marquette Hall, the adjacent Thomas Hall, and the Most Holy Name

of Jesus Roman Catholic Church, the design of which was inspired by Canterbury Cathedral in the UK.

The statue of Jesus with uplifted arms in front of Marquette is referred to locally as "Touchdown Jesus," for obvious reasons.

Tulane University **⑯**

6823 St. Charles Ave. **Map** 6 B2. **Tel** 865-5000. 🚋 St. Charles. 🚌 22, 15. ◯ 9am–5pm daily. ▨

Founded in 1834 as a medical college, the precursor of Tulane University was given its present name in 1882 after it received a substantial gift from Paul Tulane, a native of Princeton, New Jersey. He made a fortune from a merchandising business, which he launched in New Orleans in 1822. Tulane's School of Business is the oldest college of commerce in the country.

The University moved to its current location in 1894. The 110-acre campus has 79 buildings, designed in a variety of styles. The Howard Tilton Memorial Library houses the Hogan Jazz Archive, plus other special collections. About 12,000 students attend the university.

Amistad Collection **⑰**

Tilton Hall, Tulane University. **Map** 6 B3. **Tel** 862-3222. 🚋 St. Charles. 🚌 15, 22. ◯ 8:30am–4:30pm Mon–Fri. 📷

This research center is named for the famous slave mutiny aboard the Cuban slave ship *Amistad* in 1839. After a trial in Hartford, Connecticut, the slaves were acquitted and allowed to return home. The American Missionary Association, an organization formed to defend the slaves, established the center's archive, which moved to New Orleans in 1969. It consists of documents, photos, pamphlets, and oral history records. A small gallery shows the works of artists including such names as Henry O. Tanner and Elizabeth Catlett.

Newcomb Art Gallery **⑱**

Tulane University. **Map** 6 B2. **Tel** 865-5328. 🚋 St. Charles. 🚌 22, 15. ◯ noon–5pm Tue–Sun. ● public hols and summer months. 📷

In 1886 Josephine Le Monnier Newcomb founded a women's college that was allied with Tulane University. Initially she donated $100,000 in memory

Stately Tulane University's Gibson Hall, built in Richardson-Romanesque style

Taking a rest on a hot day in Audubon Park

of her daughter Harriot Sophie Newcomb, who died at the age of 15 in 1870. When Josephine herself died, she left an additional estate of more than $2.5 million to the college.

The Woldenberg Art Center houses the Newcomb Art Gallery and a smaller space to display student and faculty works. The Newcomb Gallery focuses on presenting traveling shows and also curates its own exhibitions.

The name of Newcomb is more familiarly associated with the arts-and-crafts style of pottery that was made at the Newcomb College of Art from 1895 to 1940. The gallery has some typical pieces on display.

Audubon Park ⓳

6500 Magazine St. **Map** 6 B3.
🚋 *St. Charles.* 🚌 *22, 11.* 📷 ♿
www.auduboninstitute.org

This park was carved out of the plantations owned by the Foucher and Boré families in 1871. The 1884 World's Industrial and Cotton Exposition was held here. New Orleans was still recovering from the double devastations of the Civil War and Reconstruction *(see pp18–19)*, and the exposition helped boost the city's morale. The main building

alone covered almost four times the surface of the Superdome *(see p95)*. The first streetcar was introduced at the Expo, and it so entranced Thomas Lipton of tea company fame that he became a motorman. The Mardi Gras Krewe of Rex *(see pp28–9)* arrived at the Expo aboard a yacht, establishing a tradition that survives to this day. Inside the park there is a fine executive golf course, several ponds, recreation areas, sport facilities, and the Audubon Zoo, which occupies 58 acres of the grounds. The park was named for naturalist John James Audubon, whose statue stands in its grounds. Audubon, the artist of *Birds of America*, was born in the West Indies. He came to New Orleans and rented his first studio in 1821 at 706

Bronze statue in Audubon Park

Barracks Street. He stayed only four months before taking off for another brief sojourn as tutor to a young girl at Oakley Plantation in West Feliciana Parish *(see p151)*. Here, in this rich ornithological environment, he began many of his bird portraits, but he stayed only a short time because of a dispute with his employer. He returned to New Orleans and took up residence at a studio at 505 Dauphine Street.

Audubon Zoo ⓴

See pp112–13.

Riverbend ㉑

Riverfront of St. Charles Ave.
Map 6 A1. 🚋 *St. Charles.* 🚌 *34.*

With more than 300 billion gallons of water flowing by the city each day, New Orleans lives under the constant threat of flood. A system of spillways, pumps, and levees, like this one along the St. Charles Avenue Riverfront, forms a line of defense against the Mississippi. Still, certain sections of the city are prone to flooding, particularly after heavy rains. The pumping system was installed soon after 1927 when the city was so threatened that the authorities cut the levee below the city in St. Bernard Parish to forestall urban flooding. This part of the levee has been adapted as a recreation area, where visitors can enjoy a beautiful view of the river.

Riverbend, a popular place for outdoor recreation

Audubon Zoo ⑳

Elephant giving
a show

This appealing 58-acre zoo, landscaped with fountains and water gardens, can be toured easily in a few hours. It opened in 1938 but was completely redesigned in the 1980s; today most of the animals are living in open paddocks that replicate their natural habitats. Only a few of the 1930s buildings remain. The swamp exhibit is one of the most engaging, showcasing Louisiana white alligators, as well as Acadian culture and music. The world-class zoo is part of Audubon Park *(see p111)*, one of the loveliest urban parks in the country. Originally, the 340-acre park was the sugar plantation of Jean Etienne Boré, who developed the commercially successful sugar granulation process. It was also the location of the 1884 World Exposition.

★ **Louisiana Swamp**
Alligators bask along the banks or float like logs in the muddy lagoon.

Primates, such as orangutans and gorillas, play here.

The African Savannah
Rhinos, hippos, marabou storks, zebra, kudu, and white pelicans all live together with a host of opportunistic visitors such as ibis, heron, and egrets.

Tropical Bird House

Sea Lions
The sea lion pool is one of the oldest features of the zoo. Feeding time draws the crowds.

Reptile Encounter
King cobra, python, boa constrictors, and the impressive Komodo dragon hold court here.

★ Jaguar Jungle
Sloths, spider monkeys, and anteaters cohabit with jaguars in this exhibit, which is built around a replica of Mayan ruins set in a super-lush jungle.

VISITORS' CHECKLIST

6500 Magazine St. **Map** 6 B3.
Tel 581-4629. 🚌 11. 🚋 St.
Charles. ☐ 10am–4pm Tue–Sun
(to 5pm Sat, Sun). ● first Friday
in May, Thanksgiving, Dec 24–25,
Mardi Gras. 🖼 ♿ 🎁 🍴

Flamingos
Near the river cruise landing, a peaceful lake is home to dozens of beautiful flamingos.

Elephant Plaza
An elephant show is presented in front of the plaza, while children are able to enjoy the unique experience of touching one.

Main entrance

St. Charles Streetcar free shuttle stop

Australian Outback
This area recreates the Australian out-back with its kangaroos and kookaburras.

STAR FEATURES

★ Jaguar Jungle

★ Louisiana Swamp

Evocative statue at the New Orleans Botanical Gardens

SIGHTS AT A GLANCE

Museums & Galleries
Degas House ⑩
Longue Vue House and
  Gardens ⑬
New Orleans Museum of Art
  pp120–23 ①
Pitot House ⑦
Storyland and Carousel
  Gardens ③

Parks and Gardens
Bayou St. John ⑥
Dueling Oaks ②
New Orleans
  Botanical Garden ④

Cemeteries
Cypress Grove
  Cemetery ⑪
Metairie Cemetery ⑫
St. Louis Cemetery
  #3 ⑧

Entertainment
Fair Grounds ⑨
Sports Facilities
  in City Park ⑤

KEY

▨	Street-by-Street map *See pp116–17*
🚃	Streetcar stop
⊠	Post office
✚	Church

GETTING THERE
Routes 22, 46, 48, 54, 90.
The Canal Streetcar runs from
the Mississippi River to City
Park Ave. A spur line goes to
City Park itself.

Rose garden entrance, Botanical Gardens

MID-CITY

Extending from the French Quarter toward Lake Pontchartrain, Mid-City is the greenest part of New Orleans, with the largest swath of land taken up by City Park. This is carved out of an old plantation that was donated to the city in 1850 by bank director John McDonogh on the provision that the funds from its sale be used for public schools. The city bent the rules a little and created a park instead. The other green areas in Mid-City are given over to various cemeteries such as Greenwood, Metairie, St. Louis Cemetery #3, and Cypress Grove. The major streets in the area are Canal Street and Esplanade Avenue. Canal connects downtown with the cemeteries, while Esplanade is lined with Creole mansions. Mid-City suffered from flooding in the aftermath of Hurricane Katrina. While portions of it are above sea level, other areas were under water for weeks. Tremendous strides have been made toward reconstruction, and today the bright-red Canal streetcar rumbles through this charming area once again.

Angel statue in Greenwood cemetery

Street-by-Street: City Park

This 1,500-acre park is the tenth-largest urban park in the US. Hurricane Katrina caused damage to the grounds, trees, infrastructure, and facilities, but most of the park has now reopened and is thriving. Visitors flock to the spectacular Botanical Gardens and the New Orleans Museum of Arts, while kids love the carousel and Storyland, a theme park with rides and fairy tale exhibits. Eight miles of lagoons allow for fishing and boating. The park's latest addition, the Besthoff Sculpture Garden, showcases 30 major 20th-century sculptures.

Sculpture at NOMA

Storyland and Carousel
The wooden carousel is one of the main attractions in this children's park ❸

Sports Facilities
The Pan-American Stadium hosts many high-school football games ❺

VICTORY AVENUE

DREYFOUS DRIVE

CITY PARK AVENUE

Popp's Bandstand
Named after lumber magnate John Popp, this bandstand is often used by jazz bands and mime artists.

0 meters	100	**KEY**
0 yards	100	- - - Suggested route

The Peristyle
An entrance to a building that was never erected, the Peristyle formerly functioned as a dancehall. Today it is a picnic area.

★ New Orleans Botanical Gardens
Botanical exhibits and themed gardens – including the famous rose gardens – cover 10 acres of this ever-popular park. Statues by Mexican artist Enrique Alferez stand among the trees ④

LOCATOR MAP
See Street Finder map 1

★ New Orleans Museum of Art
A Beaux-Arts building houses a collection of American and international art ①

ROOSEVELT MALL

Besthoff Sculpture Garden

LELONG DRIVE

Dueling Oaks
As many as ten duels a day were once fought here. The last one was a challenge with sabers and took place in 1939 ②

The Casino (1912)
Originally a casino, this Mission Revival building houses a visitors' center, offering tourist information, a gift shop, and food concessions.

STAR SIGHTS

★ New Orleans Botanical Gardens

★ New Orleans Museum of Art

The Flute Player, by Enrique Alferez, at the Botanical Gardens

New Orleans Museum of Art ❶

See pp120–23.

Dueling Oaks ❷

City Park. **Map** 2 A1. 🚌 *46, 48, 90.* 🚋 *Canal.* ♿

Behind the famous statue of Confederate General P. G. T. Beauregard *(see p71)*, which guards the entrance to City Park, Lelong Avenue approaches the New Orleans Museum of Art. To the left is a grand, solitary oak, still commonly called the Dueling Oaks although there is now only one.

Many duels were fought in New Orleans, and most of these took place in the bosky acres of what has since become City Park. Under the massive branches of live oaks, as many as ten duels a day were fought. Reports indicate that one particular dueler called for the use of whaling harpoons, after which the offended party decided he wasn't so offended after all. The last duel was fought in 1939 between two students from a local fencing academy. The owner of the original plantation from which City Park was carved, Louis Allard, is rumored to be buried at the foot of the oaks.

Storyland and Carousel Gardens ❸

City Park. **Map** 2 A1. *Tel* 482-4888. 🚌 *46, 48, 90.* 🚋 *Canal.* ◗ *10am–3pm Tue–Fri, 11am–6pm Sat & Sun.* ● *Dec 25.* 📷 ⬛ **www**.neworleanscitypark.com

Storyland, a beguiling theme park for children, is filled with all kinds of entertainments derived from traditional folk tales and well-known nursery rhymes. Kids can enjoy Jack and Jill's slide, climb around Miss Muffet's spider web, or challenge Captain Hook to a duel. Along the way, they may also encounter fairytale characters such as Jack (of the Beanstalk), Puss in Boots, Rapunzel, and many others. There is also story reading, puppet shows in the Puppet Castle, and face painting.

The carousel, situated in the southwest corner of the gardens, was built in 1906 and is one of the few antique wooden carousels left in the US. Nearby, visitors can climb aboard a miniature train, which has run around the park since 1896. A large Ferris wheel offers a birds-eye view of the park.

New Orleans Botanical Garden ❹

Victory Ave, City Park. **Map** 2 A1. *Tel* 483-9386. 🚌 *46, 48, 90.* 🚋 *Canal.* ◗ *10am–4:30pm Tue–Sun.* ● *Jan 1, Dec 25, Mardi Gras.* 📷 ⬛ ♿ **www**.neworleanscitypark.com

This 10-acre public garden was created in the 1930s. Back then, it was mainly a rose garden, but today there are also spring and perennial gardens featuring azaleas, camellias, and magnolias, as well as tropical plants and trees. Several statues by Mexican artist Enrique Alferez, including his *Women in Huipil* and *The Flute Player*, stand among live oaks.

The Garden Study Center and the Pavilion of the Two Sisters are reminiscent of European garden architecture. The Conservatory houses orchids and two major exhibits: Living Fossils, showcasing plants that grew on the earth before flowering plants, and the impressive Tropical Rainforest exhibit.

Much of the plant collection was lost as a result of Hurricane Katrina, but the gardens have now been completely rebuilt.

The carousel in City Park, one of the oldest enclosed carousels in the United States

For hotels and restaurants in this region see pp167–8 and pp183–4

Sports Facilities in City Park ❺

Map 2 A1 B1. *Riverfront. Tel 482-4888.* 🚌 *46, 48, 90.* 🚋 *Canal.*
www.neworleanscitypark.com

The majestic City Park contains many excellent sports facilities. The Wisner Tennis Center has 34 lighted courts, which can be reserved by phone 30 days ahead of time. The Bayou Oaks Golf Club has a 100-tee lighted driving range. Its three golf courses, however, were severely damaged by Hurricane Katrina and have yet to reopen to the public.

The park's 8 miles (13 km) of lagoons provide ample opportunities for boating, and for fishing for bass and trout. Egrets, heron, and the occasional alligator also inhabit the lagoons. Fishing permits can be obtained at the Administrative Center. There is also a stable, offering riding lessons and trail rides.

Bayou St. John ❻

Map 2 B1. 🚌 *46, 48, 90.* 🚋 *Canal.*

The French recognized this bayou as a key strategic asset, providing access to the Gulf of Mexico via Lake Pontchartrain.

The Wisner Tennis Center, City Park

As New Orleans grew, so did plantations along the bayou and a canal was dug, linking it to the downtown, ending in Basin Street at Congo Square. Today, the canal is filled in, but the name Basin Street survives.

In the 18th and 19th centuries the bayou was the scene of voodoo ceremonies. Marie Laveau (*see p83*) was the most infamous practitioner.

Pitot House ❼

1440 Moss St. **Map** 2 B2. *Tel 482-0312.* 🚌 *46, 48, 90.* 🚋 *Canal.*
🕙 *10am–3pm Wed–Sat.* ● *Major hols.* 🖼 **www**.pitothouse.org

This classic West Indian-style raised house was built in 1799, on the banks of Bayou St. John. Once a working plantation, it was carefully moved in the 1960s a block upstream to this location. In 1810, the house was purchased by James Pitot, who had been the second mayor of the city five years earlier. He had arrived from Haiti in 1796 after the slave uprising led by Toussaint L'Ouverture. Pitot went on to direct a bank and run the New Orleans Navigation Company before being appointed to a judgeship.

In 1904, the house was bought by Mother Cabrini, who was later to become America's first saint, and converted into a convent. It is now a museum and contains the original antiques and furnishings from the house.

Bayou St. John, where plantations developed a unique way of life

New Orleans Museum of Art ❶

Together, the New Orleans Museum of Art (NOMA) and the adjacent Sydney and Walda Besthoff Sculpture Garden comprise of one the most important cultural destinations in the Gulf South. Housed in a classic Beaux-Arts building, NOMA's impressive collections include the Fabergé gallery; works by Picasso, Degas, Miró, Rodin, and Pollock; a 7,000-piece photography exhibition; and Asian, African, and American art. In a beautiful 5-acre site, the sculpture garden showcases pieces by world-renowned artists, such as Henry Moore and Barbara Hepworth.

Aztec maize goddess

Third floor

Japanese Suit of Armor
This is 18th-century Domaru-style one-piece body armor manifests the moral and spiritual traditions of the Samurai warriors.

Stairs to third floor

Stairs to first floor

← To sculpture garden

★ **Portrait of a Young Woman** (1918)
This is one of Italian Expressionist Amadeo Modigliani's most famous paintings, and the oval face and elongated lines are typical of his style.

Museum shop

Art storage

First floor

STAR EXHIBITS

- ★ Portrait of a Young Woman

- ★ Reclining Mother and Child

- ★ Serpent about to Strike

Melanesian Ancestor Figure
This carved-wood figure from the Abelan peoples in Papua New Guinea is one of the finest representations of the religious art of Melanesia.

Lousiana Indians Walking Along the Bayou (1847)
Alfred Boisseau portrayed the Choctaw Indians engaged in everyday activities.

★ Serpent about to Strike
(1889–1908)
This Fabergé silver snake rests on a piece of Persian turquoise. It was created by Johan Aarne, one of the firm's talented work-masters, and is regarded by many as his masterpiece.

Stairs to third floor

Second floor

GALLERY GUIDE
The main entrance leads to three European art collections. The second floor houses the American Art, the Fabergé, and three further European collections. The third floor offers African, Oceanic, and Native American exhibits.

KEY TO FLOOR PLAN

- ☐ African and Oceanic Art
- ☐ American Art
- ☐ Asian Art
- ☐ Contemporary Art
- ☐ Decorative Arts
- ☐ European Art
- ☐ Prehispanic/Native American Art
- ☐ Photography and Graphics
- ☐ Non-exhibition space

★ Reclining Mother and Child (1975)
A gift of the Sydney and Walda Besthoff Founda-tion, this Henry Moore sculpture depicts the bond between mother and child.

Main entrance

Stairs to second floor

Exploring the New Orleans Museum of Art

The major collections displayed in the museum's 46 galleries include a vast selection of European art, from 12th-century Italian Florentine to 20th-century French and Spanish works. There are specialized collections of Latin American and Prehispanic art; Native and modern American works; arts of Africa and Asia; photography; and decorative arts. The Sydney and Walda Besthoff Sculpture Garden displays an eclectic array of works in a landscaped park.

Portrait of a Bijin (courtesan), Yamaguchi Soken (1800)

AFRICAN AND OCEANIC ART

Yoruba mounted warrior

This is one of the finest African art collections in the country. Established in 1953, it now represents Sub-Saharan Africa's five major art-producing regions, including works by the Baman and Dogon peoples of Mali and the Benin, the Yoruba, the Ibo, and the Ekoi peoples of Nigeria, Cameroon, and the Ivory Coast. Among the highlights is a rare palace veranda post carved in the shape of an equestrian warrior figure by Yoruba artist Olowe of Ise. Another gem is a terra-cotta head from the Nok culture dating from around 500 BC–AD 200. *The Head of an Oba* (late 18th century) is a striking bronze funerary portrait, which might have been placed on an altar in the Benin royal palace to commemorate the deceased.

The Oceania gallery includes wooden figures from Papua New Guinea; nephrite (a hard green jade-like stone) weapons, tools, and ornaments from the Maoris; and a standing Malanggan figure, also from New Zealand.

AMERICAN ART

This collection includes some fine examples of early American artists such as John Singleton Copley, Gilbert Stuart, Charles Willson Peale, Benjamin West, and John Singer Sargent. An entire gallery is devoted to a collection of Louisiana paintings, including *Louisiana Indians Walking Along the Bayou (see p121)* by Alfred Boisseau, *Back of Algiers* (1870–73) by Richard Clague, and *Blue Crab and Terrapins* (1880) by Achille Perelli. The *Portrait of Mme. René de Gas, née Estelle Musson*, painted in 1872–3 by Edgar Degas during a visit to New Orleans, is also displayed.

ASIAN ART

One of the finest collections of Edo (1600–1868) Japanese paintings can be seen in these galleries. All the major Japanese schools are represented, and it is particularly strong on the Nanga, Zenga, and Maruyama-Shijo schools. The collection also includes a wide variety of ceramics, lacquer, textiles, prints, photographs, and armor. The Chinese collection

Portrait of a Young Girl, Joan Miró (1935)

has ceramics from the Neolithic to the modern era. There are stone, wood, and bronze sculptures, plus miniatures, and religious art from India.

CONTEMPORARY ART

A great variety of sculpture, paintings, and mixed- media works, such as Joseph Cornell's intricate small-scale shadow boxes, are included in the Contemporary Art collection, which is divided into Contemporary European Art and the American Art exhibits. The European collection features works from such artists as Miró and Picasso. The American exhibit ranges from Georgia O' Keefe's *My Back Yard* (1937) and Hans Hofmann's *Abstraction with Chair and Miró* (1943), to Jackson Pollock's *Composition (White, Black, Blue, and Red on White)* (1948) and Roger Brown's *California Hillside* (1988).

DECORATIVE ARTS

The museum has a fabulous glass collection consisting of more than 6,000 items, including ancient glass and Tiffany vases. The pottery collection features a large group of pieces from New Orleans' own Newcomb Pottery. There is also a rare collection of "Old Paris" porcelain, plus examples of Sevres and Limoges. The silver collection contains some lustrous pieces by English silversmith Paul Storr.

EUROPEAN ART

The European collection spans a period of 600 years and features examples from the major national schools.

The Kress Collection, donated to the museum by the American philanthropist Samuel H. Kress, includes sublime Italian Old Master paintings from the early Renaissance to the 18th century. French art is also well represented, with works from the 17th to the 20th centuries. The Hyams Gallery features lesser-known 19th-century Salon and Barbizon painters, in contrast with the more familiar Impressionist and Post-Impressionist painters

Morning Glory Tiffany vase

represented in the adjacent Forgotston Gallery.

Other highlights include gems such as Picasso's *Woman with Tambourine* (1938), Miró's *Lady Strolling on the Rambla in Barcelona* (1925), Degas' *Dancer in Green* (1878), Rodin's *The Age of Bronze* (1876), and works by other European masters.

PREHISPANIC/ NATIVE AMERICAN ART

These galleries display a strong collection of material from Mayan culture, including some impressive sculptures and ceramics. Artifacts from Central American cultures are also represented, such as Olmec and Mixtec, along with the later Aztec civilization.

The Native American collections include Kachina dolls from the Hopi and Zuni, pottery from the Acoma Santo Domingo and San Ildefonso pueblos, Apache and Pima baskets, and Percé beadwork and textiles from the northwest coast.

The museum also has a special collection of Latin American colonial art, much of it from Cuzco in Peru. It includes an early 18th-century portrait of an archangel with a musket.

Native American kachina dolls representing a family (1958)

PHOTOGRAPHY AND GRAPHICS

This collection of more than 7,000 vintage photographs is one of the finest of its kind in the Southeast. It includes works by all the known masters, such as William Henry Fox Talbot's *View of the Paris Boulevards* (1843), André Kertész's *Théâtre Odeon* (1926), Man Ray's *Portrait of Berenice Abbott in front of Man Ray Composition* (1922), and Diane Arbus's *A Young Brooklyn Family Going on a Sunday Outing* (1966). In his 1946 *Elegy for the Old South (No. 6)*, Clarence John Laughlin captures the nostalgia of the old South in surrealistic images of decay. His photographs of abandoned plantation homes and the South in the early 20th century are justly famous.

SCULPTURE GARDEN

The dynamic sculptures of Henry Moore, Barbara Hepworth, Louis Bourgeois, George Segal, and other renowned artists are displayed among the ancient oaks, magnolias, and tranquil lagoons of the Sydney and Walda Besthoff Sculpture Garden.

This five-acre site, adjacent to the museum building, was opened in 2003 to provide a beautiful natural space for more than 50 modern and contemporary sculptures. Visitors are free to wander around the park, or join one of the daily tours.

The Cardinal's Friendly Chat, Jehan Georges Vibert (1880)

Miniature train passing through the oaks at City Park ▷

Some of the city's most poignant tombs at St. Louis Cemetery #3

St. Louis Cemetery #3 ⑧

3421 Esplanade Ave.
Map 2 B1. **Tel** 482-5065.
📷 48, 90. ⬜ 8am–4:30pm daily.
⬤ Mardi Gras.

This pristine cemetery, with its beautiful wrought-iron gates, opened in 1856. Among the notables buried here is Antoine Michoud, the original owner of a plantation which is now the site of the NASA plant where the Saturn rockets were built in the 1960s. There is also a memorial to architect James Gallier, Sr. *(see p95)* and his wife, who are buried in Metairie Cemetery. Both were killed when the steamer *Evening Star* sank en route from New York to New Orleans in October 1866.

Other famous figures here include Father Rouquette, missionary to the Choctaw, and black Creole philanthropist Thomy Lafon, owner of the old Orleans Ballroom,

Period furniture in the dining room at Degas House

where the famous "quadroon balls" were held. Lafon also sponsored an orphanage for African-American children.

Fair Grounds ⑨

1751 Gentilly Blvd. **Map** 2 C1.
Tel 944-5515. 📷 48. 📷 ♿
www.fgno.com

In the mid-1800s, New Orleans was a leading center for horse racing. The Creole Racecourse operated during the 19th century on what is now the Fair Grounds. When Metairie Racecourse closed, the Louisiana Jockey Club took over and purchased the Luling Mansion just off Esplanade as a clubhouse. The name change occurred when the Fair Grounds Corporation took over in 1940. Races are run here from November to March, and in April the Fair Grounds host the New Orleans Jazz Fest *(see p41)*. The clubhouse lost its roof to Hurricane Katrina but reopened in 2007.

Marble statue at Cypress Grove

Degas House ⑩

2306 Esplanade Ave. **Map** 3 D3.
Tel 821-5009. 📷 48.
⬜ by appointment only.
📷 📷 **www.**degashouse.com

Calling himself "almost a son of Louisiana," Impressionist painter Edgar Degas (1834–1917) visited his uncle, Michel Musson *(see p107)*, at this house from October 1872

until March 1873. Degas was charmed with America and especially New Orleans. Several important paintings evolved from his sojourn here, despite the fact that he did not venture far from the house for fear of the intense New Orleans sun affecting his eyesight. *The Cotton Buyer's Office* (1873) shows his uncle with several members of his family, including the artist's own brothers René and Achille, who both worked in the cotton business.

The Esplanade house, which dates from 1854, has Greek Revival details and cast-iron balconies. The house is beautifully maintained throughout and offers bed and breakfast accommodations *(see p167)*, as well as welcoming visitors during the day. Many reproductions of Degas' work are on display.

Cypress Grove Cemetery ⑪

120 City Park Ave. **Map** 1 C2.
Tel 482-3232. 📷 40, 46.
⬜ 8am–4:30pm daily. ♿

This cemetery, established by the Firemen's Charitable Association, was laid out in 1841. The impressive Egyptian-style gate leads into a graveyard filled with handsome memorials. Many of the tombs are dedicated to individual firefighters, such as Irad Ferry, who lost their lives in the line of duty. Ferry's tomb, which features a broken column, was designed by the famous architect J. N. B. de Pouilly *(see p83)*.

The cemetery also contains a large number of rich Protestants, who were buried here after Girod Cemetery began to deteriorate. Many of the tombs have remarkable ironwork, like the weeping cupid gate which is crowned with lovebirds and set between inverted torches.

An extension to Cypress Grove was built right across the street to fulfil a need for space after the yellow fever epidemic of 1853. Known as Greenwood Cemetery, it was the first in New Orleans to be built without a boundary wall. It is the site of the city's first Civil War Memorial.

Metairie Cemetery ⓬

5100 Pontchartrain Blvd. **Map** 1 B1.
Tel 486-6331. 🚌 40, 46.
🕐 8am–5pm daily. ♿

This is the most attractively landscaped cemetery in New Orleans, and the final resting place of many of its blue-bloods. In the 19th century, the city was the premier venue for horseracing, and the Metairie Racetrack was the most famous. After the Civil War, mismanagement afforded Charles T. Howard the opportunity to take revenge on the racetrack members who had refused him admission. He purchased it in 1872 and converted it into a cemetery. The oval racecourse became the cemetery's main drive.

Many magnificent tombs are located here, and near the entrance stands the massive 85-ft (26-m) high Moriarty monument, which required the laying of a special railroad to bring it into the cemetery. Daniel

Egan Family tomb, modeled after the ruins of an Irish chapel

Moriarty was an Irish immigrant and saloonkeeper who had succeeded financially but was scorned socially. He was determined to avenge his wife, Mary, and designed this tomb so that in death she could look down on all those who had snubbed her.

The tomb of legendary madam Josie Arlington bears a bas-relief of a young girl knocking on a door. Orphaned at the age of four, Josie went into business for herself as a teenager. She became a notorious whore and brawler, and once bit off half an ear and the lower lip of a fellow prostitute.

A large bell from his boat *America* marks the grave

of Captain Cooley, who ran several steamboats until his death in 1931. Other denizens include P. B. S. Pinchback, a free man of color who became Louisiana's only black governor in 1872–3, and William C. C. Claiborne *(see p17)*, first governor of Louisiana. David C. Hennessy, the police chief who was assassinated in 1891, also has an impressive tomb.

Longue Vue House and Gardens ⓭

7 Bamboo Road. **Map** 1 A2.
Tel 488-5488. 🚌 34, 39.
🕐 10am–4:30pm Mon–Sat, 1–5pm Sun. ● public hols. 📷 🎥 ♿ 🎁
www.longuevue.com

Cotton broker Edgar Stern and his wife Edith Rosenwald, heiress to the Sears fortune, established this estate between 1939 and 1942. The interiors are exquisitely decorated with antiques, Oriental carpets and fine art, including works by Jean Arp, Pablo Picasso, and Barbara Hepworth. The gardens, which contain 23 fountains created by Ellen Biddle, are exceptional examples of landscape design. The largest garden is modeled on Spain's 14th-century Alhambra gardens; others are inspired by French and English designs.

One of Ellen Biddle's fountains gracing the gardens of Longue Vue House

THREE GUIDED WALKS

These three walks take visitors through landmark districts and also into the heart of elegant residential areas that showcase the unique make-up of New Orleans' historic neighborhoods. The walk along the Mississippi riverfront has sweeping views of the city, and the short ferry ride to Old Algiers Point provides a fascinating glimpse of the workings of this powerful natural waterway. The Faubourg St. John walk explores an area with deep historic ties to the city's colonial origins, with its French West Indies-style raised houses and

Garden District ironwork detail

distinctive cemetery, circling around a lesser-known waterway, the Bayou St. John. The third walk heads uptown to the Lower Garden District, a diverse and bustling area full of interesting shops, historic churches, and fine architecture, with literary connections. In addition, each of the five neighborhoods covered in the *Area by Area* section of this book has a walk marked on its *Street-by-Street* map. Several organizations also offer guided walks through the French Quarter, Garden District, and other areas in the city *(see pp198–9)*.

CHOOSING A WALK

The Three Walks
This map shows the location of the three guided walks in relation to the main sightseeing areas of New Orleans.

Faubourg
St. John
(pp134–5)

Mid City

Lower French
Quarter

Upper French
Quarter

Mississippi
Riverfront
(pp130–31)

Warehouse
and CBD

Garden District
and Uptown

Mississippi

Mansion on Esplanade Avenue,
Faubourg St. John

Steam boat
Natchez

KEY

••••• Walk route

0 kilometres   4

0 miles   2

Lower Garden
District
(pp132–3)

St. Charles Avenue
streetcar

◁ An elegant residence on Esplanade Avenue

A Walk Around the Mississippi Riverfront

New Orleans owes its very existence to the Mississippi River, one of the world's great waterways and an iconic feature on the cultural, historic, and economic landscape of America. This walk provides superb vistas from both sides of the river, explores a portion of the levee system and, thanks to a free ferry ride, gives you a chance to experience its swirling waters up close.

Cannon, Washington Artillery Park ①

The steam boat *Natchez*, crossing the wide Mississippi River ④

Jackson Square to the Aquarium

Begin at Washington Artillery Park ① *(see p77)*. This raised platform features a 19th-century cannon and has excellent views of Jackson Square *(see p54)* and the river. Descend the stairs on the river side of the platform and cross the railroad tracks to

TIPS FOR WALKERS

Starting point: *Washington Artillery Park near Jackson Square.*
Length: *1 mile (1.6 km), plus the ferry ride.*
Getting there: *The riverfront area is within easy walking distance of downtown or French Quarter hotels. The Riverfront streetcar also runs along here.*
Stopping-off points: *The renovated Jackson Brewery has a coffee shop and food court. There are many outdoor vendors in the Spanish Plaza near the Canal Street ferry terminal. Adjacent to the plaza is the Riverwalk Marketplace, which has a large food court with a branch of the famous Café du Monde (see p76 and p176). Across the river in Algiers, drop into the Dry Dock Café and Bar opposite the ferry terminal for gumbo, or "po'boys" and plenty of atmosphere.*

reach the Moonwalk ②, a paved walkway named for former New Orleans mayor Maurice "Moon" Landrieu. Take the set of steps leading down to the water. This is a popular place for visitors to watch passing vessels, while street musicians performing for tips add to the ambience. Follow the Moonwalk upriver (toward Canal Street), passing the Jax Brewery ③, which at one time was the largest brewery in the South and is now a shopping mall. You also pass the berth for the Steamboat *Natchez* ④ *(see pp64–5)*, a paddle wheeler that offers river trips and enlivens the riverfront with music from its steam calliope prior to each departure. Just upriver is Woldenberg Riverfront Park ⑤ *(see p88)*, named for a local philanthropist. Once occupied by rusting river warehouses, the park now provides an open green area that's popular for picnics, outdoor games, and jogging, as well as a bandstand. The park is also the setting for a collection of sculptures and monuments, including the white marble *Monument*

Monument to the Immigrant, Woldenberg Riverfront Park ⑤

to the Immigrant and the city's Holocaust memorial. Coast Guard cutters or tugboats often temporarily tie up along this stretch of the river, giving walkers a close-up view of the vessels. Just past Woldenberg Park is the Audubon Aquarium of the Americas *(see pp90–91)* and Entergy IMAX Theater ⑥. This area is filled with whimsical sculptures of marine life, shady park benches, and outdoor vendors serving refreshments.

Canal Street ferry to Old Algiers Point

Next to the aquarium is the terminal for the John James Audubon ⑦ *(see p217)*, a state-run commuter ferry providing free rides for

The façade of St. Louis Cathedral

arms. The ferry ride is brief but offers excellent views of the New Orleans skyline, St. Louis Cathedral *(see pp56–7)*, as well as the various craft

that ply the river, including the gigantic cruise ships berthed just upriver. The ferry docks in Old Algiers Point ⑨, a village established in 1719. After leaving the Algiers terminal,

turn left and follow the trail of crushed shells that top the grassy levee. This manmade embankment is part of a system of levees along thousands of miles of riverfront that protects communities from the Mississippi's floodwaters. On the right, you can see the Algiers Courthouse ⑩, a grand Romanesque Revival structure built in 1896 after a devastating fire wiped out much of the neighborhood.

Looking toward the river, you can watch huge ships from around the globe make the dramatic hairpin turn round Algiers Point. This curve in the river suggested New Orleans' most enduring nickname, the Crescent City.

Follow the levee path for about 1,640 ft (500 m), then descend the set of colorfully painted concrete steps down to Patterson Road. Turn left on Patterson Road and continue walking one block to Olivier Street. Turn right and walk two blocks past some of the area's beautifully restored Creole townhouses and shotgun-style homes *(see p35)*. Turn right on Pelican Avenue, a tree-shaded residential street with more distinctive architecture. At the end you reach Bouny Street, turn right here and continue up the levee to the ferry terminal for the return trip.

KEY

•••	Walk route
🚊	Streetcar stop
⛴	Ferry boarding point

0 meters   300

0 yards   300

foot passengers across the Mississippi. If the ferry is not in dock at the terminal, you could use the waiting time to explore the adjacent Spanish Plaza ⑧ *(see p88)*. Dedicated in 1976, the plaza was a gift from Spain in a gesture of friendship to its one-time colony and features a fountain ringed by tile mosaics of Spanish coats of

The fountain at the center of the Spanish Plaza ⑧

A Walk Around the Lower Garden District

The Lower Garden District offers visitors a diverse sampling of the ethnic, historical, and economic dynamics at work in the area through the last two centuries. Although this area is not as opulent as the neighboring Garden District (see pp100–1), it has seen a tremendous amount of revitalization since the 1990s. The walk takes you past buildings with fascinating histories, ornate churches, an antebellum mansion, and a cut-down Eiffel Tower.

Interior of St. Mary's Assumption ⑤

St. Charles Avenue fuses the old with the new

blocks toward the river to Coliseum Park ②, an irregular space that was laid out in 1806. The park's name refers to an outdoor arena that was planned here but never realized. Follow the path along Camp Street beneath the spreading branches of oak trees for three blocks and turn left on Race Street. Continue one block then turn right on Magazine Street.

Dominating the corner here is St. Vincent's Guesthouse, a sweeping structure with fanciful wrought-iron balconies ③. The inn was originally built as an orphanage in 1861, a time when yellow fever left many children without parents. The orphanage was a beneficiary of Margaret Haughery, an Irish immigrant and orphan herself who made an enormous fortune operating bakeries around the city. Continue up Magazine Street, where homes give way to rows of boutiques and restaurants with large balconies shading the sidewalks beneath. After four blocks on Magazine Street, turn left on St. Andrew Street and continue for one block before turning right on Constance Street.

proximity for separate Irish and German parishes during the immigration boom of the mid-19th century. The Irish worshipped at St. Alphonsus ④, located on the left side of the street. Now deconsecrated, St. Alphonsus is open as an arts and cultural center with tours available (Tuesday, Thursday, and Saturday) to view its frescoes, stained glass, and a small exhibit on the early Irish experience in New Orleans.

Coliseum Square to Magazine Street

Begin at the streetcar stop at St. Charles Avenue and Melpomene Street ①, which is one of a collection of parallel streets in the area, named for the Nine Muses of Greek mythology. Walk two

TIPS FOR WALKERS

Starting point: The streetcar stop at the corner of St. Charles Avenue and Melpomene Street.
Length: 1.75 miles (2.8 km)
Getting there: By streetcar to the Melpomene Street stop; or a cab ride from Canal Street.
Stopping-off points: Rue de la Course Coffeehouse at Magazine and Race streets is a popular spot. Further down Magazine, Sophie's Ice Cream Parlor has the ambience of an old-fashioned soda fountain, while Juan's Flying Burrito serves Tex-Mex fare with rock and roll flair. On St. Charles Avenue, near Jackson Avenue, Igor's Lounge and Game Room has big burgers.

St. Alphonsus and St. Mary's Assumption

This single block on Constance Street is home to two historic Catholic churches built in close

Former home of Anne Rice, a prominent New Orleans author ⑦

It was consecrated on the same day in 1858 that the cornerstone was laid across the street for St. Mary's Assumption ⑤. This German Baroque Revival church has an altar, statues, and stained glass all imported from Munich and is considered one of the most ornate churches in New Orleans. Regular services continue at St. Mary's Assumption, which is also home to the National Shrine of Blessed Francis Xavier Seelos. Known as "the Cheerful Ascetic," Father Seelos died of yellow fever in 1867 and was beatified by the Church in 2000. The shrine houses his remains, a collection of religious art, and a gift shop.

First Street to St. Charles Avenue

Leaving the church of St. Mary's Assumption, turn right on Josephine Street and continue for one block. Turn left on Magazine Street and continue for three blocks past more boutiques. Turn right on 1st Street, one of the first streets in the Garden District proper. On the left, at No. 1134, is the privately-owned Payne-Strachan House ⑥ (see p107), where Jefferson Davis, president of the

American Confederacy, died in 1889. One block up at No. 1239 ⑦ (see p107), is the Brevard-Wisdom-Rice House, the private home previously owned by novelist Anne Rice and used as a setting for her book *The Witching Hour.*

Continue walking three blocks to St. Charles Avenue and turn right. This avenue is the main route for Mardi Gras parades (see pp28–9) and, if you look up, the remnants of colorful beads thrown from the floats can often be seen tangled in the branches of the oaks along the street.

One block down, at No. 2220 St. Charles Avenue, is the House of Broel ⑧, an antebellum mansion that is open to the public for tours.

A further two blocks down St. Charles Avenue you'll find the striking metal structure known locally as the Eiffel Tower building ⑨. It was built from pieces of the Paris land-mark that were removed during its 1980 renovation and shipped here. Originally a restaurant, it is now the banquet facility for the famed New Orleans Culinary Institute.

The familiar sight of a St. Charles streetcar

On the next block is the visitors' center of the New Orleans Metropolitan Convention and Visitors' Bureau ⑩, which is a good place to pick up maps, and information on tours, restaurants, and attractions across the city. Outside, at the corner of St. Andrew Street, is a streetcar stop for the return trip downtown and the walk's end.

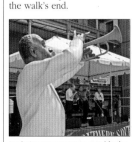

Louis Armstrong statue, outside the New Orleans Visitors' Bureau ⑩

KEY
• • • Walk route
🚋 Streetcar stop

0 meters 300
0 yards 300

A 90-Minute Walk Around the Faubourg St. John

This walk circles a portion of Bayou St. John, an historically strategic waterway where some of the city's earliest colonial development took place. It also showcases a beautiful residential neighborhood with original Creole mansions and the distinctive above-ground St. Louis Cemetery #3. The area is easily accessible from downtown via the Canal streetcar and is close to the attractions in City Park *(see pp116–17).*

The banks of the Bayou St. John waterway

Pitot House, a West Indian-style raised house ②

Around the Bayou

Begin at Beauregard Circle ①, where a statue honors Confederate general P. G. T. Beauregard, nicknamed "the Mighty Creole" *(see p71),* who directed the opening battle of the Civil War at Fort Sumter in South Carolina. Cross N. Carrollton Avenue to the Esplanade Avenue bridge and, once across, turn right on Moss Street. Follow the sidewalk or the grassy footpath around the bend of Bayou St. John *(see p119).* Local Choctaw Indians first showed

this waterway to French explorers in 1699, and it quickly became an important shipping route that connected the early trading posts on the Mississippi River with Lake Pontchartrain and the Gulf of Mexico. Later, the bayou was extended to the French Quarter by a canal that has since been filled. Today, the bayou is an informal recreational area. The banks of the waterway have also historically been connected with voodoo rituals *(see p83),* including those led by Marie Laveau in the 19th century. Although voodoo practice is much less in public evidence today, some practitioners still congregate at Bayou St. John on holidays, especially St. John's Eve on June 23.

In the 18th and early 19th centuries French colonists built country homes in this area and these can still be seen in the French West Indies-style houses here. An outstanding example is Pitot House ② *(see p119),* a Creole raised country house that is

TIPS FOR WALKERS

Starting point: *Beauregard Circle, at the gates of City Park.*
Length: *2 miles (3.2 km).*
Getting there: *From Canal Street, take the Canal streetcar marked City Park to the end of the line. RTA bus #48 runs from N. Rampart Street at Esplanade Avenue to Beauregard Circle.*
Stopping-off points: *There are many casual and upscale restaurants and cafés clustered around Esplanade Avenue and Ponce de Leon Street, including the French bistro Café Degas, the Fair Grinds Coffeehouse, and the Spanish restaurant Lola's.*

KEY

••• Walk route

now a museum. Named for James Pitot, New Orleans' first American mayor, construction of the house started in 1799. It is filled with period antiques, and offers a glimpse of life in early 19th-century New Orleans.

Next to Pitot House is Cabrini High School ③, a private school named for Mother Frances Cabrini who had originally established an orphanage on the spot in 1905. Mother Cabrini later became America's first canonized saint.

Cross the bayou on the steel pedestrian bridge ④ directly across from the school, then turn left to wander along the grassy bank of the bayou until you arrive at the next bridge located at Dumaine Street ⑤. Take the bridge to the other side of the bayou and turn left again, continuing along the opposite bank. Small concrete embankments and steps here-abouts provide

One of several impressive Victorian mansions on Esplanade Avenue ⑦

good places to sit and admire the wildlife and views. Fish often leap from the water after insects and, in the cooler months, the bayou attracts large pelicans, which plunge down dramatically to scoop their own meals from the water.

From Ursulines to Esplanade

Strolling on along Moss Street, turn right on Bell Street, which becomes Ursulines Street ⑥ after one block. This broad avenue, named for the order of nuns who came to New Orleans from France in 1727, was laid out around 1860 after the marshy lands surrounding the bayou were drained. Today, all kinds of beautiful homes can be seen here, including Victorian houses, bungalows, and cottages trimmed with gingerbread woodwork. Three blocks down Ursuline Avenue, turn left on N. Lopez Street at a small triangular park and walk three blocks to Esplanade Avenue ⑦. Turn left here and walk up this impressive avenue, with its mansions that were built in the late 19th and early 20th

An angel at prayer, St. Louis cemetery ⑪

centuries. If you would like a break, on Ponce de Leon Street ⑧ you will come across a cluster of charming restaurants, cafés, and small boutiques. Near here, each spring, the New Orleans Jazz and Heritage Fest is held at the Fair Grounds Race Course ⑨ (see pp41 and 126). Two blocks further on, on the left, is Our Lady of the Holy Rosary ⑩, a Catholic church built in 1925 with Classical columns and a dome that's visible from the bayou. One block further up on the right, is St. Louis Cemetery #3 ⑪ (see p126), which has well-maintained examples of New Orleans' distinctive tombs and funerary art. Continue along Esplanade Avenue, crossing Bayou St. John again, to end the walk back at Beauregard Circle.

A view of the altar, Our Lady of the Holy Rosary church ⑩

0 meters   200

0 yards   200

Old oaks line the road to Oak Alley Plantation ▷

BEYOND NEW ORLEANS

BEYOND NEW ORLEANS

*T*he countryside around New Orleans is a land full of history and tradition. The beautiful plantations of the Mississippi River, Baton Rouge (the capital of Louisiana), and the famous Cajun Country are full of cultural and entertainment interest. Venturing beyond New Orleans allows you to experience the unique mixture of Louisiana's cultures in all their various accents.

The lifeblood of New Orleans was, and still is, the Mississippi River. In the 18th and 19th centuries, the river banks were lined with large plantations producing all kinds of commodities, including sugar, tobacco, and cotton, which were shipped around the world via New Orleans. Today only a handful of plantation homes survive along the River Road, but many are open to visitors, and some offer accommodation.

Sculpture at the Louisiana State Capitol

Prior to Hurricane Katrina, the state capital, metropolitan Baton Rouge, had a population of about 600,000; however, as people resettled away from low-lying areas, numbers rose to close to 700,000. An oil-refining center, Baton Rouge has several attractions associated with its role in state government, including the State Capitol, the Old State Capitol, and the Governor's Mansion. Other sights include the Rural Life Museum, the World War II destroyer the USS *Kidd*, and the Louisiana State University. To the west of Baton Rouge lie the massive Atchafalaya Swamp and Cajun Country. The latter is famous for its Francophone culture, Cajun and zydeco music, and its robust, spicy cuisine. Visitors can explore Cajun culture in a number of towns in this area – Eunice, Lafayette, and Opelousas – as well as along the bayous of New Iberia, and Avery Island. To get a feel for life on the bayous, you can attend a *fais do-do* (dance), try the local cuisine, or tour the McIlhenny Tabasco Sauce Factory. For an insight into the Cajun way of life, visitors can drift among age-old cypress trees in the swamps, or visit museums and historic villages.

Original Cajun house in the Acadian Village near Lafayette

◁ **St. John the Evangelist cathedral in Lafayette**

Exploring Beyond New Orleans

An excursion to the bayous and small towns a few hours away from New Orleans will show visitors just how different the city is from its Louisiana surroundings. Upriver, the Cajun heritage is evident in the architectural styles, the food, and even the language, since French is spoken almost everywhere. Only a few hours' drive from New Orleans, it is possible to visit more than a dozen Creole and American plantations along the Mississippi River and to get a taste of life as it used to be. The city of Baton Rouge, the state capital, makes an interesting modern counterpoint.

KEY

═══ Interstate highway

▭▭▭ State highway

━━━ Major road

╼╾ Main railway

──── Minor railway

SEE ALSO

• **Where to Stay** pp168–9

• **Where to Eat** pp184–5

Vermilionville
This restored 19th-century Cajun-Creole settlement is peopled by costumed staff. Traditional ways of life are enacted.

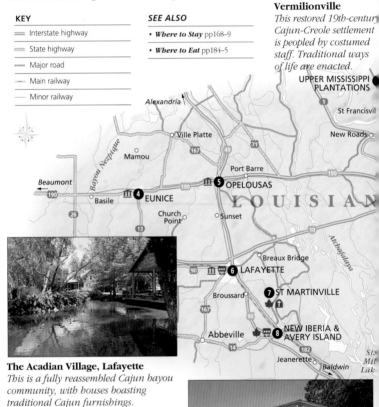

UPPER MISSISSIPPI PLANTATIONS

St Francisvil

Alexandria

New Roads

Ville Platte

Mamou

Port Barre

Beaumont

Basile

5 OPELOUSAS

4 EUNICE

Church Point

Sunset

L O U I S I A N A

Atchafalaya

Breaux Bridge

6 LAFAYETTE

7 ST MARTINVILLE

Broussard

Abbeville

8 NEW IBERIA & AVERY ISLAND

Jeanerette

Baldwin

The Acadian Village, Lafayette
This is a fully reassembled Cajun bayou community, with houses boasting traditional Cajun furnishings.

GETTING AROUND

All of the sights can be reached easily by road from New Orleans. Interstate 10 (I-10) connects the city directly to Baton Rouge. Some exits from route I-10 also lead to the River Road Plantations and to Cajun Country. From New Orleans, several guided tours to the bayous are available *(see p221)*, which offer a convenient way to explore life on the bayous.

Cajun Music Hall of Fame, Eunice
A country store dating from the 1930s now houses a museum of local music.

Nottoway
Built in 1859, Neo-Classical Nottoway Planta-tion has 64 rooms. Today it operates as a bed and breakfast and has a fine restaurant.

Old State Capitol, Baton Rouge
This Gothic Revival castle, built in 1847, was burned by the Union Army and repaired in 1882. Today it houses a museum of local history.

Swamp canal near Baton Rouge
Numerous canals cross the swamps, providing access to the area.

SIGHTS AT A GLANCE

Lower Mississippi Plantations ❶

Old plantation water pump

The River Road meanders along both banks of the Mississippi River, changing route numbers as it goes. It runs behind the levee, past petrochemical plants, towering live oaks draped with Spanish moss, and magnificent plantation homes. Creole families once owned and operated the plantations located between New Orleans and Baton Rouge. Some of the old plantation residences have been given a new lease on life as small museums.

Restored Plantations
Many plantations are carefully restored and are open to the public as bed and breakfast hotels.

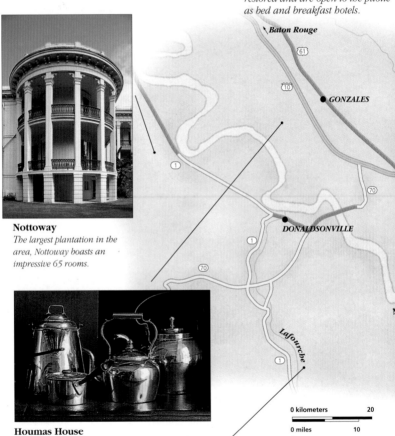

Nottoway
The largest plantation in the area, Nottoway boasts an impressive 65 rooms.

Houmas House
The country's largest sugar plantation in the 19th century, this grand house now displays a fine antiques collection.

Madewood Plantation
This Greek Revival style plantation house is one of the best preserved in the area and is also a bed and breakfast.

LOCATOR MAP

Oak Alley

A glorious double row of live oak trees lines the drive to this mansion, which was built in 1836.

San Francisco

"Steamboat Gothic" style is displayed in all its glory at this plantation.

Laura

The slaves who worked this typical Creole-style plantation are the source for the Brer Rabbit folktales.

Destrehan

This French-style mansion was constructed with a combination of wood and brick.

KEY

▦	Freeway
▬	Major road
▭	Minor road

Exploring Lower Mississippi Plantations

By 1850, two-thirds of America's millionaires lived on plantations located along the Great River Road. The economic relationship between the plantations' production and the trade from New Orleans to the rest of the world made it one of the wealthiest regions of the nation. The treasures of this glory are displayed in homes from New Orleans to Baton Rouge, with colorful French and Spanish Creole architecture and beautiful natural surroundings.

Destrehan plantation

Destrehan

13034 River Rd, Destrehan. **Tel** (985) 764-9315. 9am–4pm daily. major holidays.

Charles Pacquet, a free man of color, built this home for Robert de Logny in 1787. The original Creole cottage was modified in 1810 and 1840. Union troops housed freed slaves here during the Civil War (see pp18–19).

San Francisco

2646 Hwy 44, River Rd, Garyville. **Tel** (985) 535-5450. 10am–4pm daily. Jan 1, Easter, Thanksgiving, Dec 25, Mardi Gras.

www.sanfranciscoplantation.com

The term "Steamboat Gothic" has been applied to this ornate plantation home built for Edmond Bozonier Marmillion in 1856. Originally it was painted in flamboyant purples, blues, and greens, and the structure was decorated with plenty of ornate grillwork and gingerbread trim. The interiors feature some splendid ceiling paintings completed by Dominique Canova (cousin of the famous sculptor) featuring cherubs, trailing vines, flying parrots, and exquisite faux marbling and graining. Commissioned by Edmond's son, Valsin, and his daughter-in-law during major renovations in 1860, they were so expensive that Valsin named the house Saint Frusquin, from the French *sans fruscins*, meaning "without a penny." The name eventually became corrupted to "San Francisco." Valsin died before he could enjoy the house he had imagined, and shortly after the Civil War his widow sold it to a Colonel Bougere. The grounds of the original plantation have been reduced by several levee setbacks over the years, and so today it stands very close to the road.

Laura

2247 Hwy 18, Vacherie. **Tel** (225) 265-7690. 10am–4pm daily. major holidays.

www.lauraplantation.com

Revolutionary War veteran Guillame Duparc was given a large land grant and built the classic raised Creole plantation house in 1805. After he died, four generations of women ran the plantation. In 1891, Laura Locoul sold the property in order to marry and move with her husband to St. Louis.

The plantation gained notoriety for the stories told by the French-speaking slaves, later tenant farmers, living there. Folklorist Alcée Fortier first translated these Senegalese stories about Brer Rabbit, which later inspired Joel Chandler Harris's *Uncle Remus* and *Brer Rabbit* books.

In 2004 the main house was devastated by fire. It has now been meticulously rebuilt under the guidance of architectural historians, and guided tours are offered.

Oak Alley

3645 Hwy 18, Vacherie. **Tel** (225) 265-2151. 9am–4pm daily (to 5pm Sat, Sun). Jan 1, Thanksgiving, Dec 25, Mardi Gras.

www.oakalleyplantation.com

Oak Alley's name comes from the 28 magnificent live oaks that line the entrance to this plantation home. They were planted about 300 years ago,

San Francisco plantation, the ultimate in "Steamboat Gothic" style

The Great White Ballroom at Nottoway plantation

even before the house was built for Jacques Telesphore Roman III in 1837. The house and grounds are so striking that it has been used as a location for several movies, including *The Long Hot Summer* (1985) and *Interview with the Vampire* (1994). A slave gardener developed the first commercial variety of pecan nut, the "Paper Shell," on the property.

🏛 Nottoway

30970 Hwy 405, White Castle. *Tel* (225) 545-6884. ⬜ 9am–4pm daily. ⬤ Dec 25. 🖼 ▦

This is the largest plantation on this stretch of the Mississippi. It was designed by architect Henry Howard to accommodate John Hampden Randolph, his wife, and a family of 11 children, and completed in 1859. Randolph was a wealthy sugar planter originally from Virginia. The mansion occupies 53,000 sq ft (18,000 sq m), with 64 rooms, 16 fireplaces, 200 windows, and 165 doors. At the time it was built, it incorporated some innovative conveniences such as indoor plumbing, gas lighting, and coal fireplaces. In the Great White Ballroom, which is 65 ft (22 m) long, seven of Randolph's daughters celebrated their weddings. It is the largest and most impressive room in the house. It survived the Civil War due to the intervention of a Union

Antique clock at Nottoway

gunboat officer, who asked that it be spared because he had once been a guest of the Randolphs. It now operates as a bed and breakfast.

🏛 Madewood

4250 Hwy 308, Napoleonville. *Tel* (985) 369-7151 or (800) 375-7151. ⬜ 10am–4pm daily. ⬤ Jan 1, Thanksgiving, Dec 25. 🖼 ▦

Built in the prosperous times of pre-Civil War Louisiana, Madewood is unusual among south Louisiana plantation houses. It is a classic Greek Revival house, uninfluenced by the raised Creole villa style that predominates in the region. It was the first significant building by architect Henry Howard and erected between 1840–48 for sugar planter Thomas Pugh using construction materials from his holdings. Bricks for the exterior were made on the plantation and then covered with stucco

to give the illusion of masonry. In 1964 New Orleans preservationist Naomi Marshall saved the house from ruins after it lay neglected for years. She and her family then spent 13 years restoring the building and grounds. It now serves as a year-round bed-and-breakfast inn, and the site for many events, such as classical music recitals, local art fairs, and holiday celebrations.

🏛 Houmas House

40136 Hwy 942, River Rd, Darrow. *Tel* (225) 473-7841. ⬜ 9am–5pm Mon–Tue, 9am–8pm Wed–Sun. ⬤ Jan 1, Dec 25. 🖼 ▦ www.houmashouse.com

With its grand two-story verandas and monumental Tuscan columns, Houmas House is one of the most recognizable plantation villas in the South. As well as sprawling gardens, there is also a second house, a two-story French Colonial-era structure, which is attached to the main house by a carriageway. The main house, dating from 1840, is furnished in high antebellum style with a fine collection of period antiques. It survived the Civil War because its Irish owner, John Burnside, claimed immunity as a British subject. A wealthy merchant, Burnside amassed several sugar mills and at the end of the 19th century, this plantation was producing as much as 20 million pounds (9 million kg) of sugar each year.

Embroidery stand

Houmas House, a fine example of Greek Revival style

Baton Rouge ❷

In 1719, the French established Baton Rouge as a fort designed to control access to the Mississippi and the interior. It was so named by Jean Baptiste Le Moyne, Sieur de Iberville *(see p19)*, after he observed the spikes (red sticks) hung with bloody fish heads that were arranged along the river bluffs. In 1762, the French ceded it to the British. During the American Revolution, the Spanish took the opportunity to seize the garrison, which remained under their control until 1810. After that, the local American population took the fort and proclaimed the Republic of West Florida. The area was claimed for the United States and it was incorporated into the Union in 1817. It has been the state capital since 1849.

Lantern at LSU

The graceful interior of Louisiana Old State Capitol

🏛 Louisiana Old State Capitol

100 North Blvd. *Tel* (225) 342-0500. ◻ 10am–4pm Tue–Sat, noon–4pm Sun. ⬤ Mon, public hols. 🖼 ♿
James Harrison Dakin designed this striking castle-like building in 1847. William Freret conceived the soaring iron spiral staircase, installed during a renovation in 1882, which winds from the foyer toward the stained-glass dome. It was here, in the House Chamber, that Louisiana's state representatives voted in 1861 to secede from the Union. Seven decades later, in 1929, impeachment proceedings were begun here against Huey "Kingfish" Long. Today, this magnificent building serves as the state's Center for Political and Government History. Visitors can view and listen to many of the state's colorful political orators expressing their views.

🏛 Louisiana State University

Nicholson Drive btw Highland Rd and W Chimes St. *Tel* (225) 578-5030.
With its 31,000 students, this is the state's flagship university. The tree-shaded campus is attractively landscaped and boasts some unique features. In the northwest corner, for example, two mounds rise some 20 ft (6 m) high. Archeologists believe that they are 5,000-year-old Native American mounds built before the first Egyptian pyramids.

The university's sports teams are some of the hottest tickets in college sports. In baseball, the Tigers have won national titles for several consecutive years, and the enthusiasm generated by the football team is legendary.

The university also has two cutting edge research facilities; the Pennington Biomedical Research Center, devoted to nutritional medicine, and the Center for Microstructures

and Devices. The collections at the Museum of Natural Science in Foster Hall (225-578-2855) are also worth seeing. The visitor information center is at Dalrymple Drive and Highland Road.

🏛 Magnolia Mound Plantation

2161 Nicholson Dr. *Tel* (225) 343-4955. ◻ 10am–4pm Mon–Sat, 1–4pm Sun. ⬤ public hols. 🖼
John Joyce built this plantation home in 1791. In the 19th century it stood at the center of a 900-acre farm, producing indigo, cotton, perique tobacco, and sugarcane. The building has been carefully restored to reflect the antebellum era.

🏛 Old Governor's Mansion

502 North Blvd. *Tel* (225) 387-2464. ◻ 10am–4pm Tue–Fri. ⬤ public hols. 🖼 📷 only (last tour 3pm). ♿
Governor Huey Long had this mansion built in 1930. He modeled it on the White House, even down to the office, which is a smaller version of the Oval Office. The building has been carefully restored, and the rooms have even been repainted in their original colors, some of which are outlandish; Huey Long apparently loved hot pinks, purples, and greens, which appear in several bathrooms. Many of the furnishings in the library and the master bedroom are original to the house. There is also memorabilia from other governors, including the singing governor, Jimmie Davis, who wrote *You Are my Sunshine*.

Façade of the Greek Revival Old Governor's Mansion

The House Chamber, State Capitol

State Capitol

State Capitol Dr at N 3rd St.
Tel (225) 342-7317. ☐ 9am–4pm
daily. ● Jan 1, Easter Sunday,
Thanksgiving, Dec 25. ☐
Huey Long worked hard to
persuade the legislators to
approve the $5 million
funding for this Modernist
34-story building, erected in
1932. It is the tallest capitol
in the United States. Both
the House and Senate
chambers are impressive, as
are the murals in Memorial
Hall. Visitors can still see
the bullet holes in the
marble walls of the first-floor
executive corridor, where
Long was assassinated on
September 8, 1935, by Dr.
Carl A. Weiss, the son-in-law
of a political enemy, Judge
Benjamin Pavy. The grounds
contain Long's grave in a
sunken memorial garden.

There are excellent
views of the Mississippi
and the city from
the 27th-floor observa-
tion deck.

🏛 USS Kidd

305 S River Rd. *Tel (225)
342-1942.* ☐ 9am–5pm
daily. ● Thanksgiving,
Dec 25. ☐ ☐
Commissioned in
1943, this World War
II destroyer saw action
in the Pacific, where she
suffered a kamikaze attack on
April 11, 1945, and 38 of the
crew were killed. She also
served in the Korean War and
other missions until 1964,
when she was decommi-
ssioned. Visitors can see the
anti-aircraft guns and
other equipment
on the ship, and
tour the cramped
quarters shared by
the 330-man crew
below decks.

🏛 Rural Life Museum and Windrush Gardens

4560 Essen Lane at I-10. *Tel (225)
765-2437.* ☐ 8:30am–5pm daily.
● Jan 1, Easter Sunday, Thanksgiving,
Dec 24, Dec 25. ☐ ☐
Ione Burden and her brother,
Steele, who landscaped
Louisiana State University,
assembled this collection of

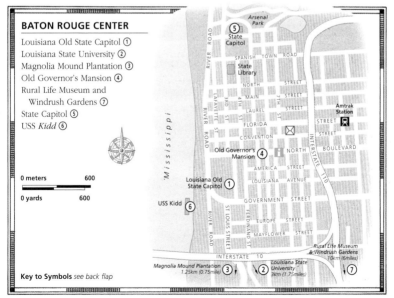

Old tractor at the Rural Life Museum

buildings and 19th-century
tools and artifacts. Each building is filled with fascinating
objects – a washing machine
dating from 1900, pirogues
(a type of boat used on the
bayous), cockfighting spurs,
and a tobacco press, to name
a few. Steele Burden's paintings and ceramic figures are
also displayed,
along with other
collectibles. In
the time before it
was fashionable to
preserve African
American culture,
Steele also rescued
all the buildings from nearby
Welham Plantation and
re-erected them in a typical
plantation layout. Today,
visitors can gain some insight
into how such a plantation
functioned as a self-contained
community. Crape myrtle,
azaleas, and other plantings
fill the adjacent gardens.

BATON ROUGE CENTER

Louisiana Old State Capitol ①
Louisiana State University ②
Magnolia Mound Plantation ③
Old Governor's Mansion ④
Rural Life Museum and
Windrush Gardens ⑦
State Capitol ⑤
USS Kidd ⑥

0 meters   600
0 yards   600

Arsenal Park
State Capitol ⑤
SPANISH TOWN ROAD
State Library
NORTH STREET
MAIN STREET
LAUREL
FLORIDA STREET
Amtrak Station
CONVENTION STREET
Old Governor's Mansion ④
NORTH BOULEVARD
AMERICA STREET
Louisiana Old State Capitol ①
LOUISIANA AVENUE
GOVERNMENT STREET
USS Kidd ⑥
EUROPE STREET
MAYFLOWER STREET
Rural Life Museum & Windrush Gardens 10km (6miles)
INTERSTATE 10
Magnolia Mound Plantation ③ 1.25km (0.75mile)
Louisiana State University ② 3km (1.75miles) ⑦

Mississippi

Key to Symbols see back flap

Upper Mississippi Plantations ❸

The West Feliciana Parishes, to the north of Baton Rouge, were not included in the Louisiana Purchase *(see p17)* and remained part of the Spanish domain until 1810. The plantations in this area differ from the southern Creole-style plantations. They were established by British immigrants or by Americans from North Carolina and Virginia, who made

Weather vane their fortunes here and brought their own culture and architectural styles. These beautiful plantations, with exceptional surrounding gardens, are well worth visiting.

Living Traditions
Many of the original work-shops and tools have been reconstructed and are in use.

Greenwood Plantation
One of the largest and most beautiful plantation houses in the area, Greenwood was built in 1830 by William Ruffin Barrow in classic Greek style.

Butler Greenwood
Built in 1790, this house is thoroughly Victorian, both in its architecture and furniture.

Mississippi

← Alexandria

NEW ROA

The Myrtles
Built between 1796 and 1830, The Myrtles plantation is exceptionally well preserved. Its 120-ft (40-m)-long cast-iron gallery is its most extravagant exterior feature.

Cottage Plantation
With its original 14-karat gold wallpaper in the parlor, this offers one of the best stays in the area. Andrew Jackson stayed here after the Battle of New Orleans (see p17).

LOCATOR MAP

```
0 kilometers        5
0 miles             3
```

Natchez

Catalpa
This little Victorian cottage is surrounded by 30 acres of splendid gardens. Tours of the interior reveal numerous interesting historic family heirlooms.

ST FRANCISVILLE

Baton Rouge

Oakley House
Naturalist John James Audubon (see p111) tutored James Pirrie's daughter, Eliza, at this plantation. Many of Audubon's original prints are on display. Fascinating nature trails are also available.

Rosedown
This plantation has remarkable original furnishings, plus fine formal gardens.

KEY

— Major road
— Minor road

Exploring the Upper Mississippi Plantations

The French established Baton Rouge in 1719, when they built a fort to control access to the Mississippi River and the interior *(see pp146–7)*. After being controlled by the Spanish and the British, this city was finally incorporated into the United States in 1817, and became the state capital in 1849. North of Baton Rouge the plantations were established by British or Americans, who held on to their Anglo-Saxon heritage. A different architecture with Greek Revival influences is dominant in this area. Many of these plantations have been restored and are now charming B&Bs.

Butler Greenwood, surrounded by beautiful gardens

Old slave cabin at Cottage Plantation

🏛 Butler Greenwood

8345 Hwy 61, St. Francisville. *Tel* (225) 635-6312. ◯ 9am–5pm daily. 🖼 🎫 www.butlergreenwood.com
Pennsylvania Quaker physician Samuel Flower founded this plantation in 1796. His daughter, Harriet, ran it for most of the 19th century as a cotton-producing plantation. Today it is still a working plantation operated by the eighth generation of the family. Family portraits hang throughout the house, which contains many of the original 19th-century furnishings, including a fine 12-piece parlor set made of rosewood and upholstered in the original scarlet-colored fabric. The plantation also offers lovely B&B-style accommodation.

🏛 Catalpa

9508 Hwy 61, St. Francisville. *Tel* (225) 635-3372. ◯ by appointment only. ● Dec 15–Jan 31. 🖼 🎫
The current building is a reconstruction of the original, which was destroyed in a fire in 1885. Carolinian William J. Fort established the plantation in the early 1800s. He was famous for his hospitality

and for the many parties he gave in the gardens, which were landscaped with a pond complete with an island for picnics, a deer park, and several summer houses. He also maintained greenhouses filled with exotic tropical plants including banana, guava, and mandarin.

🏛 Cottage Plantation

10528 Cottage Lane, St. Francisville. *Tel* (225) 635-3674. ◯ 9:30am–4:30pm daily. ● major holidays. 🖼 🎫 www.cottageplantation.com
The land on which this house stands was granted to John Allen and Patrick Holland in 1795. Judge Thomas Butler purchased the original cottage and property in 1810. He was the son of Colonel Thomas Butler, one of the five fighting Butlers who served under General Washington during the American Revolution (1775–83). He extended the house to accommodate his family. The interiors are lavishly decorated with 14-karat gold-leaf wallpaper and plenty of *faux bois*.

Exhibit at Butler Greenwood

The property includes several outbuildings, one of which has been converted into a restaurant. Overnight lodging is also offered.

🏛 Greenwood Plantation

6838 Highland Rd, St. Francisville. *Tel* (225) 655-4475. ◯ Nov–Feb: 10am–4pm; Mar–Oct: 9am–5pm. ● Jan 1, Jul 4, Thanksgiving, Dec 25. 🖼 🎫 ♿ www.greenwoodplantation.com
In 1830, James Hammon Coulter designed this majestic Greek Revival home for William Ruffin Barrow, who had migrated from the Carolinas. It stood on 12,000 acres, which were worked by 750 slaves. Some 40 outbuildings housed workshops that made the plantation completely self-sufficient. The Barrows became one of the most prominent families in the area, but anticipating the Civil War they sold the plantation. It survived the war serving as a hospital, but afterward it deteriorated rapidly. In 1906 Mr. and Mrs. Frank Percy restored it,

Greenwood Plantation, furnished with impressive antebellum pieces

For hotels and restaurants in this region see pp168–9 and pp184–5

salvaging the marble mantels and silver hinges and doorknobs. Tragically, in 1960 lightning destroyed the entire structure, except for the 28 massive Doric columns. It has since been restored, and visitors can once again see the splendor of the 70-ft (21-m)-long central hall and the rest of the interior. Greenwood runs a B&B and is a popular venue for weddings.

Greenwood Plantation, one of the largest American-style plantations

🏛 The Myrtles

7747 Hwy 61, St. Francisville. **Tel** (225) 635-6277. ◯ 9am–5pm daily. ● major hols. 🅿 💳 ♿
www.myrtlesplantation.com

A leader of the Whiskey Rebellion (1794) in Pennsylvania, Judge David Bradford fled south and established this plantation in 1796. He built the north wing of the house and in the early 1800s, his daughter and her husband, Judge Clark Woodruff, added the 107-ft (36-m)-long gallery. Ruffin Gray Stirling bought the house in 1834, and added the south wing. Local legend says that several murders were committed here and that the house is haunted. Special tours on Friday and Saturday nights highlight its haunted history. Bed-and-breakfast accommodation is also available.

The handsome cast-iron veranda surrounding The Myrtles

🏛 Rosedown Plantation

12501 Hwy 10, St Francisville. **Tel** (225) 635-3332. ◯ 9am–5pm daily. ● Thanksgiving, Dec 25, Jan 1. 🅿 💳

Rosedown is one of the largest and most complete of the plantations along the river. The gabled central structure, built of cedar and

cypress, has a double gallery supported by Doric columns. Other sections of the house feature Georgian details.

The Turnbull family owned and operated the plantation from 1835 to 1955. Practically all of the contents of the house are original, including rosewood furniture by Mallard and Seignoret, portraits by Thomas Sully, brocade draperies, and marble mantels. Daniel and Martha Turnbull, who established the plantation in 1835, purchased most of the furnishings on their initial Grand Tour of Europe in 1834 and on subsequent trips abroad. The grounds contain a kitchen building, the doctor's office, a barn, and a gardener's tool house. The 28 acres of French-style gardens are exquisite too. Martha Turnbull was a well-known horticulturist, who introduced the first azaleas and camellias to the region.

In 2000 the state of Louisiana purchased the plantation from a private owner, who had unfortunately sold some of the original furnishings. The estate has been renovated and now offers a fascinating 45-minute tour of the house and grounds.

🏛 Oakley House and Audubon State Historic Site

Hwy 965, St. Francisville. **Tel** (225) 635-3739. ◯ 9am–5pm daily. ● Thanksgiving, Dec 25, Jan 1. 🅿 💳

Wealthy Scottish immigrant James Pirrie built this house between 1808 and 1810, and it is a splendid example of the way colonial architecture was adapted to the Louisiana climate. Since then, it has been surrounded by a bosky paradise inhabited by numerous species of birds.

In 1821, naturalist John James Audubon *(see p111)* and his assistant arrived to teach daughter Eliza Pirrie dancing, music, drawing, and math. He and his assistant received room and board and $60 a month. The arrangement did not last, and he left after only four months, having quarreled with his employer. Still, in that brief time he began at least 32 bird portraits, which later appeared in *The Birds of America*. Today, visitors can see the room Audubon stayed in and wander the trails around the property. Magnolias, beeches, and poplars still shelter abundant bird life in the state park surrounding the house.

Study used by John James Audubon in Oakley House

The Liberty Theater, home of the *Rendez-Vous des Cajuns* radio show

Eunice ❹

Cajun Country. 🚶 *11,000.*
🚌 *1238 W Landry St.* ℹ 200 South
CC Duson Dr, *(337) 457-2565.*

Every weekend there is a
Cajun music celebration in
this picturesque Louisiana
town, where most of the
main attractions are in the
downtown area. The town
was founded by C. C. Duson
in 1893, who named it in
honor of his wife. **The Liberty
Theater** is the keeper of the
flame of Cajun music – the
Grand Ole Opry of Cajun
music. It opened in the 1920s
as a movie and vaudeville
theater. Every Saturday from
6 to 8pm the theater hosts a
live broadcast of the *Rendez-
Vous des Cajuns* radio show.
It is filled with Cajun and
zydeco music and plenty
of good Cajun humor. The
master of ceremonies makes
introductions in both English
and French.

Visitors to **The Prairie
Acadian Cultural Center**,
located just behind the
theater, can observe musical
instruments and other items
being made in the craft room.
Other displays focus on
aspects of Acadian culture,
including the *Courir.* Literally
"the race," this is the Cajun,
and distinctly medieval,
version of Mardi Gras.
Participants wear a *capuchon*
(a tall, cone-shaped hat,
which covers the face as well
as the head) and ride on
horseback from farm to farm
begging for the ingredients
for a community gumbo,

which will be eaten at the
end of the day. The key
ingredient, a chicken, has
to be chased down and
caught live.

Located nearby are
two other cultural
centers. **The Cajun
Music Hall of Fame
& Museum**, which
opened in 1997,
honors the ori-
ginators of Cajun
music and the
artists who have
kept the tradition
alive. It displays
memorabilia,
instruments such as
accordions and violins,
photographs, and biographies
of the 40 inductees.

Cajun music is a blend of
several traditions – German,
Scottish, Irish, Spanish, Afro-
Caribbean, and Native
American – which have been
laid over a base of French
and French-Acadian folk

Cajun accordion in The
Savoy Music Center

tradition. Zydeco developed
from the same traditions but
incorporates much more Afro-
Caribbean rhythm and style.

The Hall of Fame features
the great names in Cajun
music, from such early
musicians as Amédé Ardoin,
Alphé Bergeron, Dennis
McGee, Joe Falcon, Amédé
Breaux, Iry Lejeune, and
Lawrence Walker, to more
recent interpreters, including
Michael Doucet, Zachary
Richard, and Wayne Toups.

Heading from Eunice to
Opelousas along Highway
190, there is **The Savoy
Music Center**, the informal
headquarters for Cajun
musicians in the area. The
store is owned by accordion-
maker-musician Marc Savoy
and his wife, Ann. It sells
musical instruments,
CDs, and books on
Cajun culture and
music. On Saturday
mornings local
musicians assemble
in the front of the
store for a jam
session around the
upright piano. They
bring accordions,
triangles, and
fiddles, and play
together. People
can bring beer, boudin, and
other snacks. Visitors are
welcome to listen and join in.

🏛 **The Prairie Acadian
Cultural Center**
250 West Park Ave.
Tel *(337) 457-7700.*
🕐 *8am–5pm Tue–Fri, 8am–6pm
Sat.* ⚫ *25 Dec.* ♿

Mardi Gras costume and memorabilia at The Prairie Acadian Cultural Center

Opelousas Museum and Interpretive Center

🏛 The Cajun Music Hall of Fame & Museum
240 South CC Duson Dr. **Tel** *(337) 457-6534.* ☐ *summer: 9am–5pm Tue–Sat; winter: 8:30am–4:30pm Tue–Sat.* ◉ *major hols.* &

🎵 The Liberty Theater
200 Park Ave. **Tel** *(337) 457-7389.* ☐ *4pm Sat.* 📷 &

🎵 The Savoy Music Center
Hwy 190 East, Savoy. **Tel** *(337) 457-9563.* ☐ *9am–5pm Tue–Fri, 9am–noon Sat.* ◉ *major hols.* &

Opelousas ❺

Cajun Country. 👫 *11,000.* 🚉 *828 E Landry St, (800) 424-5442.* **www.**cityofopelousas.com

This city, the capital of Confederate Louisiana during the Civil War *(see pp18–19)*, was named after the Native American tribe that lived in this area before the Europeans arrived. It was founded as a French trading post settlement during the 1700s, and today it is one of the liveliest towns in this district, thanks to its excellent cuisine and music.

The major collections of the **Opelousas Museum** focus on the local culture and history of the town. The museum's two main exhibit areas are devoted to the prehistory of the area, its agricultural and commercial development, and to the people of different races and religions who developed the region and contributed to its culture. One room is devoted to memorabilia from the Civil War, while another houses a fascinating collection of more than 400 dolls.

The **Opelousas Museum of Art** stands in the oldest part of the city, in a historic Federal-style brick building, built originally as a one-story tavern. The second story was added in 1828. Today, the museum mounts several shows each year featuring art on loan from major museums and private collections. Recent shows have focused on paintings by Louisiana's African American folk painter, Clementine Hunter, jazz photographs taken by William P. Gottlieb, and the wood engravings made by Winslow Homer for *Harper's Weekly*.

A slice of Opelousas life is on view at **Le Vieux Village**, a collection of buildings dating from the 1700s, including a church, schoolhouse and doctor's office, that offers visitors an opportunity to view the historic local architecture. A tourist information center is also located here, as well as a small museum devoted to native son Jim Bowie, who was the hero of the Alamo and the namesake of the well-known frontier knife.

Evangeline Downs Racetrack & Casino is a state-of-the-art racing facility that opened in 2003. The track offers both quarter horse and thoroughbred racing (on separate dates). It is a "racino," that is, a racetrack with a full casino component, which is a growing institution among US racetracks. The casino consists primarily of slot machines.

🏛 Opelousas Museum
315 N Main St. **Tel** *(337) 948-2589.* ☐ *9am–5pm Mon–Sat.* ◉ *major hols.* 📷 &

🏛 Opelousas Museum of Art
106 North Union St. **Tel** *(337) 942-4991.* ☐ *1–5pm Tue–Fri, 9am–5pm Sat.* ◉ *major hols.* 📷 &

🏕 Le Vieux Village
28 East Landry St. **Tel** *(337) 948-0561, toll-free 800-424-5442.* ☐ *8am–4pm daily.* ◉ *major hols.* 📷 &

Evangeline Downs Racetrack & Casino
2235 Creswell Lane Extension. **Tel** *(866) 472-2466, toll-free 800-424-5442.* ☐ *Feb–Sep (racetrack); 24 hrs daily (casino).* 🍴 🍸 & **www.**evangelinedowns.com

Main façade of the Opelousas Museum of Art

Lafayette ⑥

When the first Acadians arrived in 1764, they settled along the bayous and in the prairie lands west of New Orleans. Being rural people, they worked as farmers and made a living from the swamps. Lafayette is Cajun country's largest city. It is at the heart of the Cajun culture, because of the strong Arcadian family traditions and cultural heritage. Community centers, restaurants, several detailed reconstructions of Cajun villages, and its own local architectural style have imprinted this city with a unique atmosphere and the distinctive feeling of being in the Cajun Country.

Harp on display at the Alexandre Mouton House

🏛 Acadian Cultural Center

501 Fisher Rd, Lafayette. **Tel** (337) 232-0789. 8am–5pm daily. Dec 25.

A 37-minute film dramatizes the British deportation of the Acadian population from Canada's Acadie, and charts their diaspora to France and to places along the east coast of North America, before their final arrival in Louisiana. In an adjacent display area, informative exhibits, featuring photographs and artifacts, focus on every aspect of Acadian culture, including language, music, architecture, religion, cuisine, the *Courir* festival (*see p152*), and all kinds of handcrafts.

Old-fashioned Cajun plough

🏛 Vermilionville

300 Fisher Rd, Lafayette. **Tel** (337) 233-4077. 10am–4pm Tue–Sun (last admission 3pm). major hols. www.vermilionville.org

This fascinating living-history museum features a collection of buildings dating from 1790 to 1890 assembled into a typical Cajun village on 23 acres. Its name, Vermilionville, was the original name for the city of Lafayette. Costumed artisans demonstrate the skills that were needed to survive in 18th- and 19th-century Louisiana; woodworking, blacksmithing, spinning, weaving, and cooking. It is pleasant to wander from building to building imagining what traditional Cajun life was like. A performance hall, where Cajun bands regularly entertain, is open in the afternoon.

🏛 Lafayette Museum/ Alexandre Mouton House

1122 Lafayette St, Lafayette. **Tel** (337) 234-2208. 9am–4:30pm Tue–Sat, 1–4pm Sun. major hols.

Jean Mouton, founder of Lafayette, built the original house around 1800. He and his wife Marie and their 12 children used it only on Sundays when they came from their plantation in Carencro to attend church and socialize. In 1825 the sixth son, Alexandre, moved his family and law practice into the house. He later became a United States senator and governor of Louisiana – a notable example of Cajun success. The house contains furnishings, paintings, maps, and documents relating to the city's history, plus some glittering Mardi Gras costumes and regalia.

🏛 University Art Museum

1710 East St. Mary Boulevard, Lafayette. **Tel** (337) 482-2278. 10am–5pm Tue–Sat. major hols. www.louisiana.edu/uam

This small art museum is located on the campus of the University of Louisiana at Lafayette, an institution with

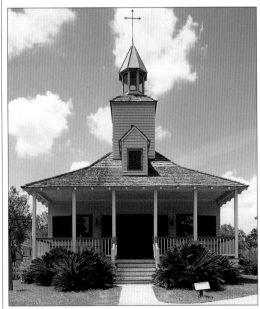

Original Acadian chapel in Vermilionville

The University Art Museum, a 2001 design in steel, stone, and glass

17,000 students, which has an excellent Computer Science department and is also home to both the National Wetlands Research Center and the Center for Louisiana Studies. The University Art Museum was founded in 1968 and has a permanent collection of more than 1,500 works including paintings, sculpture, folk art, and textiles. The emphasis is on the cultural heritage of Louisiana. In 2001, the museum moved to a bold new building of glass and steel with state-of-the-art exhibition spaces. It has many outstanding works of art, including European and American art from the 18th, 19th, and 20th centuries, and a wide assortment of 2nd century BC Egyptian artifacts. This permanent exhibition also includes an excellent collection of African American folk art. Diverse architectural drawings, as well as student works, are displayed along with temporary exhibits all year long.

🏛 The Acadian Village
200 Greenleaf Dr, Lafayette.
Tel *(337) 981-2364.* ⭘ *10am–4pm daily.* ⬤ *Jan 1, Thanksgiving, Dec 25, Mardi Gras.* 🖼 ♿

At this version of a recreated 19th-century village, most of the buildings are original, although they have been moved here from other locations. The houses are furnished with typical Cajun furniture and tools, and are tended by costumed guides who demonstrate such skills as spinning, weaving, and blacksmithing. One of the residences was the birthplace of state senator, Dudley LeBlanc, the creator of a cure-all tonic called Hadacol, which was still in use as recently as the 1950s.

THE ACADIANS
Driven by the British from Acadia, in Nova Scotia, Canada, the Acadians (or "Cajuns") settled along the bayous of Louisiana in 1764, working as farmers. For generations they were disparaged, and in the 20th century their culture came under threat, first when compulsory education was introduced in 1916 and the French language was forbidden, and later in the 1930s when Huey Long *(see p146)* built roads across the swamps, opening their communities to a wider world. When oil was discovered, the transformation intensified; outsiders flooded in and the Francophone culture was endangered. The culture survived largely because Cajuns have a strong sense of family and attachment to place. Today Cajun Country is the largest French-speaking community in the United States. In the 1960s, Cajun pride was restored when the teaching of French returned to the classrooms. At the same time, Cajun and zydeco music started growing in popularity among a broader audience, and Cajun cuisine, promoted by chef Paul Prudhomme *(see p177),* spread across the country.

Traditional Acadian dress

Dentist's chair at the Acadian Village's infirmary

The Acadian Memorial in St. Martinville

St. Martinville ❼

Cajun Country. 👥 8,000. ℹ️ 215 *Evangeline Blvd, (337) 394-2233.* www.cityofsaintmartinville.com

This small picturesque town on a natural levee of the Bayou Teche, was founded in 1765 as a military outpost. It became known as "Petit Paris" (little Paris) because many French noblemen settled there after fleeing the French Revolution.

Acadian Memorial

Located in the main square of this town is the **Acadian Memorial**, which houses the mural painted by Robert Dafford, *The Arrival of the Acadians in Louisiana*, which portrays some 40 people, who arrived in Louisiana between 1764 and 1788. The painter went so far as to model some of the portraits on contemporary descendants. Opposite the painting, the Wall of Names lists about 3,000 early Acadians. Behind the mural, an eternal flame burns in a small courtyard garden overlooking Bayou Teche.

Nearby stands the **Evangeline Oak**, marking the spot where the two famous Acadian lovers, Gabriel and Evangeline, supposedly encountered each other. Gabriel confessed that after three years in exile he had despaired of ever seeing her again and married another. She went mad and died soon after. Longfellow's poem changes the ending, placing her as a nurse at his bedside as he lay dying.

St. Martin de Tours Church is the focal point of St. Martinville. Established in 1765 by French missionaries, it was the first church to serve the Acadian community. Fairly plain inside, it contains a baptismal font, which was a gift from Louis XVI, and a replica of the grotto at Lourdes. The grave of Evangeline Labiche (mythologized as Longfellow's Evangeline) and a bronze statue of her are located in the garden behind the church. The monument was donated by actress Dolores del Río, who played the role of Evangeline in the silent movie filmed here in 1929. Also on the church square there is the **Petit Paris Museum and Gift Shop**, which houses the historical records of the most important events in the town's life. The **Longfellow-Evangeline**

St. Martin de Tours church at the center of St. Martinville

State Commemorative Area is a 180-acre state park that stretches along Bayou Teche. It offers pleasant picnicking and walking trails among 300-year-old oaks. At the center of the park stands a reconstruction of a typical Acadian cabin representative of the 1790s. This can be contrasted with the Olivier House, a plantation home built in 1815. The cypress and brick structure has 14-inch (36-cm) thick walls. There is also a museum, which focuses on Acadian history and culture.

🏛 **Acadian Memorial**
121 South New Market St.
Tel *(337) 394-2258.* ⏱ *10am–4pm daily.* ⬤ *major hols.* ♿ 📷

🏛 **Petit Paris Museum and Gift Shop**
103 S Main St. **Tel** *(337) 394-7334.* ⏱ *9:30am–4:30pm daily.* ⬤ *Dec 25.* ♿ 📷

✝ **St. Martin de Tours Church**
133 S Main St. **Tel** *(337) 394-7334.* ⏱ *8am–6pm daily.* ⬤ *Fri noon–6pm.* ♿

🏛 **The Longfellow-Evangeline State Commemorative Area**
1200 N Main St. **Tel** *(337) 394-3754.* ⏱ *9am–5pm daily.* ⬤ *Thanksgiving, Dec 25, Jan 1.* ♿ 📷

New Iberia and Avery Island ❽

Cajun Country. 👥 32,000. 🚉 *1103 E Main St.* ℹ️ *2513 Highway 14, (888) 942-3742.* www.cityofnewiberia.com

New Iberia is notable for its many sugar cane plantations. The area also owes its wealth to oil drilling and salt mining. In fact, the so-called "islands" in the region, such as Avery and Jefferson, are not actually surrounded by water: rather they are domes located atop salt mines.

At the plantation home known as **Shadows on the Teche**, 40 trunks were found in the attic, filled with 17,000 letters, photographs, receipts, and papers relating to the family who lived here. This documentation is used as background for the fascinating tour of the house. A native of Maryland, David Weeks, built the plantation home in 1831. He died shortly thereafter, leaving his wife, Mary Clara, to run it. During the Civil War *(see pp18–19)*, when Union General Nathaniel P. Banks seized it and made it his headquarters, Mary Clara retired to the attic where she died in 1863. The last owner, Weeks Hall, was a well-known artist and scholar, who restored the house and entertained many famous visitors in it, including director Cecil B. DeMille and writer Henry Miller. Their names are inscribed in the foyer.

On Avery Island the **McIlhenny Company Tabasco Factory and Jungle Gardens** is the source of the famous hot sauce, which is an essential ingredient in Bloody Marys and in local cuisine. Approximately 75 acres of pepper plants blaze their bright red color from August to November. A brief film explains the process in which the red chili peppers are crushed and combined with salt and vinegar to make the zesty sauce. Visitors can also tour the bottling factory.

The founder considered himself a botanist-naturalist and the Jungle Gardens that he assembled are spectacular. In addition to abundant camellias and azaleas, there are such exotica as Latin American papaya. The

Moss-draped oaks and spring-flowering plants in the Jungle Gardens

gardens also shelter a diverse population of egrets, herons, peacocks, as well as the beaver-like nutria. In winter, wild fowl stop here too.

The **Rip Van Winkle House and Gardens** are located on the salt dome called Jefferson Island. It was built by the actor Joseph Jefferson in 1870 and named after the role he played 4,500 times. Architecturally, it is a hodgepodge of Moorish, Steamboat Gothic, and Victorian. The house is surrounded by 25 acres of beautiful gardens, which are on the banks of Lake Peigneur.

After Jefferson died in 1905, J. Lyle Bayless of the Salt Island Mining Company purchased the house. Shortly afterward, oil was discovered on the property. It was soon producing up to 250,000 barrels of oil a week from 30 wells. In

1972, the Texaco Oil Company mistakenly drilled through the salt dome, causing an explosion that set off a minor tidal wave on the lake. Miraculously, no one was killed.

Shadows on the Teche
317 E Main St, New Iberia. *Tel (337)* 369-6446. ◯ *9am–4:30pm daily (from noon Sun).* ◉ *major hols.* www.shadowsontheteche.org

McIlhenny Company Tabasco Factory and Jungle Gardens
Hwy 329, Avery Island. *Tel (337)* 365-8173. ◯ *9am–4pm daily.*
Jungle Gardens *Tel (337) 369-6249* ◯ *9am–5pm daily.* ◉ *major hols.* www.tabasco.com

Rip Van Winkle House and Gardens
5505 Rip Van Winkle Rd, Jefferson Island. *Tel (337) 359-8525.* ◯ *8am–5pm daily.* ◉ *public hols.* www.ripvanwinklegardens.com

Shadows on the Teche in New Iberia

Food stalls in the French Market, New Orleans ▷

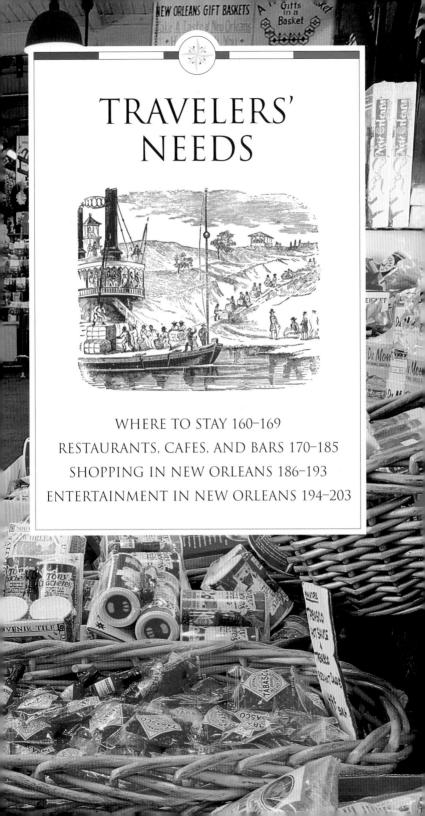

TRAVELERS' NEEDS

WHERE TO STAY

New Orleans is a big convention town, with many well-known hotel chains, including the Hyatt, Hilton, Marriott, and Sheraton. It also has some elegant hotels, like the Windsor Court, the Ritz Carlton, and Le Pavillon, and lovely boutique offerings, such as International House and Soniat House. Some of the best lodgings can be found in

Bellman

bed and breakfasts, like the House on Bayou Road, or in small inns such as the Maison de Ville and Audubon Cottages. The Fairmont, which closed after Hurricane Katrina due to damage, was reborn in 2009 as The Roosevelt, a return to its historic name and the name locals remember. It has undergone extensive renovation, and is now a Waldorf Astoria property.

Le Pavillon Hotel in the Business District *(see p165)*

WHERE TO LOOK

Most hotels are located in the French Quarter or in the Central Business District along Canal Street, the latter being within walking distance of both the Quarter and the Convention Center. Bed and breakfasts (B&Bs) are scattered throughout the city, uptown in the Garden District, and on the fringes of the Quarter in the Faubourgs Marigny and Treme.

HOTEL PRICES AND SERVICES

New Orleans has accommodations to fit any budget, from the least expensive motel to the fabulous French Quarter hotels and guest houses. Prices vary according to the location and the level of luxury; many boutique hotels are as expensive as the splendid high rises, and if the hotel or B&B is in the French Quarter, the price will reflect this sought-after location.

Prices can rise more than 50 percent during Mardi Gras and special events, and be prepared for a three- to five-day minimum stay.

All hotel accommodations, unless otherwise stated, include air-conditioning, elevators, non-smoking rooms, and full bathrooms.

During major holidays, such as Christmas, many hotels require a three- or four-night minimum stay. In the off-season, such as the summer, special rates and vacation packages offer amazing discounts.

BED AND BREAKFAST

Guest houses and boutique hotels are usually in renovated historic homes, and B&Bs are rooms in a private residence. All offer some meals, full breakfasts or just coffee and croissants, and often, afternoon tea or cocktails are provided. All have a limited number of rooms, so advance reservations

are necessary. Some of the budget-priced guest houses and B&Bs have shared bathrooms, and facilities for disabled guests can be limited.

HIDDEN EXTRAS

Taxes will add 13 percent to the bill plus an additional $1–$3 for "room night tax". Valet parking will cost from $12 to $25 a day. Some motels and B&Bs have free parking, so always ask ahead. Hotel telephone charges are often very high. It is always cheaper to use a pay phone in the lobby or use your cell phone, particularly when calling overseas. You will also pay a premium on products in your minibar. A tip of $1 to $2 per bag is usually paid to the bellman for carrying bags. Room-service waiters expect the standard 15 percent tip. If staying more than one night, you should leave $1 to $2 a day for the housekeeping staff.

Lobby of the Omni Royal Orleans hotel *(see p162)*

A perfect welcome at the Monteleone Hotel *(see p162)*

FACILITIES

Most establishments offer full facilities, such as well-appointed rooms, cable TV, phone, modems, mini-bars, and full bathrooms. Often the larger hotels have one or two fine restaurants, several bars, a fitness room, a swimming pool, and a business center. At virtually every hotel, you will find complimentary toiletries, a morning newspaper delivered to your door, room service, and wake-up and reservation services.

Because the weather in New Orleans is semi-tropical, all accommodations are air-conditioned. B&Bs generally do not offer all these amenities, but the ambience in these homes makes up for any lack.

HOW TO BOOK

If you want to visit the city during Mardi Gras or the Jazz and Heritage Festival, you will need to book six months to a year in advance. At other times, a few months' advance booking is recommended. You can make telephone or online reservations using a credit card. A deposit of one night is usually required, and there are specific cancellation policies that guests should clarify at the time of booking. If you anticipate arriving after 6pm, ask for guaranteed late arrival. Most hotels have toll-free reservation numbers, and many take reservations by fax or e-mail.

SPECIAL RATES

When making reservations, it won't hurt to ask for special AAA, AARP, or senior citizen rates. Some chains offer discount rates, and look at hotel websites for special deals. You can reserve by using a major credit card. Package tours may also offer savings from hotel or B&B accommodations to airport/hotel transportation. Check the newspapers for specials.

A four-poster bed in one of the upscale bed and breakfasts

DISABLED TRAVELERS

Since 1992 all hotels in the United States have been required by law to provide wheelchair-accessible accommodations. However, older, listed, and historic properties are exempt from this provision, but most establishments have at least one room equipped for disabled guests. If you or any of your traveling companions have special needs, it is wise to call the hotel in advance to confirm suitability.

TRAVELING WITH CHILDREN

Most hotels welcome children, although New Orleans may not be an ideal destination for the young. Children aged up to 12, 16, or 18 (depending on the place) can usually stay free in their parents' room.

YOUTH AND BUDGET ACCOMMODATIONS

New Orleans has a few hostels, as well as some guest houses with rooms with shared bathrooms that are modestly priced. Many motels on the outskirts of the city are also fairly inexpensive.

Choosing a Hotel

These hotels have been selected across a wide price range for their good value, excellent facilities, and location. This chart lists the hotels by area of the city in the same order as the rest of the guide. Within each area, entries are listed alphabetically within each price category, from the least expensive to the most expensive.

PRICE CATEGORIES
For a standard double room per night in the tourist season, including tax and service:

$ $50–$100
$$ $100–$150
$$$ $150–$200
$$$$ $200–$250
$$$$$ over $250

UPPER FRENCH QUARTER

Grenoble House
P 🏊 $$
323 Dauphine St, 70112 **Tel** *(504) 522-1331* **Fax** *(504) 524-4968* **Rooms** *17*   **Map** *4 C2*

All the rooms are suites in this little-known French Quarter hotel. Kitchens and ample living space make this the perfect place for a family or a group (but no children under 12). Furnishings are utilitarian. The courtyard and small pool are lovely, and the staff are attentive and welcoming. **www.grenoblehouse.com**

Prince Conti Hotel
P 🍴 $$
830 Conti St, 70112 **Tel** *(504) 529-4172* **Fax** *(504) 581-3802* **Rooms** *73*   **Map** *4 C2*

Generations of Southern families have stayed at the Prince Conti. Rooms vary in size and are handsomely furnished with antiques and art. The friendly, long-term staff make a point of getting to know guests. The hotel's bar, the Bombay Club, is renowned for its martinis. **www.princecontihotel.com**

Iberville Suites
P 🍴 🏊 📺 $$$
910 Iberville St, 70112 **Tel** *(504) 523-2400* **Fax** *(504) 524-1321* **Rooms** *230*   **Map** *4 C2*

This is the downscale segment of the Ritz-Carlton but it is still pretty luxe. All the rooms are junior suites with small fridges, coffeemakers, two TVs, and much more. Decor is chintz and mahogany. The famed Ritz service is good even for the not-so-rich guests who bunk here. **www.ibervillesuites.com**

Olivier House
🏊 $$$
828 Toulouse St, 70112 **Tel** *(504) 525-8456* **Fax** *(504) 529-2006* **Rooms** *58*   **Map** *4 C2*

Three townhouses and several other buildings compose this Quarter hotel. The entrance parlors are formal, but there is a free spirit about the Olivier House. Rooms range from no-frills options to shabby-chic suites. The courtyard is small but pretty. Pets are welcome. **www.olivierhouse.com**

Maison de Ville & Audubon Cottages
P 🍴 🏊 $$$$
727 Toulouse St, 70130 **Tel** *(504) 561-5858* **Fax** *(504) 528-9939* **Rooms** *24*   **Map** *4 C2*

The Maison de Ville is a beautiful Creole townhouse compound with richly decorated, if smallish, rooms. The even more expensive Audubon Cottages are a block away: idyllic private cottages in a tropical garden with a pool. This is how visitors dream their Quarter hotel will be. **www.hotelmaisondeville.com**

Monteleone Hotel
P 🍴 🏊 📺 $$$$
214 Royal St, 70130 **Tel** *(504) 523-3341* **Fax** *(504) 681-4491* **Rooms** *655*   **Map** *4 C3*

The Monteleone has been a French Quarter landmark since 1886. This family-owned hotel has undergone a major renovation, revamping its rooms with new fabrics, furniture, and amenities. Try booking one of the "literary rooms," named for writer guests such as Truman Capote and Ernest Hemingway. **www.hotelmonteleone.com**

Omni Royal Orleans
P 🍴 🏊 📺 $$$$
621 St. Louis St, 70130 **Tel** *(504) 529-5333* **Fax** *(504) 529-7089* **Rooms** *346*   **Map** *4 C2*

One of the largest hotels in the French Quarter, the Omni Royal is known for its attentive service. Rooms have an old New Orleans look but are fully equipped with dataports, Wi-Fi, and dual phones. Ask for a "get fit" guest room and get your own treadmill and supply of healthy snacks. **www.omniroyalorleans.com**

The Ritz-Carlton
P 🍴 🏊 📺 $$$$
921 Canal St, 70112 **Tel** *(504) 524-1331* **Fax** *(504) 524-7675* **Rooms** *527*   **Map** *4 B3*

This hotel actually comprises three hotels in one place (Iberville Suites and Maison Orleans are the other two). The largest segment is the Ritz-Carlton, which lives up to its reputation for luxury. Rooms are large with marble baths. The hotel spa, which is one of the best in the US, is pure bliss. **www.ritzcarlton.com**

Royal Sonesta Hotel
P 🍴 🏊 📺 $$$$$
300 Bourbon St, 70130 **Tel** *(504) 586-0300* **Fax** *(504) 586-0335* **Rooms** *535*   **Map** *4 C2*

Covering almost a block in the Quarter, this hotel is like a little village with its own shops, cafés, courtyards, and personalities. Rooms range from basic to suites, all handsomely appointed. Ask to be as far away from Bourbon Street as possible to avoid street noise. **www.royalsonestno.com**

Key to Symbols *see back cover flap*

Maison Orleans

904 Iberville St, 70112 **Tel** *(504) 670-2848* **Fax** *(504) 670-2849* **Rooms** *75*

Map *4 C2*

The Ritz-Carlton goes over the top with the supremely luxurious Maison Orleans. It feels like a private club with your own staff rather than a hotel. Rooms have dreamy beds, gilt-encrusted furniture, and soaking tubs. Guests are served food and drink almost continually. **www.ritzcarlton.com**

W French Quarter

316 Chartres St, 70130 **Tel** *(504) 581-1200* **Fax** *(504) 522-3208* **Rooms** *99*

Map *4 C3*

W tries to find a middle ground between postmodern and French Quarter non-modern in this stylish hotel. Rooms have all the W signatures: most important, the lush bed. All the rooms are small, which is typical of the Quarter. The hotel restaurant Bacco is a top New Orleans spot. **www.whotels.com**

LOWER FRENCH QUARTER AND MARIGNY

Bon Maison Guesthouse

835 Bourbon St, 70116 **Tel** *(504) 561-8498* **Rooms** *4*

Map *5 D1*

On lower Bourbon Street, Bon Maison is an 1833 Creole townhouse with slave quarters. It is convenient to the gay bar scene, although non-gays also like the B&B for its historic ambience, well-appointed rooms, and great prices. Rooms have fridges and microwaves. The guesthouse doesn't accept children. **www.bonmaison.com**

Pierre Coulon Guesthouse

714 Spain St, 70117 **Tel** *(504) 943-6692* **Rooms** *1*

Map *5 F1*

Staying at this Marigny home is like living in New Orleans. Guests reside in the restored two-story slave quarters, equipped with a small kitchen. The rooms open out into a tranquil courtyard, shared with the main house. The hosts know the city intimately and cheerfully share tips. **www.pierrecoulonguesthouse.com**

Andrew Jackson Hotel

919 Royal St, 70116 **Tel** *(504) 561-5881* **Fax** *(504) 596-6769* **Rooms** *22*

Map *5 D1*

This fine little hotel sits on a tranquil corner of Royal Street in a 19th-century villa. The best rooms are the balcony suites overlooking the street. It is worth the extra charge for the fine view. Rooms are traditional in style, with basic amenities. Most rooms open onto the courtyard. **www.frenchquarterinns.com**

Chateau Hotel

1001 Chartres St, 70116 **Tel** *(504) 524-9636* **Fax** *(504) 525-2989* **Rooms** *45*

Map *5 D2*

The Chateau is a hotchpotch of several historic and newer buildings cobbled together in the Lower (quieter) Quarter. Rooms come in a variety of sizes, some with antique pieces. The hotel has a long list of regulars who return year after year, giving it a clubhouse feel. **www.chateauhotel.com**

Cornstalk Hotel

915 Royal St, 70116 **Tel** *(504) 523-1515* **Fax** *(504) 522-5558* **Rooms** *14*

Map *5 D1*

Named for its charming cornstalk-shaped cast-iron fence, this hotel is a converted 19th-century home. Some of the rooms are tiny, but all are furnished with antiques. The second-story verandah is a favorite gathering place for sipping drinks while watching the Quarter pass by. **www.cornstalkhotel.com**

Frenchmen Hotel

417 Frenchmen St, 70116 **Tel** *(504) 948-2166* **Fax** *(504) 948-2258* **Rooms** *28*

Map *5 E1*

This hotel is just steps away from the French Quarter and the Frenchmen Street music scene. It's a compound of several 19th-century buildings. Rooms can be on the dark side, and the pool is tiny. Pluses include the friendly, helpful staff and the bohemian ambience. **www.frenchmenhotel.com**

Hotel Provincial

1024 Chartres St, 70116 **Tel** *(504) 581-4995* **Fax** *(504) 581-1018* **Rooms** *115*

Map *5 D2*

Popular with business travelers and families, the family-owned Provincial's rooms have a vintage look, with antiques and exposed brick. There are several courtyards, two pools, parking, and access to the motel's acclaimed eatery, Stella! **www.hotelprovincial.com**

Hotel Villa Convento

616 Ursulines St, 70116 **Tel** *(504) 522-1793* **Fax** *(504) 524-1902* **Rooms** *25*

Map *5 D1*

This is a family-owned inn of the old school: modest in amenities but rich in service and ambience. Rooms are basic and clean. The inn is on a quiet street in the Quarter and is a quick walk to clubs and attractions. Singer Jimmy Buffett lived here in the 1970s when it was a rooming house. **www.villaconvento.com**

Le Richelieu Hotel

1234 Chartres St, 70116 **Tel** *(504) 529-2492* **Fax** *(504) 524-8179* **Rooms** *86*

Map *5 D1*

A Quarter favorite, this hotel is forever famous for Paul McCartney and his family staying here for months in the 1970s. Rooms have a vintage look, and suites are also available. The courtyard and pool are very pretty, and the large, park-it-yourself parking lot is a rarity in the Quarter. **www.lerichelieuhotel.com**

Lions Inn Bed & Breakfast ⬛ ⬚ $$

2517 Chartres St, 70117 **Tel** *(504) 945-2339* **Fax** *(504) 944-4927* **Rooms** *10*   **Map** *5 F1*

The engaging house-party atmosphere makes this gay-friendly inn popular with straight people as well. The B&B's two adjoining houses open onto a large, jungle-like courtyard with a pool. Rooms vary in size from tiny to apartment with kitchenette. Two rooms have shared baths. **www.lionsinn.com**

Maison Dupuy Hotel ⬚ P ⬛ ⬚ ⬚ $$

1001 Toulouse St, 70112 **Tel** *(504) 586-8000* **Fax** *(504) 525-5334* **Rooms** *200*   **Map** *4 C2*

This hotel is at the "back of the Quarter" (opposite from the river). It is built around a courtyard, and some rooms have overlooking balconies. Rooms are decorated with local art and soothing colors. Dominique's, one of the city's top *haute cuisine* restaurants, is part of the hotel. **www.maisondupuy.com**

Nine-O-Five Royal Hotel $$

905 Royal St, 70116 **Tel** *(504) 523-0219* **Fax** *(504) 525-3905* **Rooms** *13*   **Map** *5 D2*

This small hotel in the French Quarter is a little-known jewel. Set in a large Victorian house on a quiet corner, it offers the best kind of basic stay – a good place to sleep and regroup in attractive surroundings with a helpful staff. Ask for one of the suites with a balcony. **www.905royalhotel.com**

Claiborne Mansion ⬚ P ⬚ $$$

2111 Dauphine St, 70116 **Tel** *(504) 949-7327* **Fax** *(504) 949-0388* **Rooms** *7*   **Map** *3 E4*

This is one of New Orleans's best-kept secrets. The 1858 villa has been imaginatively restored using a subtle color palette and contemporary furniture. The rooms are airy and luxurious. The gardens feature a lap pool and a small cottage. A favorite of visiting celebrities. **www.claibornemansion.com**

Hotel de la Monnaie ⬚ P ⬚ ⬚ $$$

405 Esplanade Ave, 70116 **Tel** *(504) 947-0009* **Fax** *(504) 945-6841* **Rooms** *53*   **Map** *5 E1*

Built in the 1980s, this Beaux-Arts style hotel is an ideal blend of the historic and the new. Rooms are clean, modern, and stylishly decorated. The Monnaie is across Esplanade Avenue from the French Market and Old Mint museum. The hotel is a time-share but rents to non-owners. **www.hoteldelamonnaie.com**

Lafitte Guesthouse $$$

1003 Bourbon St, 70116 **Tel** *(504) 581-2678* **Fax** *(504) 581-2677* **Rooms** *14*   **Map** *5 D1*

Ask for one of the two rooms with balconies overlooking Bourbon Street for a special experience. The 1840s Creole townhouse feels like the 19th century but with modern conveniences. On the minus side, the bathrooms are small, and there's no elevator for the house's four stories. **www.lafitteguesthouse.com**

Sunburst Inn ⬚ P $$$

819 Mandeville St, 70117 **Tel** *(504) 947-1799* **Rooms** *2*   **Map** *3 F1*

Located six blocks from the French Quarter, in an area full of popular restaurants, live-music venues, and gay bars, this small inn is housed in a 1905 building that has been lovingly restored and painted in vibrant, cheerful hues. It offers high-end amenities and a welcoming atmosphere, with hosts who love to entertain. **www.sunburstinn.net**

Lanaux Mansion ⬚ P ⬚ $$$$

547 Esplanade Ave, 70119 **Tel** *(504) 330-2826* **Rooms** *4*   **Map** *5 D1*

Esplanade Avenue, formerly known as "The Creole Promenade," has some of the grandest architecture you will see in the city. The mansion housing the Lanaux was built in 1879, and has been lovingly restored with stunning, wrought-iron balconies. Rooms feature antiques and Oriental rugs. The garden is also lovely. **www.lanauxmansion.com**

Soniat House ⬚ P $$$$$

1133 Chartres St, 70116 **Tel** *(504) 522-0570* **Fax** *(504) 524-0810* **Rooms** *33*   **Map** *5 D1*

The Soniat House is a favorite with visiting celebrities and millionaires. The service is sublime and the rooms are beautifully appointed with Louisiana antiques, Oriental rugs, and big, enveloping beds. The hotel is located in restored Creole townhouses that face each other across Chartres Street. **www.soniathouse.com**

WAREHOUSE AND CENTRAL BUSINESS DISTRICTS

O'Keefe Plaza Hotel ⬚ P ⬚ ⬚ $

334 O'Keefe Ave, 70112 **Tel** *(504) 524-5402* **Fax** *(504) 524-5450* **Rooms** *129*   **Map** *4 B3*

If you can get past the homely big-box look and dreary streetscape, this hotel has some lovely features. The prices are astoundingly low, and it's a clean, well-run facility. Rooms are plain but have all the basic necessities. The O'Keefe Plaza is close to the French Quarter and CBD offices. **www.okeefeplazahotel.com**

Hampton Inn ⬚ P ⬚ ⬚ $$

226 Carondelet St, 70130 **Tel** *(504) 529-9990* **Fax** *(504) 529-5453* **Rooms** *187*   **Map** *4 B3*

This hotel is housed in a handsome historic office building in the Central Business District. Some rooms have four-poster beds. Business travelers will find everything they need here. The pool, courtyard, and breakfast buffet are especially good features. **www.neworleanshamptoninns.com**

Key to Price Guide *see p162* **Key to Symbols** *see back cover flap*

La Quinta Inn & Suites

301 Camp St, 70130 **Tel** *(504) 598-9977* **Fax** *(504) 598-9978* **Rooms** *182*   **Map** *4 C3*

This handsome business hotel blends into the streetscape. While it may be short on charm, this branch of the La Quinta chain is big on efficiency, cleanliness, and good prices. A few blocks from the Quarter and close to the St. Charles Avenue streetcar, this hotel is also well placed. A large breakfast is included. **www.lq.com**

Royal St. Charles Hotel

135 St. Charles Ave, 70130 **Tel** *(504) 587-3700* **Fax** *(504) 587-1704* **Rooms** *143*   **Map** *4 C3*

The slick exterior and boutique label make this hotel sound a little more exciting than it really is. The rooms are small but clean and comfortable. The hotel is suitably located on the St. Charles Avenue streetcar line and barely a block from the French Quarter. **www.royalsaintcharleshotel.com**

Staybridge Suites

501 Tchoupitoulas St, 70130 **Tel** *(504) 571-1818* **Fax** *(504) 571-1811* **Rooms** *182*   **Map** *4 C4*

Convenient to the Convention Center, the museum district, and the casino, this chain hotel delivers on all its promises. Rooms are bright and clean, and the breakfast is unusually fresh and abundant. The pool is a bit on the small side, but the fitness center covers the basics. **www.staybridgesuites.com**

Lafayette Hotel

600 St. Charles Ave, 70130 **Tel** *(504) 524-4441* **Fax** *(504) 523-7327* **Rooms** *44*   **Map** *4 B4*

Right on the St. Charles Avenue streetcar line, the Lafayette recalls the elegant residential hotels of an earlier era with its classic decor, friendly staff, and handsome Beaux-Arts building. Rooms are retreats with marble baths, soothing colors, and polished wood furniture. **www.thelafayettehotel.com**

Le Pavillon Hotel

833 Poydras St, 70112 **Tel** *(504) 581-3111* **Fax** *(504) 620-4130* **Rooms** *226*   **Map** *4 B3*

One of the city's grande dames, Le Pavillon wears its crown lightly. The courtly staff evoke the days of gracious hotel service. Rooms are decorated with fine art and period furniture. The rooftop pool, late-night lobby snacks, and cool bar add to the hotel's special allure. **www.lepavillon.com**

Lowe's Hotel

300 Poydras St, 70130 **Tel** *(504) 594-3300* **Fax** *(504) 595-3310* **Rooms** *273*   **Map** *4 C4*

This stylish hotel in the city's business and entertainment district is within a short walk of many galleries and restaurants. Rooms are luxurious, and some have views of the nearby Mississippi River; the hotel's Grand Luxury Suite is the largest in the city. There is also a popular bar and restaurant. Pets are welcome. **www.loweshotels.com**

Renaissance Arts Hotel

700 Tchoupitoulas St, 70130 **Tel** *(504) 613-2330* **Fax** *(504) 613-2331* **Rooms** *217*   **Map** *4 C4*

This hotel in the Warehouse District lives up to the "arts" in its name with a gallery and cutting-edge art works everywhere. The large, airy rooms use bold colors and contemporary design. The hotel restaurant and bar, LaCote Brasserie, is on the local list of hot spots. **www.marriott.com**

Renaissance Pere Marquette Hotel

817 Common St, 70130 **Tel** *(504) 525-1111* **Fax** *(504) 525-0688* **Rooms** *272*   **Map** *4 B3*

The sophisticated Pere Marquette was built in 1925 as one of New Orleans' first "skyscrapers." There is a strong jazz theme throughout the hotel, and every room features luxurious amenities, whimsical decor, spacious baths, and Herman Miller Aeron chairs. The in-house restaurant MiLA is wonderful. **www.marriott.com**

W Hotel

333 Poydras St, 70130 **Tel** *(504) 525-9444* **Fax** *(504) 581-7179* **Rooms** *423*   **Map** *4 C4*

This seriously hip hotel has more going for it than design. Rooms have super-luxurious beds and all the electronic amenities. The rooftop pool and cabanas are very trendy. The lobby is a popular meeting spot for beautiful 20-somethings who love the Whiskey Blue bar. **www.whotels.com**

Windsor Court Hotel

300 Gravier St, 70130 **Tel** *(504) 523-6000* **Fax** *(504) 596-4513* **Rooms** *324*   **Map** *4 C4*

Everything English is worshipped here. The hotel even does an authentic afternoon tea service. Luxury is the starting point for the Windsor Court, where rooms are magical retreats, and the lobby is truly palatial. The service is almost omniscient without being intrusive. **www.windsorcourthotel.com**

International House

221 Camp St, 70130 **Tel** *(504) 553-9550* **Fax** *(504) 553-9560* **Rooms** *119*   **Map** *4 C3*

Staying here is an adventure – of the pleasant kind. Most months there's an elaborate voodoo altar in the lobby. Rooms are furnished with Louisiana-themed items. The marble bathrooms are extra large and have dual shower-heads, and big soaking tubs. The Loa bar is a local hot spot. **www.ihhotel.com**

The Roosevelt

123 Baronne St, 70112 **Tel** *(504) 648-1200* **Fax** *(504) 585-1295* **Rooms** *504*   **Map** *4 B3*

This historic hotel, which was once the New Orleans headquarters of Louisiana political boss Huey Long, fully embraces its colorful past. After years as the Fairmont Hotel, it reopened in 2009 as the Roosevelt Hotel – its prior name. Today it stands under a new flag, the esteemed Waldorf Astoria brand. **www.therooseveltneworleans.com**

GARDEN DISTRICT AND UPTOWN

Avenue Inn B&B   P   ⑤

4125 St. Charles Ave, 70115 **Tel** *(504) 269-2640* **Fax** *(504) 269-2641* **Rooms** *17*   **Map** *7 E4*

You see this 1891 mansion almost as its first occupants did; it has never been remodeled, only restored. Rooms are on all three floors, some with period pieces, all with private baths. The house is near Tulane and Loyola, right on the St. Charles Avenue streetcar line. **www.avenueinnbb.com**

Garden District Hotel   🔲 P ⚊ 🍸   ⑤

2203 St. Charles Ave, 70130 **Tel** *(504) 566-1200* **Fax** *(504) 581-1352* **Rooms** *141*   **Map** *8 A3*

The St. Charles Avenue streetcar stops right in front of this hotel, which is only a short ride away from the French Quarter. It is a reliable, mid-size establishment with unremarkable but comfortable, spacious rooms. It specializes in arrangements for group travel, from transportation to catering and tours. **www.gardendistricthotel.com**

Maison St. Charles Inn   P ⚊ ⚊   ⑤

1319 St. Charles Ave, 70130 **Tel** *(504) 522-0187* **Fax** *(504) 529-4379* **Rooms** *130*   **Map** *8 A2*

Although this inn is not located in the most elegant part of the Garden District, it is still on the St. Charles Avenue streetcar line. The rooms have a traditional decor and basic amenities. The central courtyard with pool, evening happy hour, and billiard table add to the conviviality. Special deals for cruise-ship travelers. **www.maisonstcharles.com**

Marquette House   P   ⑤

2249 Carondelet St, 70130 **Tel** *(504) 523-3014* **Fax** *(504) 529-5933* **Rooms** *25*   **Map** *8 A3*

A loose-limbed hostel (not part of the international association), Marquette House has typical dormitory rooms for budget travelers. Apartments are also available in adjacent historic buildings and offer one of the best deals in town. The compound is a block from the St. Charles Avenue streetcar. **www.neworleansinternationalhouse.com**

Prytania Park Hotel   P   ⑤

1525 Prytania St, 70130 **Tel** *(504) 524-0427* **Fax** *(504) 522-2977* **Rooms** *74*   **Map** *8 A3*

One block from St. Charles Avenue, this compound of old and new buildings is a collection of suites and rooms. Furnishings are from the upscale furniture store across the street (owned by the same family). Kids will love the lofts in some suites, while everyone else will love the affordable rates. **www.prytaniaparkhotel.com**

St. Charles Guest House   ⚊   ⑤

1748 Prytania St, 70130 **Tel** *(504) 523-6556* **Fax** *(504) 522-6340* **Rooms** *35*   **Map** *8 A3*

Once a seamen's boarding house, the inn has grown to include several buildings near St. Charles. It's a friendly family-run place where guests get to know each other and return year after year. All rooms are different, ranging from no-frills to a few frills. No phones or TVs in the rooms. **www.stcharlesguesthouse.com**

Avenue Plaza   🔲 P ⚊ ⚊ 🍸   ⑤⑤

2111 St. Charles Ave, 70130 **Tel** *(504) 566-1212* **Fax** *(504) 525-6899* **Rooms** *258*   **Map** *8 A3*

This hotel is all suites (two sizes) with kitchens. The St. Charles Avenue streetcar stops at the front door. The hotel is a time-share and has recently undergone a refurbishing sequence. The main attraction is the courtyard pool, where guests can relax and enjoy a massage. **www.avenueplazahotel.com**

Chimes Inn   ⑤⑤

1146 Constantinople St, 70115 **Tel** *(504) 899-2621* **Fax** *(504) 488-4639* **Rooms** *5*   **Map** *7 E4*

Guests stay in the four private rooms and one cottage in this Uptown home. Nicely decorated and perfectly maintained, the B&B is a good homebase for travelers. The hosts serve a deluxe Continental breakfast and are enthusiastic guides to the city. **www.chimesneworleans.com**

Columns Hotel   🔲 P ⚊   ⑤⑤

3811 St. Charles Ave, 70115 **Tel** *(504) 899-9308* **Fax** *(504) 899-8170* **Rooms** *20*   **Map** *7 E4*

This small hotel is famous as the set for the Louis Malle film *Pretty Baby* and has plenty of fans for its laid-back ambience. The 1883 mansion's rooms are quirky and decorated with antiques and secondhand chic. The lounge, the Victorian Bar, is one of the city's best bars. **www.thecolumns.com**

Creole Gardens Guesthouse   P   ⑤⑤

1415 Prytania St, 70130 **Tel** *(504) 569-8700* **Fax** *(504) 895-2231* **Rooms** *25*   **Map** *8 B2*

Bright tropical blues and yellows signal a Caribbean mood for this lively guesthouse, popular with Europeans and younger travelers. Rooms are in various shapes and sizes. All three 19th-century buildings that constitute the hotel open onto the courtyard. Breakfast is included. **www.creolegardens.com**

The Green House Inn   P ⚊   ⑤⑤

1212 Magazine St, 70130 **Tel** *(504) 525-1333* **Fax** *(504) 525-1383* **Rooms** *9*   **Map** *8 B2*

This historic bed and breakfast in the Lower Garden District offers great access to downtown without the hustle and bustle. A tropical theme pervades the premises, and the surrounding neighborhood is bejeweled with architectural gems. The Green House is a pet-friendly establishment too. **www.thegreenhouseinn.com**

Key to Price Guide *see p162* **Key to Symbols** *see back cover flap*

Hubbard Mansion

🅿 $$

3535 St. Charles Ave, 70115 **Tel** *(504) 897-3535* **Fax** *(504) 899-8827* **Rooms** *5* **Map** *7 E4*

This Greek Revival house is actually a new building, designed as a replica of a Natchez mansion. It's furnished with beautiful antiques, including rare Louisiana armoires. The host, Don Hubbard, is a New Orleans insider. Rooms are of different sizes, and all have marble baths. **www.hubbardmansion.com**

Josephine Guest House

🅿 $$

1450 Josephine St, 70130 **Tel** *(504) 524-6361* **Fax** *(504) 523-6484* **Rooms** *7* **Map** *8 A3*

Popular with romantics and those who enjoy a relaxed pace, the Josephine Guest House is located in an 1870 Italianate villa off St. Charles Avenue. The rooms are decorated with antiques and period pieces. Traditional *café au lait* is served in the morning, along with fresh breads. **www.josephine.us**

St. Charles Inn

🔲 🅿 🔳 $$

3636 St. Charles Ave, 70115 **Tel** *(504) 899-8888* **Fax** *(504) 899-8892* **Rooms** *40* **Map** *7 E4*

The hotel is a wallflower on glamorous St. Charles but it is well worth seeking out, especially for the budget traveler. Rooms are motel ordinary, and there's no lobby to speak of, but it's safe, comfortable, and on the streetcar line. Pluses are free parking, Continental breakfast, and a fitness room. **www.bestwestern.com**

Sully Mansion

$$

2631 Prytania St, 70130 **Tel** *(504) 891-0457* **Fax** *(504) 269-0793* **Rooms** *8* **Map** *7 F3*

This 1890 Queen Anne-style mansion is wonderfully intact with stunning stained-glass windows and interior moldings. Rooms are furnished with antiques and tasteful accessories. All rooms have modern baths. The B&B is in the Garden District, a block from the St. Charles Avenue streetcar. **www.sullymansion.com**

Terrell Guesthouse

🔳 🅿 $$

1441 Magazine St, 70130 **Tel** *(504) 237-2076* **Fax** *(504) 247-0565* **Rooms** *7* **Map** *8 B3*

This charming inn is an 1858 villa in the Lower Garden District. Rooms are furnished with antiques and art, all with private baths, and there is a spacious courtyard. A full breakfast is served. The neighborhood is undergoing a renaissance of sorts. **www.terrellhouse.com**

Grand Victorian Inn

🅿 $$$

2727 St. Charles Ave, 70130 **Tel** *(504) 895-1104* **Fax** *(504) 896-8688* **Rooms** *8* **Map** *7 F3*

This meticulously restored Queen Anne-style mansion led the way for other B&Bs on St. Charles Avenue. The house is beautifully decorated with antiques and art. Bedrooms have four-poster and canopy beds along with private baths. Some rooms overlook the avenue, which is always a plus. **www.gvbb.com**

Hampton Inn

🔲 🅿 🏊 🔳 $$$

3626 St. Charles Ave, 70115 **Tel** *(504) 899-9990* **Fax** *(504) 899-9908* **Rooms** *100* **Map** *7 4E*

Well placed on St. Charles Avenue, this hotel has a cheery pastel exterior that sets the tone for the helpful staff and sunny lobby. Rooms are spacious and attractive. Big pluses are the free, non-valet parking and the ample breakfast buffet. The St. Charles Avenue streetcar stops almost in front of the hotel. **www.hamptoninn.com**

Laurel Street Bed & Breakfast

🅿 $$$

5127 Laurel St, 70115 **Tel** *(504) 269-5002* **Fax** *(504) 269-5309* **Rooms** *4* **Map** *6 C5*

Built in 1891 for the treasurer of the New Orleans Grand Opera House, this lovely B&B is housed in an old Eastlake cottage with a garden and a large porch with an attractive view. It is located in a quiet neighborhood, but close to the Mardi Gras parade routes and Audubon Park. Children are welcome.

Magnolia Mansion

🅿 $$$

2127 Prytania St, 70130 **Tel** *(504) 412-9500* **Fax** *(504) 412-9502* **Rooms** *9* **Map** *8 A3*

This is one of New Orleans's great antebellum houses. Now restored as a B&B, the grandeur remains. Guests must abide by a long list of rules (no children, no red wine, etc), and sometimes have to dodge weddings and camera crews. Rooms are lavishly decorated. **www.magnoliamansion.com**

McKendrick-Breaux House

🅿 $$$

1474 Magazine St, 70130 **Tel** *(504) 586-1700* **Fax** *(504) 522-7138* **Rooms** *9* **Map** *8 B3*

Situated on a reviving part of Magazine Street, this is one of the city's premier B&Bs. Two restored 1860s townhouses are joined by a tropical garden. Rooms have antique beds, contemporary art, and private phones, reflecting the inn's masterful blending of old and new. **www.mckendrick-breaux.com**

MID-CITY

Ashton's Bed & Breakfast

🅿 $$

2023 Esplanade Ave, 70116 **Tel** *(504) 942-7048* **Rooms** *8* **Map** *3 D3*

Guests love sitting in the back garden under the ancient oak tree at this popular B&B. The 1861 mansion is situated near the Fair Grounds, making it ideal for the Jazz Fest. City Park is also nearby. Most rooms are furnished with period furniture and all have private baths. **www.ashtonsbb.com**

Degas House
2306 Esplanade Ave, 70119 **Tel** *(504) 821-5009* **Fax** *(504) 821-0870* **Rooms** *8*   **Map** *2 C3*

P | $$

Painter Edgar Degas visited his American relatives here between 1872 and 1873. Guestrooms in the 1852 Italianate house include a garret, but it's not clear exactly which room Degas stayed in during his residency. The minimalist decor serves to show off the fine lines of the house itself. **www.degashouse.com**

O'Malley House
120 S Pierce St, 70119 **Tel** *(504) 488-5896* **Fax** *(504) 483-3791* **Rooms** *8*   **Map** *2 A3*

$$

One block off the Canal streetcar line, the O'Malley House is a marvel of elaborate Queen Anne-style architecture. Restored inside and out, the inn offers antique-filled rooms, an excellent breakfast, and hosts who go out of their way to make life interesting and easy for their guests. **www.1896Omalleyhouse.com**

Block-Keller House
3620 Canal St, 70119 **Tel** *(877) 588-3033* **Fax** *(504) 483-3032* **Rooms** *5*   **Map** *2 A3*

P | $$$

This magnificently restored Neo-Classical villa is on the Canal streetcar line, just a short ride from the French Quarter. Built in 1912, it has beautiful gardens that have been restored since Hurricane Katrina. The innkeepers have two dogs, happy to be your "pets away from home." A generous breakfast is available. **www.blockkellerhouse.com**

House on Bayou Road
2275 Bayou Rd, 70119 **Tel** *(504) 945-0992* **Fax** *(504) 945-0993* **Rooms** *8*   **Map** *2 C3*

P ⑪ 🏊 | $$$

It's hard to believe you are in the city at this B&B. Called a "petite plantation," it is set on two acres of gardens. Guests stay in elegant rooms with fireplaces, four-poster beds, libraries, private verandahs, and other delights. A two-course gourmet plantation-style breakfast is offered each morning. **www.houseonbayouroad.com**

BEYOND NEW ORLEANS

BATON ROUGE Cook Hotel
3848 W Lakeshore Dr, Baton Rouge, 70808 **Tel** *(866) 610-2665* **Fax** *(225) 383-4200* **Rooms** *128*

🛏 P 🏊 🍽 | $$

Nestled in the Louisiana State University campus, this hotel is primarily for students and conference attendees, but others can stay as well. All suites have kitchens. There is a laundry facility, and a super pool and fitness center. It is fun to stay on campus, and there is easy access to highways. **www.thecookhotel.com**

BATON ROUGE Stockade Bed & Breakfast Inn
8860 Highland Rd, Baton Rouge, 70808 **Tel** *(225) 769-7358* **Fax** *(225) 769-7358* **Rooms** *5*

P | $$

Located on the grounds of a Civil War stockade, the grim name is belied by the expansive hospitality of the host. The modern Spanish-styled house is airy and light. All rooms have private baths. Breakfast can be Continental or enormous. The house is near the LSU campus. **www.thestockade.com**

EUNICE L'Acadie Inn
259 Tasso Loop, Eunice, 70535 **Tel** *(337) 457-5211* **Rooms** *14*

P 🚶 | $

The Pitre family has revamped a 1950s roadside motel into a Cajun inn. The motel rooms are strictly no-frills, but they are clean and inexpensive. All the rooms have kitchenettes, which is very helpful in this country setting. The Pitres love sharing their vast knowledge of Cajun life. **www.hotboudin.com**

LAFAYETTE Bois des Chênes Inn
338 N Sterling St, Lafayette, 70501 **Tel** *(337) 233-7816* **Fax** *(337) 233-7816* **Rooms** *5*

🛏 P | $

The town of Lafayette has grown around this 1820s French plantation house. There are two suites in the main house and three in the converted stables. All are furnished with period antiques. A full breakfast is served, and the helpful hosts are encyclopedias of knowledge about the area.

LAFAYETTE T'Frere's House
1905 Verot School Rd, Lafayette, 70508 **Tel** *(337) 984-9347* **Rooms** *8*

P | $$

Innkeepers Maugie and Pat Pastor serve lavish breakfasts in the morning and bottomless drinks in the evening. Rooms in the main house and garden cottage are furnished with antiques. Ghost sightings are reported, but these are of the amusing rather than malicious type. **www.tfreres.com**

NAPOLEONVILLE Madewood Plantation
4250 Hwy 308, Napoleonville, 70390 **Tel** *(985) 369-7151* **Rooms** *10*

P | $$$$$

Staying at Madewood is like being a houseguest during the plantation's plush years. The bedrooms are beautifully furnished with Louisiana antiques but are comfortable and welcoming. Dinner and breakfast are included, which is helpful since the house is deep in the country. **www.madewood.com**

NEW IBERIA Estorge-Norton House
446 E Main St, New Iberia, 70560 **Tel** *(337) 365-7603* **Rooms** *5*

P | $

This lovingly maintained 1910 arts and crafts villa makes a nice change from plantation sites. It is in the New Iberia historic district, close to all the main sites. Rooms are furnished with American antiques. Three of the rooms have shared baths. A lavish breakfast is served in the dining room. **www.bbhost.com**

Key to Price Guide *see p162* **Key to Symbols** *see back cover flap*

NEW IBERIA La Maison B&B P ⑤

8317 Weeks Island Rd, New Iberia, 70560 **Tel** *(337) 364-2970* **Rooms** *2*

The house looks suburban, but the atmosphere is pure Cajun. Hostess Eleanor Naquin serves heroic breakfasts and loves to arrange for guests to have a full immersion into Acadian life. Pets are welcome, but children must be at least 12 and "well behaved."

NEW IBERIA Rip Van Winkle House & Gardens P ⑤⑤⑤

5505 Rip Van Winkle Road, New Iberia, 70560 **Tel** *(337) 359-8525* **Fax** *(337) 359-8526* **Rooms** *2*

Two small but roomy houses are available for overnight guests: Servants' Quarters and Cook's Cottage. Both date from the estate's early years. Furnished with four-poster beds, luxury linens, and kitchenettes, the cottages are surrounded by acres of manicured gardens. **www.ripvanwinklegardens.com**

ST. FRANCISVILLE 3-V Tourist Court P �ⅱ ⑤

5689 Commerce St, St. Francisville, 70775 **Tel** *(225) 937-9533* **Rooms** *10*

This 1920s motor court has been restored with taste and whimsy. The cabins are small, even tiny, but have period furnishings and kitchenettes. The motor court is flanked by the excellent Magnolia Café and Birdman Coffeehouse & Books, all owned by the same family.

ST. FRANCISVILLE Butler Greenwood Plantation P ≣ ⑤⑤

8345 Hwy 61, St. Francisville, 70775 **Tel** *(225) 635-6312* **Fax** *(225) 635-6370* **Rooms** *7*

The same family has owned this plantation since 1796. The 1810 main building is an unpretentious family house with centuries of history and is open for tours. Guests stay in one of seven cottages on the grounds, all with antiques, kitchens, and individual character. **www.butlergreenwood.com**

ST. FRANCISVILLE Cottage Plantation P ≣ ⑤⑤

10528 Cottage Lane, St. Francisville, 70775 **Tel** *(225) 635-3674* **Rooms** *7*

Unlike many plantation B&Bs, visitors stay in the big house at Cottage. Indeed, it is a huge house, built in stages between 1795 and 1859. There is also a cabin for guests. Rooms are furnished with antiques and have private baths. Shopping alert – an antique store is located on the grounds. **www.cottageplantation.com**

ST. FRANCISVILLE Greenwood Plantation P ⑤⑤

6838 Highland Rd, St. Francisville, 70775 **Tel** *(225) 655-4475* **Fax** *(225) 655-3292* **Rooms** *12*

Staying in one of the modern cottages on the plantation grounds is an experience that anyone who loves solitude will enjoy. Greenwood is deep in the countryside. The cottages are comfortable and clean. A tour of the main house is occasionally included in the price. **www.greenwoodplantation.com**

ST. FRANCISVILLE Hemingbough Guesthouse P ⑤⑤

10101 Hwy 965, St. Francisville, 70775 **Tel** *(225) 635-6617* **Rooms** *8*

There's a slight tinge of Disneyland to this modern 240-acre (96-ha) Greek Revival retreat. Built in the 1990s, it hosts meetings, weddings, and cultural events. Overnight guests stay in a replica antebellum house with modern amenities and canopy beds. **www.hemingbough.com**

ST. FRANCISVILLE Shadetree Inn ≣P ⑤⑤

Royal at Ferdinand St, St. Francisville, 70775 **Tel** *(225) 635-6116* **Fax** *(225) 635-0072* **Rooms** *3*

The inn is on a small yet beautiful site, giving it a secret garden feel. The suites have a shabby-chic look that invites you to cuddle up in a canopied bed or overstuffed chair. Breakfast is delivered to the rooms, which have microwaves and fridges. Cocktails are served in the afternoons. **www.shadetreeinn.com**

ST. FRANCISVILLE The Myrtles Plantation P ⅱ ⑤⑤⑤

7747 Hwy 61, St. Francisville, 70775 **Tel** *(225) 635-6277* **Fax** *(225) 635-5837* **Rooms** *11*

The B&B at this historically and architecturally significant mansion is wildly popular because of its reputation of being haunted. Rooms in the main house and the caretaker's cottage are reputedly the ghost hangouts. Night-time tours of the house are given on weekends. **www.myrtlesplantation.com**

ST. MARTINVILLE The Old Castillo Hotel B&B P ⅱ 🖿 ⑤

220 Evangeline Blvd, St. Martinville, 70582 **Tel** *(337) 394-4010* **Rooms** *7*

A stay at the Old Castillo is an absolute bargain. Located in the heart of charming Cajun country and built in 1827, this restored building has been on the National Register of Historic Places since 1978. Each room is beautifully and luxuriously furnished with period antiques. Wi-Fi access available. **www.oldcastillo.com**

VACHERIE Oak Alley Plantation Bed & Breakfast P ⅱ ⑤⑤⑤

3645 Hwy 18 (Great River Road), Vacherie, 70090 **Tel** *(225) 265-2151* **Fax** *(225) 265-7035* **Rooms** *7*

These charming cottages, adjacent to the Oak Alley Plantation, are offered in configurations of two, three, and four bedrooms, all with private baths and kitchens. (The price range shown is for a two-bedroom cottage.) A complimentary, if forgettable, breakfast is served in the plantation's restaurant. **www.oakalleyplantation.com**

WHITE CASTLE Nottoway P ⅱ ⑤⑤

30970 Hwy 405, White Castle, 70788 **Tel** *(866) 527-6884* **Fax** *(225) 545-8632* **Rooms** *13*

At Nottoway, guests may stay in the splendid 1859 home or a restored house on the grounds. Although you'll have to be up and out by tour time, staying in one of the plush rooms facing the river is the estate's peak experience. A full breakfast is served in an austere-looking basement room. **www.nottoway.com**

RESTAURANTS, CAFES, AND BARS

Even when other major cities in the US were living in a culinary wasteland, New Orleans had a reputation for fine, flavorful Creole cuisine. Today the reputation is still intact, but it has been enhanced by the development of "modern" Creole cuisine, Cajun cuisine, and some delicious ethnic dining as well. In this city, food matters; locals

New Orleans waiter

argue about who sells the best oysters, where to secure the finest turtle soup or gumbo, who makes the best po'boy (sandwich), bread pudding, and so on. The same is true for drinks. A pharmacist in the city invented the cocktail, and bartenders here are adept at making Sazeracs, a range of mint juleps, and such hazardous concoctions as the Obituary Cocktail *(see p174)*.

Diners at the Acme Oyster House *(see p176)*

PLACES TO EAT

Top-flight restaurants are found throughout the city, particularly in the French Quarter, the Warehouse District, and Uptown. Currently such chefs as Susan Spicer, Emeril Lagasse, Frank Brigtsen, John Besh, and others who are up-dating the traditional cuisine are generating the most excitement. There are plenty

Commander's Palace *(see p182)*, one of the city's finest restaurants

of good-quality restaurants that are producing traditional Creole and Cajun dishes – gumbo, oysters Rockefeller, jambalaya, crawfish étouffée, barbecue shrimp, and other zesty specialties *(see pp172–3)*.

In addition, there are Italian, Mediterranean, and other ethnic restaurants, plus plenty of places for cheap, good food, serving po'boys, New Orleans own *muffaletta* (a special local sandwich), pizza, and the ubiquitous dish of red beans and rice with sausage. New Orleans residents also care passionately about coffee, and the city has many good coffee and pastry shops.

OTHER PLACES TO EAT

New Orleans offers a broad range of venues other than restaurants in which to eat good

food. Many hotels have excellent dining rooms open to the public, and there are various Italian deli-catessens; these are mainly in the lower French Quarter, where you can buy a salad or a sandwich. Look out for the famous Lucky Dog hot dog carts in the Quarter.

HOURS AND PRICES

Breakfast is usually available between 7 and 11am and can be inexpensive or super-expensive – the price often depends on where it is served. Jazz brunches, a New Orleans tradition, are served between 10am and 3pm on weekends and can cost anywhere between $30 and $50.

At lunchtime, you can buy a light meal for about $7 or $10, usually between 11am and 2:30pm. In the better restaurants, prices are lower at lunchtime than at dinner. Dinner is generally served from 5 to 10pm, or until 11pm on Friday or Saturday nights. At a moderately priced place, main dishes might range from $14 to $24. In the very best restaurants, like Commander's Palace or Emeril's, be prepared to spend over $100 per person. A few places are open all night.

DINING ON A BUDGET

Do not eat breakfast at your hotel unless it is complimentary. Seek out a coffee shop or deli and feast on delicious croissants and strong coffee. At lunch, you can pop into a corner grocery and order a po'boy or *muffaletta*, and picnic somewhere. If you do sit down in a restaurant, you will find prices are lower than at dinner, as many establishments offer discounted menus early in the day. Otherwise, you can save money by ordering one course only (which is usually enough) and drinking less wine. Depending on the hour, some restaurants offer fixed-price menus that are usually cheaper.

The Upperline restaurant, filled with art *(see p182)*

TAXES AND TIPPING

A sales tax of 9 percent is added to meal and beverages checks in all restaurants. In general, you should tip 15 percent of the check for service; 20 percent if the service is superb. When the service is very bad you need not tip at all, but some restaurants automatically add a tip, especially for large groups, so check.

RESERVATIONS

At the very best restaurants you will need to make reservations considerably in advance. Some restaurants, however, do not take reservations, and you will have to stand in line or enjoy a cocktail in the bar while you wait.

DRESS CODE

New Orleans is a relaxed city and most places will allow you to wear the standard attire of jeans and T-shirt. Several of the more upscale restaurants require a jacket, and can also lend you one; ties are rarely required. Just to be on the safe side, dress smart-casual.

CHILDREN

Children are welcome at any restaurant, and special facilities, such as booster seats or highchairs, are usually available. Some restaurants offer special menus for children. The legal drinking age is 21, and children are not allowed in bars.

WHEELCHAIR ACCESS

Although since 1992 all restaurants have been required by law to be wheelchair accessible, it is best to call ahead to determine precisely how accessible a particular establishment is – whether there are steps outside or inside, for example, or whether the bathrooms are downstairs or upstairs.

The Grill Room at the Windsor Court Hotel *(see p180)*

SMOKING

Smoking is prohibited in most Louisiana restaurants. Some dining establishments that qualify as bars are exempt from the smoking ban, but always ask before lighting up.

VEGETARIAN FOOD

As in the rest of the United States, there is plenty of scope for vegetarians to eat well in New Orleans. Although much Creole and Cajun food is meat-based, most restaurants have vegetarian dishes such as salads or meat-free meals, if requested.

There are also exclusively vegetarian restaurants around town, plus Vietnamese and Thai restaurants, where vegetarian dishes are offered.

People enjoying coffee and *beignets* at Café du Monde *(see p176)*

The Flavors of New Orleans

New Orleans is one of America's culinary capitals, with a unique cuisine spawned by two distinct cultures: Creole and Cajun. Creole is the legacy of refined, city-dwelling descendants of the early French settlers. From the application of classic French techniques to local produce, a rich, sophisticated new cuisine was created. The Cajuns settled in Louisiana after being ousted from both France and Acadia (Nova Scotia), living in the bayous, hunting and fishing for indigenous foods. Their traditional dishes are spicier, the fiery seasonings tempered by long-simmering. A glossary of typical dishes and ingredients can be found on page 175.

Hot chili peppers

A plate of luscious Louisiana crawfish on a bed of rice

ONLY IN NEW ORLEANS

Several dishes are unique to New Orleans. A breakfast of *beignets* (deep-fried, sugary-sweet donuts) and chicory coffee shows the French influence. The city's contributions to sandwich culture include the *muffaletta*, a large, round roll containing cold cuts of meat, Provolone cheese and a dressing of chopped olives, olive oil, onions, cauliflower, and garlic. It owes its origins to Italian dock workers. Another is the po'boy, a submarine roll piled high with roast beef, ham, shrimp, or oysters, along with mustard, pickles, onions, herbs, and spices. You may be asked if you want your sandwich "dressed", which will include the addition of tomatoes, lettuce, and mayonnaise.

LOUISIANA PRODUCE

One of the best-known Louisiana products is crawfish (called crayfish elsewhere), which are grown locally. They breed in the muddy bayous and ponds of Cajun country, and are harvested in little boats from December to May. And oyster aficionados will tell you there's nothing as good as plump, salty Louisiana oysters on the half shell.

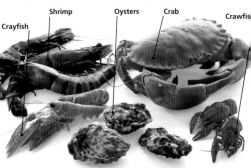

Shrimp   Oysters   Crab   Crawfis

Crayfish

Selection of the finest Louisiana shellfish

LOCAL DISHES AND SPECIALTIES

Both Cajun and Creole cooking often begin with a roux, the base of many dishes including gumbos, etouffées and sauces. A roux is simply flour and oil, stirred constantly over a flame until the right shade of brown for each dish is achieved. The darker the roux, the more intense the flavor. It is the deep, dark roux that gives a distinctive smoky, nutty flavor to gumbo. Every cook has his or her own gumbo recipe, but it always

Okra pods

begins with the roux used to thicken and flavor homemade stock, and includes sausage, a "trinity" of onion, celery, and bell pepper, scallions, cayenne pepper and a sprinkling of *filé* power (ground sassafras leaves) on the top. *Filé* is used to thicken as well as to season; another thickening is okra, which lends a silky texture to dishes.

Jambalaya *Similar to Spanish paella, this spicy rice dish may feature seafood, ham, chicken, andouille, and more besides.*

Some key ingredients of New Orleans cuisine at the French Market

Sassafras is a Native American ingredient that features strongly in New Orleans cuisine, while okra was introduced by African slaves. Two local pork products show their French origins in their names. Almost every Cajun chef has a personal recipe for *boudin* sausage, a highly seasoned pork and rice sausage. *Andouille* is another classic which, unlike its French namesake, is a hard, spicy smoked Cajun pork sausage.

OLD VERSUS NEW

The current culinary battle in New Orleans pits the old school of traditional cooking versus the new wave of chefs who want to innovate. One of the first to gain renown was Paul Prudhomme, the creator of "blackened fish," a dish that was never a part of Cajun fare but is now widely associated with it.

Emeril Lagasse is the best known of those bringing "nouveau" touches, including Asian influences, to classic dishes. Other culinary stars in the city are Susan Spicer of Bayona *(see p176)*; John Besh of Restaurant August *(see p180)*, and Donald Link at Herbsaint *(see p179)*.

Display of traditional Louisiana hot pepper sauces

HOT STUFF!

Peppery sauces are a staple of Cajun cooking and a favorite New Orleans souvenir. Food shops offer as many as 40 varieties, from mild to blazing hot, and some have "tasting bars" where you can sample before you buy. Tabasco, made on a Louisiana plantation since the 1800s, is now a favorite world-wide.

CLASSIC DINING

Antoine's Founded in 1840 and filled with memorabilia. Oysters Rockefeller was invented here *(see p176)*.

Arnaud's A maze of dining rooms decorated with theatrical panache. The jazz brunch is recommended *(see p176)*.

Brennan's Famous for turtle soup, bananas Foster and the decadently rich "Breakfast at Brennan's" *(see p176)*.

Commander's Palace A classic – don't miss the bread pudding soufflé *(see p182)*.

Galatoire's A 1905 landmark that still draws some of the city's best old families *(see p177)*.

The French Market This outdoor and covered market features superb fresh local produce *(see p70)*.

Bon Ton Café A downtown old-timer that sticks to tradition with seafood specialties and all the Creole favorites *(see p179)*.

Crawfish Etouffée *The name means "smothered," with sautéed crawfish being served in a thick, piquant sauce.*

Gumbo *Made with rice and okra, as well as chicken, seafood or* andouille, *this Creole soup is as thick as a stew.*

Bananas Foster *Bananas are sautéed in butter, sugar, and cinnamon, flamed in rum and served over ice.*

What to Drink in New Orleans

A long tradition of good drinking is one of New Orleans' trademarks. There are a wide variety of cocktails served throughout the city, some of which were invented here. Delicious and easy to drink, many are extremely potent concoctions. The local beers are also worthy: New Orleans has a top-class microbrewery. The city is a coffee-drinker's delight and has its own distinctive chicory-flavored dark roast coffee – a favorite of residents and visitors alike.

Pat O'Brien's *(see p47)*, where the popular Hurricane was created

The Sazerac   **The Hurricane**   **Mint Julep**

Vieux Carré Cocktail   **Obituary Cocktail**   **Ramos Gin Fizz**

BEER AND WINE

New Orleans is a beer town. Look for such local brews as Abita and Dixie, plus those made by the microbrewery Crescent City Brewhouse. A variety of wines are also available in the city's restaurants, particularly fine French and California vintages.

Dixie and Abita Amber, local beers   **Red and white California wines**

COCKTAILS

New Orleans was the birthplace of many cocktails. Local pharmacist Antoine Peychaud's store was located near the corner of Royal and St. Louis streets, and he is said to have invented the cocktail around 1830 when he combined cognac "Sazerac" mixed with his own bitters recipe, a drop of water, and a pinch of sugar. Peychaud mixed this in an egg cup "*coquetier,*" which his English-speaking customers mispronounced as "cocktail." Today, the Sazerac is one of New Orleans' most famous drinks: rye whiskey (or bourbon) is combined with bitters and sugar, and flavored with Pernod and lemon peel.

The Hurricane, served in a special glass, is very sweet and combines dark rum with passion fruit and other juices. The Mint Julep is made with bourbon, sugar, fresh mint, and crushed ice. The Vieux Carré mixes rye, cognac, vermouth, bitters, and a dash of Benedictine. For the Obituary Cocktail, a lethal drink created at Lafitte's *(see p78)*, add half a jigger of Pernod to a gin Martini. Bartender Henry Ramos shook the first Ramos Gin Fizz in 1888, combining sugar, orange flower water, citrus juice, gin, egg white, cream, and seltzer into a refreshing drink. Pousse Café is a mix of six cordials – raspberry and maraschino syrups, crème de menthe, curaçao, chartreuse, and cognac.

COFFEE

New Orleanians love coffee, and it comes in all roasts and styles. Community Coffee, French Market, and CDM are the three most famous Louisiana brands. The Café du Monde *(see p76)* serves "café au lait," the traditional dark roast chicory-flavored coffee with hot milk.

If you don't like the somewhat bitter taste of chicory, just ask for "pure" coffee; you'll get a tasty cup of dark or medium roast coffee. Espresso, extra-strong coffee, is also available.

"Pure" coffee

Café espresso

Glossary of New Orleans Food

The distinctive cuisine of New Orleans has its own vocabulary. Some styles and ingredients are particular to Creole and Cajun cooking; others are more common but take on that special Louisiana touch. Creole dishes often have as their base peppers, onions, and tomatoes, and can be more refined than the flavorful Cajun one-pot dishes.

Vegetables and fruit for sale in the French Market

Andouille
A hard, smoked, spicy Cajun sausage made with pork.

Bananas Foster
Bananas sprinkled with brown sugar and flambéed in rum and banana liqueur *(see p173).*

Barbecued Shrimp
Jumbo shrimp in their shells sautéed in oil and butter, garlic, peppers, and spices.

Beignet
Deep-fried square doughnut (no hole), covered in powdered sugar.

Biscuits
Flour and baking powder rolled and baked, often served with eggs at breakfast.

Boudin
Highly seasoned Cajun pork sausage combined with rice.

Bouillabaisse New Orleans-style
A spicier version of the French seafood dish.

Cajun
A style of cooking that combines French methods with local Southern ingredients.

Calas
Fried sweet rice cakes.

Chow Chow
A relish usually made with green pickles, green tomatoes, and green cayenne peppers.

Courtbouillon of Redfish
A seafood stew, prepared with local fish, spices, and white wine.

Crawfish
Also known as crayfish, these deliciously sweet, small crustaceans are prepared in various ways like stews, *étouffée,* or boiled *(see p173).*

Crawfish Boil
Crawfish boiled in water seasoned with mustard, coriander, dill, cloves, allspice, bay leaves, and the main ingredient, dried chilies.

Ripe bananas, used for desserts

Dirty Rice
Rice cooked with chicken livers and gizzards, and other seasonings.

Eggs Sardou
Eggs poached on artichoke bottoms, cradled on a bed of creamed spinach, and covered with hollandaise.

Etouffée
Literally "smothered," a method of cooking slowly with little liquid, in a covered pan.

Filé
Filé refers to the dried ground sassafras leaves used to thicken and flavor gumbos.

Grits
Ground, cooked corn grains served at breakfast with butter, salt, pepper, and eggs.

Gumbo
A spicy, thick soup containing shrimp, crawfish, oysters, okra, and served over rice *(see p173).*

Gumbo z'Herbes
A meatless version of gumbo, made during Lent.

Jambalaya
A mixture of rice, seafood, Tasso (ham), vegetables, and seasoned with onion, green peppers, and celery *(see p172).*

King Cake
A round cake made during Mardi Gras. It is sprinkled with granulated and colored sugars. A tiny doll, representing the baby Jesus, is hidden inside.

Maque Choux
A Cajun dish made with a mixture of corn, tomatoes, onions, and cayenne pepper.

Mirliton
A pear-shaped squash with prickly ribbed skin.

Muffaletta
A sandwich combining Italian deli meats, and one or two kinds of cheese on an Italian round loaf slathered with olive salad – pickled olives, celery, olive oil, carrots, cauliflower, and garlic.

Okra
A pod vegetable, originally from Africa, served as a side dish or used in Cajun gumbos and stews.

Pain Perdu
The local version of French toast (bread fried with eggs).

Po'Boy
A big French bread sandwich, with shrimp, oysters, ham, roast beef, or a combination.

Pompano en Papillotte
A sweet fish common in Gulf waters, baked in an oiled paper bag to retain its full flavor.

Pralines
A candy patty made with brown sugar and pecans.

Shrimp Cocktail

Shrimp Remoulade
Shrimp with a mayonnaise-based sauce seasoned with mustard, anchovies, gherkins, scallions, lemon, spices, and herbs.

Sweet Potato Pie
Made with sweet potatoes flavored with cinnamon, nutmeg, and ginger.

Tasso
Highly spiced smoked ham seasoned with red pepper.

Oranges and other fruits, used as ingredients in Creole food

Choosing a Restaurant

The restaurants in this guide have been selected across a wide range of price categories for their exceptional food, good value, interesting location, and attractive ambience. Within each area, entries are listed alphabetically within each price category, from the least to the most expensive.

PRICE CATEGORIES
For a three-course meal for one, half a bottle of house wine, and all unavoidable extra charges including tax:
$ under $25
$$ $25–$40
$$$ $40–$55
$$$$ $55–$70
$$$$$ over $70

UPPER FRENCH QUARTER

Café du Monde
$
800 Decatur St, 70116 **Tel** *(504) 525-4544*
Map 5 D2

You cannot visit New Orleans without sampling *beignets*, and this is their home. The charming green- and white-striped awnings beckon from blocks away, as does the smell of the chicory coffee and powdered sugar. Fried dough dunked into milky coffee never tasted so good. They are open 24 hours.

Johnny's Po-Boy
$
511 St. Louis St, 70116 **Tel** *(504) 524-8129*
Map 4 C2

This is your standard po'boy shop and really one of the only decent ones in the French Quarter. They offer all the standard stuffings such as fried seafood and cold cuts. The roast beef is especially good in a very messy way. Locals like to order takeout as there is not much ambience, and the Riverwalk provides a nearby picnic spot.

Acme Oyster House
$$
724 Iberville St, 70130 **Tel** *(504) 522-5973*
Map 4 C3

The line usually snakes out the door for this popular seafood joint, and with good reason as the raw oysters are big and fresh. A variety of dependably good fried seafood is on offer as well. However, the scene might seem a bit touristy for those wanting a more authentic New Orleans experience.

Bourbon House Seafood & Oyster Bar
$$$
144 Bourbon St, 70130 **Tel** *(504) 522-0111*
Map 4 C3

This handsome brasserie, run by the Brennan family, is firmly focused on local seafood. Oysters are served raw, topped with caviar, or broiled. The menu also includes classic renditions of New Orleans finfish and shrimp dishes, seasonal seafood salads, and a few beef dishes. The bar specializes in fine bourbons.

Antoine's
$$$$
713 St. Louis St, 70130 **Tel** *(504) 581-4422*
Map 4 C2

This old guard restaurant is the famed birthplace of Oysters Rockefeller and recalls days gone by with its beautiful tiled floors and ceiling fans. The menu offers classic *haute* Creole fare that fits the setting. Ask for a tour of the splendid private dining rooms on the other floors.

Arnaud's
$$$$
813 Bienville St, 70112 **Tel** *(504) 533-5433*
Map 4 C2

The Mardi Gras museum at this palatial dining institution really rivals the cuisine. Upstairs, you will find all the grand costumes of the former owner set amidst the finery of the many ornate dining rooms. The signature dish here is the famed shrimp remoulade. There's an excellent, unobtrusive jazz band.

Bayona
$$$$
430 Dauphine St, 70112 **Tel** *(504) 525-4455*
Map 4 C2

Renowned chef Susan Spicer lives up to all expectations here at her flagship restaurant. The service, setting, and menu embody elegance. It would be difficult to order badly, but signature dishes such as her quail salad and legendary sweetbreads are sure to please. The wine list is also excellent, so take your time going through it.

Bistro at Maison de Ville
$$$$
727 Toulouse St, 70130 **Tel** *(504) 528-9206*
Map 4 C2

Modeled after the cafés of Paris, the mirror-lined, romantic dining room here is the perfect showcase for superior, contemporary Creole cuisine with classic French and Italian touches. When the weather allows it, ask for a table in the lush courtyard, which makes a beautiful, intimate setting for a fine meal.

Brennan's
$$$$
417 Royal St, 70130 **Tel** *(504) 525-9711*
Map 4 C2

This is the original restaurant of the Brennan's dining empire, and its brunch continues to romance visitors and locals alike. You should expect a wait (even with reservations), and service can be a bit unreliable. But everyone loves the Bananas Foster cooking demonstration, which is a Brennan's creation.

Key to Symbols *see back cover flap*

K-Paul's Louisiana Kitchen
🚶 ♿ 🍴 $$$$

416 Chartres St, 70130 **Tel** *(504) 524-7394*   **Map** 4 C2

Chef Paul Prudhomme introduced the world to the cuisine of South Louisiana back in the 1980s when he reigned supreme over the New Orleans restaurant scene. This place still draws crowds, but the prices seem a bit inflated. However, this is a landmark restaurant and should be given due respect.

Nola
🚶 ♿ $$$$

534 St. Louis St, 70130 **Tel** *(504) 522-6652*   **Map** 4 C2

This is the most downscale of chef Emeril Lagasse's restaurants, but still expect *haute cuisine* and high prices. Things are a bit funkier here with more fusion dishes and less formal service. Reservations are also easier to come by as the huge space seats hundreds. An especially enjoyable table is located near the open kitchen.

Galatoire's
🚶 ♿ $$$$$

209 Bourbon St, 70130 **Tel** *(504) 525-2021*   **Map** 4 C3

The pomp and circumstance of this blue blood favorite are what make it so wonderful, and of all the old restaurants this one is the most reliable. The menu is made up of Creole classics such as trout *amandine*, which never fail to please the palate. Expect a wait to sit in the esteemed dining room downstairs.

LOWER FRENCH QUARTER AND MARIGNY

Central Grocery
🚶 ♿ $

923 Decatur St, 70116 **Tel** *(504) 620-0174*   **Map** 5 D2

This classic New Orleans grocery and deli offers just one prepared food item – the famed *muffaletta*, an Italian sandwich loaded with meat, cheese, and olive salad. You can enjoy this beauty in the store or take it to the nearby riverfront for a picnic. The walls are lined with jars filled with Italian delicacies such as roasted peppers and anchovies.

Clover Grill
🚶 ♿ $

900 Bourbon St, 70116 **Tel** *(504) 598-1010*   **Map** 5 D1

The fun never stops at this quirky diner where the flamboyant staff turns on the charm constantly. Plus, the burgers are cooked under hubcaps to juicy perfection, and they actually serve malt milkshakes, taking you back to the golden days – just set to a different tune. Expect a cabaret atmosphere.

Croissant d'Or Patisserie
🚶 ♿ $

617 Ursulines Ave, 70116 **Tel** *(504) 524-4663*   **Map** 5 D1

You will imagine that you have stepped into Paris when you enter this little bakery. Their buttery pastries are out-standing. They also serve some sandwiches and salads, but the sweets are really the way to go. The eclairs and tarts warm the heart, and the early morning sunshine casts a spell that is sure to charm. Great for an early breakfast.

The Joint
🚶 ♿ 🍴 $

801 Poland Ave, 70117 **Tel** *(504) 949-3232*

The quirky charm of the Bywater neighborhood comes across strong at this little barbecue joint. The bright decor, hip jukebox, and the smokey meats all work together. Ask about specials that might not be on the menu, such as the smoked bowl of tangy coleslaw topped with shredded pork. Also sip on a Rattler for good measure.

Verti Marte
🚶 ♿ $

1201 Royal St, 70116 **Tel** *(504) 525-4767*   **Map** 5 D1

If you need some good ol' greasy grub after an exhausting day in the Quarter, head to this corner store where take-out rules. Whether you prefer a traditional po'boy or an original creation such as the shrimp cheesesteak, you will be satisfied. The prepared salads can vary in quality, but the mac and cheese is a solid choice.

Adolfo's
$$

611 Frenchmen St, 70116 **Tel** *(504) 948-3800*   **Map** 5 E1

Perched above a bar and overlooking the lively nightlife of Frenchmen Street, Adolfo's is a funky neighborhood café where value and flavor take precedence over creature comforts. The tiny open kitchen produces a mix of classic, casual Italian fare and local seafood, with a large selection of fish.

Bennachin
🚶 ♿ $$

1212 Royal St, 70116 **Tel** *(504) 522-1230*   **Map** 5 D1

A sweet family runs this African restaurant, and they are definitely part of the charm. There is also the quaint storefront and heartwarming dishes that are sure to win you over. The menu provides plenty of vegetarian options such as the addictive plantains and sautéed spinach. Carnivores should try a meaty stew or the grilled chicken.

Coop's Place
🚶 ♿ $$

1109 Decatur St, 70116 **Tel** *(504) 525-9053*   **Map** 5 D1

This is the hidden gem of the Quarter. Here, the loaded jambalaya, enormous sandwiches, and superbly greasy cheese fries always hit the spot. The local clientele adds to the ambience with plenty of eccentric characters who have stories to tell. It is also a good watering hole.

Eat New Orleans

900 Dumaine St, 70116 **Tel** *(504) 522-7222*

Map *4 C1*

For a quick sandwich or a hearty meal of New Orleans staples like jambalaya and barbecue shrimp, this bright, stylish, and relaxed café is a solid bet and the prices are very reasonable. Eat New Orleans is also a good place for a casual Sunday brunch. A bring-your-own-bottle policy is encouraged.

El Gato Negro

81 French Market Pl, 70116 **Tel** *(504) 525-9752*

Map *5 E1*

Built in a former French Market icehouse, El Gato Negro is the spot for authentic Mexican fare. Tacos, *burritos*, and *enchiladas* are made according to traditional Mexican recipes, and fish, steak, and chicken entrées have elaborate preparations. The carrot juice margaritas are uncommonly refreshing. Mexican breakfasts are served on weekends.

Elizabeth's Restaurant

601 Gallier St, 70117 **Tel** *(504) 944-9272*

This homely diner is under new ownership, but all remains the same with their hearty breakfast and lunch fare. In the morning, try the praline, bacon, and stuffed French toast; at midday the po'boys or plate lunches are the way to go. Saturday means an all-day brunch with over-the-top egg dishes and huge lines. No reservations.

Fiorella's

1136 Decatur St, 70116 **Tel** *(504) 528-9566*

Map *5 D1*

If you are craving fried chicken in the Quarter, you should seek out this friendly, no-frills eatery. Everything on the menu is a safe bet, but highlights are the fried pickles, mac and cheese, and the stupendeous chicken. Their Italian fare is tasty as well, and they offer great deals on buckets of beer. Check out breakfast on the weekends.

Mimi's

2601 Royal St, 70117 **Tel** *(504) 942-0690*

Map *5 F1*

This tapas bar serves authentic Spanish treats such as marinated olives, sharp cheeses, and plenty of affordable wine. There are also hot dishes, but the cold fare seems of better quality. Enjoy these nibbles while gazing down onto quiet neighborhood streets. On weekends, they also have great dance parties that take place late at night.

Monaghan's 13

517 Frenchmen St, 70116 **Tel** *(504) 942-1345*

Map *5 E1*

Monaghan's offers quick and easy bar food that will fuel you for a night of dancing in the neighboring music clubs. The menu leans toward greasy vegetarian, such as a roasted vegetable sandwich or a pita pizza. The loaded Tater Tots are especially satisfying, and their Bloody Mary could well be a cure for whatever ails you.

Napoleon House

500 Chartres St, 70130 **Tel** *(504) 524-9752*

Map *4 C2*

The charming courtyard in this historic building sets the mood for sipping the café's signature drink of a Pimm's cup. While some might doubt the ability of a New Orleans bar to pull off such a decidedly British drink, here they succeed. The refreshing Pimm's perfectly complements the *muffaletta*. Other menu items pale in comparison.

Port of Call

838 Esplanade Ave, 70116 **Tel** *(504) 523-0120*

Map *5 D1*

The line usually streams out of the door at this famed burger joint. Both locals and visitors love the strong rum drinks and super thick burgers. Serious eaters also go for the loaded baked potato that rivals the burger in size. The beach bar feel seems to encourage copious eating and drinking, and there are always interesting scenes as the night progresses.

Sukho Thai

1913 Royal St, 70116 **Tel** *(504) 948-9309*

Map *5 E1*

Good Thai is hard to come by in New Orleans, and this quality Marigny place is a gem. The ingredients are always fresh, and the spice is just right. Their BYOB policy makes for a fun time with friends, especially at one of the side-walk tables. Best bets are the soups, curries, and desserts. The coconut black rice pudding really tickles the palate.

Feelings Café

2600 Chartres St, 70117 **Tel** *(504) 945-2222*

Map *5 F1*

The courtyard at this neighborhood fine-dining eatery positively seduces, especially on picturesque spring and fall evenings. The menu offers traditional New Orleans dishes such as fried oysters and barbecue shrimp. There are no surprises to blow your mind, but that's what makes this spot a classic. Try the peanut butter pie for dessert.

Meauxbar Bistro

942 N Rampart St, 70116 **Tel** *(504) 569-9979*

Map *4 C1*

With a flourish of bright Caribbean yellow on the outside and stylish Art Deco touches on the inside, Meauxbar can be either an upscale spin on the neighborhood joint serving burgers, pasta dishes, and fish and chips, or a fine dining destination for traditional French bistro cuisine, fusion-style dishes, and great homemade ice cream.

Irene's Cuisine

539 St. Phillip St, 70116 **Tel** *(504) 529-8811*

Map *5 D2*

You will smell the aroma of garlic long before you see the doors, and that's a good sign. The mostly Italian fare of this romantic Quarter hideout boasts strong flavors that really satisfy the appetite. Locals and visitors alike line up early as reservations are not taken. Try to go on a weeknight as weekends mean a long wait, but it is worth it.

Key to Price Guide *see p176* **Key to Symbols** *see back cover flap*

Marigny Brasserie 🚶♿🚻 $$$$$

640 Frenchmen St, 70116 **Tel** *(504) 945-4472* **Map** *5 E1*

Here, you will find seasonal dishes prepared with a light touch. The large windows that look out on the ever-happening Frenchmen Street provide plenty of entertainment as you enjoy a quiet meal. The wine list is ample, and the waitstaff are quick to answer any questions. The inviting bar is an ideal spot for drinks and music.

Muriel's 🚶♿ $$$$

801 Chartres St, 70116 **Tel** *(504) 568-1885* **Map** *5 D2*

The appearance of this upscale Jackson Square eatery might seem a bit much for a new guard restaurant as there is an abundance of lavish decorations. Still, devotees swear that the cuisine lives up to the look. Popular dishes include an appetizer of crawfish and goats' cheese crêpe and an entrée of pecan-crusted puppy drum.

Stella! $$$$

1032 Chartres St, 70116 **Tel** *(504) 587-0091* **Map** *5 D1*

This quaint Quarter restaurant offers excellent food and service in charming environs. The menu changes with the seasons, but expect lots of local seafood that is often prepared with an Asian twist. The risotto is a standout. The wine list might not be as extensive as some of the other major fine-dining establishments, but it is good quality.

Wolfe's ♿ $$$$

1041 Dumaine St, 70116 **Tel** *(504) 593-9535* **Map** *4 C1*

Since chef Anne Kearney sold this elegant venue to chef Tom Wolfe, the menu has changed a bit. Kearney's feminine touch seen throughout the kitchen and dining area is now shadowed by Wolfe's strong approach. His credentials go back to Emeril's, and the dishes bear that heavy signature. Order a good robust red and embrace the abundance.

WAREHOUSE AND CENTRAL BUSINESS DISTRICTS

Commerce Restaurant 📋🚶♿ $

300 Camp St, 70130 **Tel** *(504) 561-9239* **Map** *4 C3*

There is nothing like a hearty breakfast of a tasty po'boy from a bonafide lunch counter. The long narrow room with plenty of gleaming metal harks back to days of old, and many regulars could probably tell you a tale or two from that era. They could also fill you in on the best dishes such as red beans on Mondays. Closed on weekends.

Horinoya 🚶♿ $$

920 Poydras St, 70112 **Tel** *(504) 561-8914* **Map** *4 B4*

The seafood is impeccable at this hidden sushi bar. The business crowd knows the secret for lunch, but in the evening you will have the Zen environs to yourself. The rolls are excellent, and the cooked fare impresses as well. Be daring and try an exotic item as you can count on freshness. Go with a group and dine in the traditional back dining rooms.

Mother's Restaurant 🚶♿ $$

401 Poydras St, 70130 **Tel** *(504) 523-9656* **Map** *4 C4*

People stand in line for hours at this 60-something-year-old restaurant to dine on traditional po'boys such as the signature roast beef that locals call "debris." Devotees swear by the gravy on this sandwich, but detractors claim that it is not worth the wait. Just be sure to go as early as possible.

Bon Ton Café 🚶♿ $$$

401 Magazine St, 70130 **Tel** *(504) 524-3386* **Map** *4 C4*

This historic downtown restaurant is a favorite among the old-school business lunch crowd with its traditional New Orleans fare. Dishes such as shrimp Creole and crawfish *étouffée* give you a taste from the past. You can always count on fresh, Louisiana seafood and courteous servers. The dated atmosphere fits the golden age sentiment perfectly.

Grand Isle Restaurant 🚶♿🚻 $$$

575 Convention Center Blvd, 70130 **Tel** *(504) 520-8530* **Map** *4 C4*

Grand Isle focuses on local staples, such as fried seafood, grilled fish, boiled shrimp, raw oysters, and po'boys, all prepared with a higher degree of polish than other neighborhood restaurants – and with higher prices to match. A dining room decorated with cypress trees and a gleaming marble bar top gives the place a vintage feel.

Herbsaint ♿🚻 $$$

701 St. Charles Ave, 70130 **Tel** *(504) 524-4114* **Map** *4 B4*

There is simply nothing better than a menu that showcases quality ingredients paired thoughtfully, and that is the case with every dish at this elegant bistro. The "small plates" give you the opportunity to try a variety, and that's really the best plan of action as everything impresses. Their signature shrimp bisque and perfect frites are not to be missed.

Palace Café 🚶♿🎵🚻 $$$

605 Canal St, 70130 **Tel** *(504) 523-1661* **Map** *4 C3*

This Brennan's establishment is in an historic storefront that has been renovated beautifully. Appetizers include a crabmeat cheesecake and an oyster pan roast. Popular entrées are the *andouille* crusted fish and catfish pecan *meunière*. Their white chocolate bread pudding has become legendary in a short time. Brunch is always lively.

Cuvée
♿   ⑤⑤⑤⑤

322 Magazine St, 70130 **Tel** *(504) 587-9001*   **Map** *4 C4*

An excellent choice for an extravagant dinner, the menu provides many options that change with the seasons. You can always expect the focus to be on fresh local ingredients such as Louisiana seafood. The *foie gras* appetizer is supposedly a permanent fixture and a must try. The wine list also impresses both in quality and variety.

Restaurant August
♿   ⑤⑤⑤⑤

301 Tchoupitoulas St, 70130 **Tel** *(504) 299-9777*   **Map** *4 C3*

Chef John Besh deserves the accolades he receives for his flagship restaurant. He approaches all dishes with an artist's touch and demands the same attention to detail from his well-versed staff. Recommendations are difficult as the menu changes with the seasons, but there is really no chance of misordering given the level of excellence.

RioMar
🧍♿   ⑤⑤⑤⑤

800 S. Peters St, 70130 **Tel** *(504) 525-3474*   **Map** *4 C5*

Dedicated to serving delicious, fresh seafood, chef Adolfo Garcia succeeds admirably here. His Spanish heritage shines throughout the menu, but especially on dishes such as the ceviche sampler and all the paellas. The somewhat bare interior can increase the noise level, but the food makes up for any such shortcomings. Try a traditional Spanish dessert.

Tommy's Cuisine
🧍   ⑤⑤⑤⑤

746 Tchoupitoulas St, 70130 **Tel** *(504) 581-1103*   **Map** *4 C4*

There is a long story behind the connection between this Warehouse District newcomer and Irene's in the Quarter, but suffice it to say that the menus are similar. Here, you can count on Italian cuisine with a New Orleans flair (just like Irene's). The tiled floors and dark wood set the mood for a real feast.

Emeril's
♿   ⑤⑤⑤⑤⑤

800 Tchoupitoulas St, 70130 **Tel** *(504) 528-9393*   **Map** *4 C5*

This is the original location where the now celebrity chef made his name, and, consequently, utmost care is taken with every detail. Chef Emeril innovatively and deliciously blends different styles of cooking such as Southwestern and New England. The staff is efficient, and the menu should impress most.

The Grill Room
♿   ⑤⑤⑤⑤⑤

300 Gravier St, 70130 **Tel** *(504) 522-1992*   **Map** *4 C3*

The flagship restaurant of the elegant Windsor Court Hotel *(see p165)* maintains a high standard of opulence in its formal dining rooms, with elaborate floral arrangements and white-glove service. The menu is a mix of contemporary Creole cuisine and some tamer fare for less adventurous diners.

GARDEN DISTRICT AND UPTOWN

Café Reconcile
🧍♿   ⑤

1631 Oretha Castle Haley Blvd, 70113 **Tel** *(504) 568-1157*   **Map** *8 A2*

There is nothing like combining a good cause with good food, and that is just the case at this central city eatery. Local kids learn about the restaurant industry while providing you with food such as fried chicken, and mac and cheese. On Thursdays, their white beans and shrimp draw diners from all over the city. Do not skip the cornbread.

Camellia Grill
📋🧍   ⑤

626 S Carrollton Ave, 70118 **Tel** *(504) 309-2679*   **Map** *6 A1*

This landmark New Orleans diner was resurrected after Hurricane Katrina by new owners who made a few sensible behind-the-scenes upgrades but left the classic ambience and menu of omelettes and burgers unchanged. Seating is at the counter only, and the line to get in can be long, but the high-spirited servers make the wait worthwhile.

Chez Nous
🧍🏠   ⑤

5701 Magazine St, 70115 **Tel** *(504) 899-7303*   **Map** *6 C4*

The prepared food at this gourmet-to-go shop is as close to New Orleans home cooking as you can come by without knocking on someone's door. Everyday means a different special such as seafood gumbo, grillades and grits, or shrimp Creole. There are also many prepared salads and a variety of cakes and pies. Limited dining space.

Domilise's
📋🧍♿   ⑤

5240 Annunciation St, 70115 **Tel** *(504) 899-9126*   **Map** *6 C5*

Most Uptown locals swear that these are the best po'boys in town, and it is a good argument considering the fresh local seafood is fried to perfection. Plus, the family atmosphere makes you feel right at home crowded around small tables bumping elbows with regular customers. If seafood isn't your thing, try the roast beef.

Joey K's
🧍♿   ⑤

3001 Magazine St, 70115 **Tel** *(504) 891-0997*   **Map** *7 F4*

Although located on the edge of the elegant Garden District, this casual corner joint offers food from the humble but delicious traditions of Creole pot cooking. The daily blackboard specials feature comfort food classics at bargain prices. Wash them down with a beer or margarita served in a huge, frozen-schooner glass.

Key to Price Guide *see p176* **Key to Symbols** *see back cover flap*

The Grocery

2854 St. Charles Ave, 70115 **Tel** *(504) 895-9524* $

Map *7 F3*

The pressed sandwiches provide a welcome reprieve from po'boys. The Cuban is a classic, but the veggie melt is also good. Their gumbo also impresses, especially when eaten with a scoop of potato salad in lieu of rice. The salads are topped with homemade dressings, and the cookies and brownies are tempting. Lunch only and closed on Sundays.

St. James Cheese Co.

5004 Prytania St, 70115 **Tel** *(504) 899-4737* $

Map *7 D4*

An astounding array of imported and domestic artisanal cheeses has earned St. James a reputation as one of the most ambitious cheese shops in the South. Take a courtyard seat for a pressed sandwich or cheese board at lunch, or sample the imported and locally made charcuterie items. BYOB is easy with a wine shop right next door.

Casamento's

4330 Magazine St, 70115 **Tel** *(504) 895-9761* $$

Map *7 E4*

This is the quintessential oyster bar to the point that it closes when the salty bivalves are out of season in June, July, and August. The raw oysters are undoubtedly a must, but the sandwiches and stew also prove quite tasty. The atmosphere plays a major role as the spotless white tiles covering the floors and walls really set the perfect tone.

Franky & Johnny's

321 Arabella St, 70118 **Tel** *(504) 899-9146* $$

Map *6 C4*

Uptown families pile into this friendly neighborhood joint that specializes in fried and boiled seasonal seafood. There is also an element of New Orleans-Italian cuisine, but that pales in comparison to the ocean fare. Po'boys and fried platters are the best, and you must start with some fried bell pepper rings.

Saltwater Grill

1340 S Carrollton Ave, 70118 **Tel** *(504) 324-6640* $$

Map *6 A1*

Veterans of the Brennan's empire opened this seafood restaurant and oyster bar beneath the romantic Carrollton Avenue oak trees. They renovated an old building into a family eatery. The oyster bar always pleases, and the po'boys are some of the best in the area thanks to fresh local seafood. An excellent choice for those traveling with children.

Surrey's Juice Bar

1418 Magazine St, 70130 **Tel** *(504) 524-3828* $$

Map *8 B3*

Healthy eating is not a top priority in New Orleans, but this hip little café makes it fun. Their fresh fruit juices will set you straight after a late night, and the Latin-influenced brunch fare always hits the spot. There are many vegetarian options, including a stellar eggplant *muffaletta*. Open for breakfast and lunch only. Go early on the weekends.

Theo's

4218 Magazine St, 70115 **Tel** *(504) 894-8554* $$

Map *7 E4*

The pizza here is supposedly St. Louis style, meaning that the crust is somewhere between Chicago and New York. Whatever the definition, the pizza rocks, especially specialties such as the Jammer. Their wings prove an excellent starter, and root beer floats or chocolate cake make for a perfect ending. The young owners are always very friendly.

Whole Foods

5600 Magazine St, 70115 **Tel** *(504) 899-9119* $$

Map *6 C4*

If you are ever in a hunger emergency, Whole Foods can surely bail you out. Their wide variety of prepared foods run the gamut from sushi to pizza, and their bakery is exceptional. Of course, you can also stock up on some gourmet groceries and fine wine. Just beware of the parking lot at this location as the small confines can be quite tight.

Ye Olde College Inn

3000 S Carrollton Ave, 70118 **Tel** *(504) 866-3683* $$

Map *1 B4*

This 1930s stalwart has seen enormous change since a new owner took over and Hurricane Katrina forced a move to an adjacent address. Yet the down-home New Orleans feel remains intact, with the same regulars lining the bar and families still filling the dining room for foot-long oyster loaves and hamburger steaks.

Dick & Jenny's

4501 Tchoupitoulas St, 70115 **Tel** *(504) 894-9880* $$$

Map *7 E5*

There is a no reservations policy at this Uptown eatery, but the excellent, upscale, and funky food is well worth the wait. The husband and wife team offers creative local cuisine that changes with the seasons, and the staff always knows the ins-and-outs of the menu. The cheerful surroundings add to the good time evoked by the standout food.

La Crêpe Nanou

1410 Robert St, 70115 **Tel** *(504) 899-2670* $$$

Map *7 D4*

The authentic European café feel of this Uptown charmer keeps it packed. The menu is classic French bistro with excellent mussels and frites, and, in fact, the whole selection is good. They are only open for dinner, and the crowds come early. Save room for a dessert crêpe. Closed Sundays.

Brigtsen's

723 Dante St, 70118 **Tel** *(504) 861-7610* $$$$

Map *6 A1*

Earning his stripes under the tutelage of none other than Paul Prudhomme, chef Frank Brigtsen's credentials propelled his namesake restaurant into the spotlight, where it has stayed. He is an avid Louisiana sportsman and always offers an array of local seafood and game. A charming Uptown house provides the perfect setting.

Clancy's 🚶♿ $$$$

6100 Annunciation St, 70118 **Tel** *(504) 895-1111*   **Map** *6 B5*

This neighborhood fine-dining restaurant is a favorite among blue blood New Orleanians who love the dependable food and service. The menu rarely changes, which these diners love. Popular items include the oysters with brie, smoked soft shell crab, and peppermint ice cream. The highly experienced staff will be happy to assist you.

Dante's Kitchen 🚶♿🍴 $$$$

736 Dante St, 70118 **Tel** *(504) 861-3121*   **Map** *6 A1*

A Commander's Palace veteran opened this Riverbend eatery to showcase local ingredients prepared in a refined yet approachable fashion. The historic home setting provides the perfect backdrop for starters such as shrimp and grits with redeye gravy. Popular entrées include the *trois mignons* (three beef filets) and the falafel crusted fish.

Eleven79 ♿ $$$$

1179 Annunciation St, 70130 **Tel** *(504) 299-1179*   **Map** *8 B2*

This tucked away, swanky Italian restaurant feels a bit like a gangster movie set, and the cuisine lives up to these high standards. Regulars recommend the Oysters Panaré as an appetizer (*panéed* oysters topped with caviar) and the Veal Eleven79 (topped with peppers, mozzarella, and asparagus) wins as an entrée. Finish with tiramisu.

Gautreau's $$$$

1728 Soniat St, 70115 **Tel** *(504) 899-7397*   **Map** *7 D3*

This upscale neighborhood eatery always keeps a professional staff. Chefs seem to earn accolades here and then move on – making way for more young talent. The menu changes with the seasons, but your server's opinion should be trusted concerning all food and wine recommendations. Great for a date.

Jacques-Imo's Café 🍴 $$$$

8324 Oak St, 70118 **Tel** *(504) 861-0886*   **Map** *6 B1*

This popular restaurant serves Creole and Cajun specialties at reasonable prices. The chef/owner, Jack Leonardi, is a local character who is often part of the entertainment, and you can dine in the bed of a pickup truck out front. Reservations aren't taken less than 30 days in advance, so it's first come first served. Closed Sundays.

Lilette ♿🍴 $$$$

3637 Magazine St, 70115 **Tel** *(504) 895-1636*   **Map** *7 E4*

Chef John Harris received immediate and deserved recognition when he opened this stylish, *haute* eatery. The marrow toast sends shivers up the spine, and the pork belly happily overwhelms. The menu rarely changes, and faulty ordering is simply not possible as all is cooked to perfection. The cocktail menu is just as impressive.

Martinique Bistro ♿🍴 $$$$

5908 Magazine St, 70115 **Tel** *(504) 891-8495*   **Map** *6 B4*

The courtyard alone is enough to keep Uptowners coming back to Martinique again and again. The pleasant tropical setting complements the menu of approachable, eclectic French fare perfectly. Seafood dishes such as *bouillabaisse* are standouts. This is a perfect location for a romantic dinner away from the downtown bustle. Linger over dessert.

Pascal's Manale 🚶♿ $$$$

1838 Napoleon Ave, 70115 **Tel** *(504) 895-4877*   **Map** *7 D3*

This is supposedly the birthplace of the legendary barbecue shrimp and worth a visit. The beautiful old oyster bar is also notable, but don't expect too much from other parts of the menu. This would be a nice spot to tickle your appetite before enjoying entrées elsewhere. It is just a few blocks from the St. Charles Avenue streetcar.

Patois ♿🍴 $$$$

6078 Laurel St, 70115 **Tel** *(504) 895-9441*   **Map** *6 B5*

This former bar room has been beautifully transformed into an artfully designed Uptown gourmet destination. Louisiana regional dishes take center stage, but there are plenty of influences from French, Italian, and Spanish cuisines as well. The restaurant can get very loud at dinner, though Sunday brunch is a more laid-back affair.

Upperline $$$$

1413 Upperline St, 70115 **Tel** *(504) 891-9822*   **Map** *7 D4*

Everyone loves the classic Creole fare at this quirky, yet upscale restaurant. They claim to have invented the fried green tomato topped with shrimp remoulade that you see all over the city, and it is entirely possible considering how long owner JoAnn Clevenger and chef Ken Smith have been perfecting the art. Go hungry and order every course.

Commander's Palace ♿🎵🍴 $$$$$

1403 Washington Ave, 70130 **Tel** *(504) 899-8221*   **Map** *7 F3*

The Brennan family set the standard for New Orleans fine dining when they opened this culinary palace in the 1970s. An extensive renovation after Hurricane Katrina has left the restaurant looking fresher and brighter, while the cuisine remains a blend of Creole classics with innovative twists. The jazz brunch is an especially celebratory meal here.

Emeril's Delmonico ♿🎵 $$$$$

1300 St. Charles Ave, 70130 **Tel** *(504) 525-4937*   **Map** *8 A2*

This historic New Orleans restaurant came under Emeril's wing at the turn of the millennium, and he has made great strides in renovating the grand old place. Both the atmosphere and the menu offer some of the old while enlivening things with just enough new. The menu changes with the current *chef de cuisine*, but the aged steaks are a definite win.

Key to Price Guide *see p176* **Key to Symbols** *see back cover flap*

MID-CITY

Angelo Brocato's Ice Cream & Confectionary 🏃🦽 Ⓢ

*214 N Carrollton Ave, 70119 **Tel** (504) 486-1465* **Map** 2 A3

This traditional Sicilian ice-cream parlor has been a New Orleans institution for more than a century. The wide assortment of flavors includes specialties like tiramisu, pistachio, and the best-selling lemon flavor, while fresh, local fruit is made into Italian ices (a type of sorbet). An old, brass espresso-maker produces great coffee drinks.

Juan's Flying Burrito 🏃🦽▦ Ⓢ

*4724 S Carrollton Ave, 70119 **Tel** (504) 486-9950* **Map** 2 A3

A rock 'n' roll vibe and family-friendly atmosphere mix at this neighborhood cantina just off the Canal streetcar route. Fat California-style *burritos* are the specialty of the house, although local shrimp and fish, Caribbean jerk chicken, and plenty of vegetarian choices add variety to the tortilla-based menu.

K-Jean's Seafood 🏃 Ⓢ

*224 N Carrollton Ave, 70119 **Tel** (504) 488-7503* **Map** 2 A2

Amenities may be slim to nil at this take-out-only seafood market, but the heady aroma of boiling shrimp, crabs, or crawfish is enough to ensure a constant flow of customers. Get a po'boy or a few pounds of spicy, boiled, seasonal seafood, and make a picnic of it at nearby City Park.

Willie Mae's Scotch House 🗐🏃🦽 Ⓢ

*2401 St. Ann St, 70119 **Tel** (504) 822-9503* **Map** 2 C3

Located in a rather unsavoury part of town (take a taxi), this eatery is famous for its Southern soul food. The Scotch House suffered extensive damage as a result of Hurricane Katrina, but the local community rallied together for a clean-up operation, and the restaurant reopened to great fanfare in 2007. Open lunchtimes only, Mon–Sat.

Dooky Chase 🏃🦽 ⓈⓈ

*2301 Orleans Ave, 70119 **Tel** (504) 821-0600* **Map** 2 C3

Chef Leah Chase deserves utmost recognition for her famed restaurant that was considered by many as the head-quarters of the New Orleans Civil Rights movement. Her food is classic Creole cuisine and Creole soul in a welcoming, classy atmosphere. Non-natives might want to take a cab as the neighborhood can intimidate.

Liuzza's by the Track 🏃 ⓈⓈ

*1518 N Lopez St, 70119 **Tel** (504) 218-7888* **Map** 2 C2

This is the consummate neighborhood restaurant. The staff are friendly, and the menu offers an array of very original po'boys and salads. Their gumbo is reminiscent of a home kitchen, and the french fries simply must be ordered. Add gigantic frozen beers and loaded Bloody Marys to the mix, and you have got a recipe for a great time.

Liuzza's Restaurant and Bar 🏃🦽 ⓈⓈ

*3636 Bienville Ave, 70119 **Tel** (504) 482-9120* **Map** 2 A3

This is no relation to the restaurant of the same name, but they do resemble in quality of food and service. Here, you find perfectly fried seafood and hearty New Orleans-Italian fare. The fried pickles or onion rings are good starters, and you should order the stuffed artichoke. They also serve giant frozen beers, and the peanut butter pie is a must.

Lola's 🗐🏃🦽 ⓈⓈ

*3312 Esplanade Ave, 70119 **Tel** (504) 488-6946* **Map** 2 B2

The BYOB option makes this bustling spot all the more fun. They do not take reservations, and there is usually a wait, meaning plenty of time to sip wine before dinner. They serve authentic gazpacho that goes well with crusty French bread smeared with the super garlic butter. Paellas are the entrées to order, if in a group. Not open for lunch.

Parkway Bakery & Tavern 🏃🦽♫▦ ⓈⓈ

*538 N Hagan Ave, 70119 **Tel** (504) 482-3047* **Map** 2 B3

This resurrected po'boy icon resides by the picturesque Bayou St. John, which is nice to walk along before or after chewing on some fried seafood. You could even order takeout and picnic beside the waterway. Especially try the messy roast beef po'boy. After being closed for decades, this restaurant reopened in 2003.

Café Degas 🦽▦ ⓈⓈⓈ

*3127 Esplanade Ave, 70119 **Tel** (504) 945-5635* **Map** 2 B2

The white twinkle lights will catch your eye immediately, and that is just the beginning of the charm. Trees actually grow through the dining room of this little bistro where classic French café food abounds. There is French onion soup, quiche, and pâté. More substantial dishes include veal cheeks and duck. Close to the New Orleans Museum of Art.

Café Minh 🦽 ⓈⓈⓈ

*4139 Canal St, 70119 **Tel** (504) 482-6266* **Map** 2 A3

Chef/owner Minh Bui moved from Vietnam to New Orleans at a young age and spent many years working behind the scenes at the city's top Creole restaurants. His own restaurant features a deft fusion of Vietnamese and Creole cuisines, prepared with all the trappings of the city's best upscale bistros.

Crescent City Steakhouse

⬧ $$$

1001 N Broad Ave, 70119 **Tel** *(504) 821-3271* **Map 2 C3**

It doesn't get any more classic than this 1930s-era steakhouse, home to the New Orleans-style steak, served sizzling with butter. The sturdy dining room, with its tile floors and discreet dining booths with privacy curtains, has not changed for generations. The steaks are prime, the service is friendly, and the prices are reasonable.

Mandina's

$$$

3800 Canal St, 70119 **Tel** *(504) 482-9179* **Map 2 A3**

Every detail harks back to another era. Here, large families still dine together, and regulars wait at the stand-only bar, sipping on stiff cocktails. All the Creole classics are on the menu such as turtle soup, trout *amandine*, and bread pudding, and they all live up to the priceless atmosphere. No reservations – so, embrace the wait.

Ralph's on the Park

$$$$

900 City Park Ave, 70119 **Tel** *(504) 488-1000* **Map 2 A2**

Yet another specimen of the Brennan's restaurant chain that turns fine dining into an art. At Ralph's, the beautiful location overlooking City Park makes for an ideal experience. The salads are well considered, and the local seafood dishes are a must.

BEYOND NEW ORLEANS

ABITA SPRINGS Abita Brew Pub

$$

72011 Holly St, Abita Springs, 70420 **Tel** *(985) 892-5837*

You can sample limited runs of Abita beer that are not found elsewhere, while enjoying their own version of bar food such as Chicken Abitafeller – grilled chicken with fried oysters and spinach-artichoke dip. The quaint town of Abita Springs is nice to walk around, and there is even a bike trail right beside the restaurant.

AVONDALE Mosca's

$$$$

4137 Hwy 90 W, Avondale, 70094 **Tel** *(504) 436-8950*

There are all sorts of Mafia-related rumors surrounding this little Italian spot, and the rural, isolated setting certainly adds to that mystique. But the real draw is the family-style fare. Highlights are the Italian salads featuring tangy olives and sweet lumps of crabmeat and tasty chicken. Be sure to check out the jukebox that will take you back in time.

BREAUX BRIDGE Poche's

$$

3015A Main Hwy, Breaux Bridge, 70517 **Tel** *(337) 332-2108*

This is where to go for all those specialty Cajun meats such as *andouille* and *boudin*. They also serve plate lunches such as smothered rabbit, fried catfish, and crawfish *étouffée*. The Poche family has been in the meat business since the 1960s and should be able to answer any questions about the *charcuterie* tradition.

BREAUX BRIDGE Café des Amis

$$$$

140 E Bridge St, Breaux Bridge, 70517 **Tel** *(337) 332-5273*

This famed dancehall and restaurant really gives you a peek into Cajun culture with plenty of two-stepping and culinary delights such as crawfish pies and cornbread and eggplant wheels. Expect a crowd, especially on weekends in the fall and spring when plenty of tour buses bring in the masses. Still, the more the merrier.

CHALMETTE Rocky & Carlo's

$

613 W St. Bernard Hwy, Chalmette, 70043 **Tel** *(504) 279-8323*

A family restaurant, bar, and de facto community clubhouse, Rocky & Carlo's is a scruffy but beloved institution in St. Bernard Parish and the place to enjoy Creole-Italian comfort food. Impossibly gooey macaroni and cheese with brown gravy, the Italian meatloaf *bracciolini*, and hulking fried oyster po'boys are among the culinary charms.

COVINGTON The Dakota

$$$

629 N Hwy 190, Covington, 70433 **Tel** *(985) 892-3712*

Similar to its sister restaurant Cuvée in New Orleans, this fine-dining place offers excellent food and service. They are known for their fresh, seasonal ingredients and consequently, the menu changes often. The soft shell crabs are a must if in season, and the pork tenderloin is another popular entrée. Also, explore their extensive wine selection.

DARROW Latil's Landing

$$$$$

40136 Hwy 942, River Road, Darrow, 70725 **Tel** *(225) 473-9380*

A visit to Houmas House Plantation and Gardens *(see p137)* is meant to evoke Louisiana's prosperous past, but a meal at its fine-dining restaurant, Latil's Landing, is all about contemporary, cosmopolitan renditions of Creole cuisine. No expense is spared in decor or amenities, and elaborate tasting menus are available nightly.

GRETNA Kim Son

$$

349 Whitney Ave, Gretna, 70056 **Tel** *(504) 366-2489*

The west bank of the Mississippi River offers great ethnic cuisine, especially from Vietnam. Kim Son serves Chinese and Vietnamese dishes, and the latter are the standout. Claypot specialties are sure to please as are the salt-baked shrimp, lobster, and crab. There is basic Cantonese fare for the less adventurous but if you are daring, talk to the staff.

Key to Price Guide *see p176* **Key to Symbols** *see back cover flap*

LACOMBE La Provence   ⚐ $$$$

25020 Hwy 190, Lacombe, 70445 **Tel** *(985) 626-7662*

The French country home feel sets the stage for classic French fare such as leg of lamb and roasted duck. There are also some local dishes including chicken and *andouille* gumbo. Their "menu du paysan" special is a good deal featuring a reasonably priced three-course dinner. The 30-something-year history of the restaurant makes it special.

LAFAYETTE Anjo's Bakery   ⚐ $

1507 Kaliste Saloom Rd, Lafayette, 70508 **Tel** *(337) 989-1977*

This sweet spot has been treating Lafayette to its European-style pastries for years – offering tiramisu, cream puffs, eclairs, and more. They are famous for their baby king cakes during Mardi Gras, and they even offer a line of desserts for diabetics. On the savory side there are some hot sandwiches, but sugar is their real specialty.

LAFAYETTE Don's Seafood and Steakhouse   ⚐ $$

301 E Vermillion St, Lafayette, 70501 **Tel** *(337) 235-3551*

This family-owned local favorite is always bustling and has been for about 70 years. They offer terrific fresh local seafood (mostly fried), and big juicy steaks. They are known for their hushpuppies, and bread pudding is the signature dessert. A great place to eat if you are traveling with kids, thanks to the welcoming atmosphere and friendly staff.

LAFAYETTE Alesi's Italian Restaurant $$$

4110 Johnston St, Lafayette, 70503 **Tel** *(337) 984-1823*

This mom-and-pop restaurant has been hooking locals with their pizza and pasta for years. It is a sure charmer with red- and white-checked tablecloths and a friendly staff. Their steaks, sandwiches, and salads are popular alternatives to traditional Italian fare. A great place to go if you are traveling with children, thanks to the family atmosphere.

LAFAYETTE Prejean's   ⚐ $$$

3480 I-49 N, Lafayette, 70507 **Tel** *(337) 896-3247*

The focal point in this authentic Cajun dancehall is a 14-ft (4.2-m) long stuffed alligator named "Big Al." He watches over the nightly dancing and eating. The extensive menu offers many options, mostly of the Cajun variety, such as crawfish boudin balls, and seafood stuffed mushrooms as starters. Entrées include crawfish pasta and fried alligator.

LAFAYETTE Randol's   ⚐ $$$

2320 Kaliste Saloom Rd, Lafayette, 70508 **Tel** *(337) 981-7080*

This dancehall/restaurant places a strong emphasis on fresh ingredients. They raise their own crabs and crawfish and grow herbs for seasoning. Highlights of the menu are crab fingers, fried oyster Caesar salad, shrimp au gratin, and boiled crawfish and crabs when in season. They also sell their fresh seafood, which they will ship home for you.

MANCHAC Middendorf's Seafood   ⚐ $$

30160 Hwy 51 S, Manchac, 70421 **Tel** *(985) 386-6666*

There are actually two side-by-side locations of this fried seafood haven. Their specialty is catfish, and you can enjoy its crispy goodness as you relax surrounded by the waters of Lake Manchac. It is fun to go here on a Saturday or Sunday afternoon when the weather is nice and local families turn out in droves, giving you a feel for true Louisiana living.

MANDEVILLE Trey Yuen Cuisine of China   ⚐ $$

600 N Causeway Blvd, Mandeville, 70448 **Tel** *(985) 626-4476*

There is no lack of flair at this landmark Northshore restaurant, which was modeled after a Chinese palace, complete with courtyard gardens and ponds. The menu offers most of the familiar Chinese-American standards, but the kitchen also works in local ingredients like crawfish and oysters for some original dishes.

METAIRIE Andrea's   ⚐ $$$$

3100 19th St, Metairie, 70002 **Tel** *(504) 834-8583*

This Metairie mainstay does not look like much from the outside, but locals have revered it for years because of its delicious Italian fare. Popular starters are the antipasti and Caprese salad, and favorite entrées are the risotto New Orleans and veal chops. All seafood dishes are fresh, and the chef's tasting menu ensures a nice sampling.

METAIRIE Drago's   ⚐ $$$$

3232 N Arnoult Rd, Metairie, 70002 **Tel** *(504) 888-9254*

This unassuming Croatian restaurant became famous for the perfection of its grilled oysters. Topped with garlic and butter and cooked until just done, they are worth a trip to Metairie. They also offer a variety of other local seafood dishes, but the oysters are the standout.

NEW IBERIA Clementine Dining & Spirits   ⚐ $$$

113 E Main St, New Iberia, 70560 **Tel** *(337) 560-1007*

The focal point in this historic building is an antique bar made of tiger oak and mahogany; a perfect place for a pre-dinner cocktail. Dine in the courtyard and enjoy some of their signature dishes such as roasted red pepper bisque with mushrooms and crabmeat, and their addictive fried green tomatoes. Locals swear by their steaks.

RACELAND Spahr's   ⚐ $

4566 Hwy 1, Raceland, 70394 **Tel** *(985) 758-1602*

If you are looking for some road food as you drive west from New Orleans then you should definitely stop here. They are famous for their Bloody Marys and fried seafood, and with good reason. The Bloody Mary is basically a meal in itself, and their fried oysters, shrimp, and catfish are all exemplary. Be on the lookout – it is hidden in a gas station.

SHOPPING IN NEW ORLEANS

As the gateway to the Mississippi, New Orleans has long been a place for buying and selling goods, and it still maintains a talent for filling its stores with irresistible treasures. Antiques are among the city's finest buys, and it is possible to find anything from 18th-century French furniture to 1950s vintage dresses. Other specialties include imaginative masks, handmade crafts, rare books, and the best jazz records. Shopping in New Orleans is an initiation into local culture. Each of the city's many shopping areas has a unique character, with the French Quarter, Magazine Street, Carrollton, and Julia Street all offering vibrant, rich experiences. These pages highlight the best stops in the city.

Antique porcelain jar

The exterior of the upscale Canal Place shopping mall

WHEN TO SHOP

Stores in the Central Business District, along Magazine Street, and in the French Quarter tend to operate from 9am to 5pm or 10am to 6pm. Many open on Sundays, but always call in advance to avoid disappointment. Some shops in the Quarter don't open until noon, but they close late, too.

HOW TO PAY

Major credit cards are accepted everywhere, and there are plenty of Automated Teller Machines (ATMs) from which to get cash for a small fee. Traveler's checks are almost universally accepted. Some shops will also take personal checks with sufficient identification.

SALES TAX REIMBURSEMENT

If you are a foreign visitor, you can get back the 10 percent sales tax on tangible goods, but you must show the vendor your passport and ask for a refund voucher.

At the airport, go to the **Louisiana Tax Free Shopping Refund Center** and show your passport, sales receipts, refund vouchers, and air ticket (which may be up to a maximum of a 90-day trip). If you do not manage to get reimbursed at the airport, send copies of everything, along with an explanation, to the Refund Center.

SHIPPING

If you would prefer to send your purchases home rather than take them with you, ask the store to handle the task for you – New Orleans merchants are accustomed to shipping goods anywhere. For large buys such as furniture and art objects, professional packing and/or shipping is a necessity. A good source is **The Wooden Box** on South Peters Street. For smaller items, a reliable company is the **Royal Mail Service**.

MALLS AND SHOPPING CENTERS

New Orleans currently has only two traditional in-town malls. **Canal Place** (see p94), on the edge of the French Quarter, has upscale shops such as Ann Taylor, Williams-Sonoma, Saks Fifth Avenue, and Coach. The unique **Riverwalk Marketplace**, which stretches alongside the Mississippi River from Canal Street up to the Convention Center, has dozens of small shops and a liberal share of chains such as Chico's, Nine West, and others. Outside there is a concrete deck above the river, which has lovely views, and useful information plaques pointing out places of interest.

Jax Brewery, in the French Quarter, is a former beer factory that has been transformed into a sprawling, three-story retail space.

Visitors who want a more traditional mall experience can venture into the suburbs. **Lakeside Shopping Center** in Metairie is the biggest mall in

A band outside Riverwalk Marketplace

the metropolitan area. It has three anchor stores, Dillard's, J. C. Penney, and Macy's, and more than 100 other shops, including 15 shoe stores.

ART AND ANTIQUES

Since its earliest days, New Orleans has been a treasure trove of artistic and vintage luxuries. The locals' knack for dealing in rare and remarkable objects continues to this very day. Another big advantage of shopping for antiques in New Orleans is relative affordability. While prices may still be steep for rare and highly sought-after pieces, they are usually lower than in other US cities. Even when shipping costs are taken into consideration, buyers do very well for themselves. Vintage art can be found in abundance here, though it leans toward the pretty and comfortable; visit Julia Street for more cutting-edge works.

There are antiques shops all over the city, but the biggest concentrations can be found on Royal Street in the French Quarter and along Magazine Street in Uptown. The former is a fabulous showcase of high-end antiques, while the latter leans more toward the fun and funky. Many of the shops in the Quarter are family-run enterprises, often several generations in. This history has contributed to their developing a comfortable, easy atmosphere for all customers, especially novices.

Established in 1912, **M. S. Rau** is internationally known for its range of American, English, and French antique furniture. **Keil's Antiques** is a family-run business dating from 1899. It stocks superb antique jewelry, as well as chandeliers, furniture, and mirrors. On Chartres Street, **Lucullus** focuses on kitchen antiques, ranging from china and linens to 200-year-old French farm tables, while on Decatur Street, **Bottom of the Barrel Antiques** is a must for treasure hunters. Their motto is "This ain't

your Grandma's antique shop," and the tattoo-covered employees confirm this. Jammed with all manner of things from the region, the store is best known for unbelievably affordable prices on bedroom suites,

Linke cabinet crafted with kingwood and doré bronze, at M. S. Rau

armoires, and chandeliers. Sometimes the prices seem so cheap you think there must be a mistake.

The antiques shops on Magazine Street tend to be heavier on 20th-century wares than those in the French Quarter. **Bush Antiques** has a large range of eye-popping vintage beds, many of which come from France. Celebrities who happen to be in town can often be spotted here. **Simon of New Orleans** has a changing stock of offbeat tables, chairs, and metalwork. However, the shop is best known for proprietor and chef-turned-artist Simon Hardeveld's charming faux folk-art signs.

New Orleans also offers a wide selection of art galleries, the most famous of which is probably the **Rodrigue Studio**, in the French Quarter.

It's home to Cajun artist George Rodrigue and his distinctive *Blue Dog* paintings. Make sure you look at his other works too, such as the scenes from Cajun community life. Also in the Quarter is the **Stone & Press Gallery**, with dazzlingly detailed works on paper, etchings, lithographs, wood carvings, and mezzotints.

The artist James Michalopoulos, who owns the eponymous gallery **Michalopoulos**, has become popular for his idiosyncratic depictions of New Orleans architecture. The exaggerated silhouettes are true-to-life representations of the city.

When you are in the French Quarter, don't forget to check out the artists who hang their works on the fence around Jackson Square. While some of the pieces on display are amateur at best, there are also some very talented artists who choose this one-on-one interaction with the public rather than taking the more formal gallery route.

Julia Street, in the Warehouse District, is New Orleans' genuine gallery neighborhood. Most of the galleries here concentrate on local and regional artists, which means that you'll have a chance to see exceptional work by painters, sculptors, and photographers not well known outside of Louisiana.

LeMieux Galleries shows both emerging and established artists from Louisiana and the

Bush Antiques interior displaying a vintage sleigh bed

An array of Louisiana hot sauces to recreate the magic of Creole cuisine

Gulf Coast, often with strong New Orleans themes in their work.

Quite a few non-Louisiana artists are represented by **Arthur Roger**, including big names such as Dale Chihuly, with his art glass, and film-maker John Waters, with his quirky photographs. The **Steve Martin Studio** is an all-white space above a 19th-century storefront. The starkness shows off owner Steve Martin's wire sculptures to great advantage, and acts as an ideal backdrop for the large canvases that his emerging artists seem to favor. For avant-garde work that explores exciting installation and conceptual art, the **Jonathan Ferrara Gallery** is the place to go.

The **Stella Jones Gallery** in the CBD is the city's premier African and African-American showplace. Modern masters such as Elizabeth Catlett are on the gallery's list of artists. The **New Orleans School of Glassworks** has an exhibition space for the art glass created by its members. If possible, time your visit to observe one of the daily demos of the highly skilled artists blowing glass.

If you happen to be in New Orleans on the third Saturday of any month, a visit to the outdoors **Bywater Art Market** is a must. Join the locals as they wander among the 50-plus painters, jewelry-makers, photographers, textile artists, and woodworkers who set up for the special one-day event, come rain or shine.

JEWELRY

The oldest jewelry store in New Orleans is **Adler's**, which dates back to 1898. This is the best place for traditional rings, necklaces, and other precious items. **Mignon Faget** has become the standard for contemporary jewelry, producing handcrafted pieces in gold and silver. There are three Faget shops in the metropolitan area. **Katy Beh Contemporary Jewelry** is a stylish store that represents more than 30 modern jewelry-makers. The line of "commitment rings" is a romantic's dream come true.

Many of the antiques shops also carry an extensive stock of vintage earrings, bracelets, necklaces, and decorative pieces. **New Orleans Silversmiths** is a big favorite with many collectors.

FOOD

If you fall in love with Cajun and Creole cuisine during your stay in New Orleans,

A gifts and souvenirs stand at the popular French Quarter Flea Market

it is possible to take those unique flavors home with you. The distinctive spices, sauces, and mixes used in local dishes are readily available in jars and bottles. You'll see them all over the French Quarter in souvenir shops, but these are often wildly overpriced, so try a regular grocery store instead for *beignet* mix, coffee with chicory, crab boil, and other products – the quality is the same, but the prices are far lower. Try **Rouse's Market**, which is almost a full-service grocery store in the French Quarter, or the historic **Central Grocery** (*see p76*), another Quarter outlet that, besides its famous *muffaletta* (*see p172*), also stocks sauces, mustards, and all kinds of Italian delicacies. Pralines are a must-try for many visitors. The greatest fun is to sample the different outlets before hitting upon a favorite. The tastiest bets are **Laura's Candies** and **Aunt Sally's Praline Shop**.

If you want to take home crawfish, crab, or andouille sausage, head for the **Big Fisherman** on Magazine Street, where the locals go for their fare. An advantage is that the staff are expert at packing these meaty perishables for travel.

CRAFTS

For a wide selection of items made out of ceramics, wood, paper, metal, and glass, try the third floor of Canal Place, where **Rhino Contemporary Craft Co.** features crafts from a range of regional artists. The **Idea Factory** is filled with handmade woodcrafted toys, games, vases, sculptures, boxes, and all sorts of other collectibles. The Idea Factory manages to be both primitive and sophisticated.

The fun **French Quarter Flea Market** (*see p70*) is host to a number of vendors selling all sorts of strange and alluring crafts. These include wood carvings that, in spite of their questionable African origins, make delightful gifts. Quirky handmade toys and jewelry are also available here.

GIFTS AND SPECIALTY STORES

Located in a handsome old-fashioned store, **Hové Parfumeur** has been sweetly scenting New Orleanians since 1931. At **Santa's Quarters**, it is Christmas all year round. You will find lovely holiday ornaments and decorative objects at this store, which is a real boon for those who prefer to finish their Christmas shopping before winter.

If you wish to buy one of the gas lamps that flicker in the Quarter for your own front door, stop by **Bevolo Gas and Electric Lights**, while **Scriptura** is the place to go for beautiful paper products, from journals and sketch books to handmade paper and calligraphy sets.

New Orleans has strong links with the Caribbean, and there are several cigar-making stores in the city. At the **Cigar Factory**, visitors can watch the cigars being rolled and cut, then proceed to select their stogie of choice from the humidor.

Mardi Gras souvenirs such as masks and other regalia are available at several stores. The best place to find a flattering art mask is at the fair before Mardi Gras, but if you're not in town at that time of year, then stop by **Rumors**. They also sell quaint

A flamboyant Mardi Gras mask from Rumors, sold all year round

voodoo dolls that have purportedly been inspired by the Louisiana swampland. There are quite a few tarot readers in Jackson Square, but for a private session in rather unusual surroundings, opt for the **Bottom of the Cup Tea Room**.

Located within the same eclectic block of Magazine Street, **Winky's**, **Metro Three**, and **Aidan Gill for Men** all offer unusual items. **Winky's** is known for everything from

Colorful fashion feathers at Funky Monkey

surrealist arty items for the home to naughty adult gag gifts. Metro Three has area art and T-shirts reflecting local culture, while Aidan Gill is an old-fashioned gentlemen's parlor with a fine range of wristwatches, lapel pins, and grooming items.

FASHION

For mainstream apparel for men, women, and children, you can rely on department stores such as Dillard's, Macy's, and J. C. Penney, in the shopping malls. However, it is the depth and variety of formal clothing that makes New Orleans different from most other cities in the US. Everyone here attends Mardi Gras balls, from street cleaners to bank presidents, so numerous shops also carry frilly ball gowns, dancing slippers, evening purses, and other accessories.

New Orleans is the perfect place to pick out a tuxedo, since there's a wide selection and the salespeople know all about fittings. **Perlis** is almost a New Orleans tradition in formal clothing for men. The shop's signature fashion is a polo shirt with a crawfish logo (note that Perlis does also have departments dedicated to women's clothing). Another old-line store that caters to men is **Rubenstein's**. **Style Lab**, featuring fashionable casual clothing, is also an oft-frequented place for menswear.

Mimi, on Magazine Street, is the top designer-fashion

shop for women, carrying Michael Kors and Vera Wang among others. It also has a popular cosmetics counter. While Mimi's sleek and stylish look represents reigning fashion trends, New Orleans continues its love affair with overstated apparel that is characterized by ruffles, flounces, and other such flourishes. Despite the similarity in name and style, **Fleur de Paris** and **Yvonne LaFleur** are unrelated shops. The former is a lush temple to femininity in the French Quarter. Hats are the store's signature items, and they feature frothy decorations of feathers, fruits, flowers, and ribbons. Back in the Riverbend area of Uptown, Yvonne LaFleur offers lavish evening gowns and romantic hats that Scarlett O'Hara would have loved. The shop even has its own tiara department. Designer Harold Clarke's French Quarter outlet, **Harold Clarke Couturier**, is much loved by debutantes and Mardi Gras royalty. His dreamy ball gowns are always on display thanks to the full-length windows in his shop.

Magazine Street is home to a number of happening shops that specialize in funky outfits for club nights and bohemian days. **Trashy Diva** and **Funky Monkey** both stock wild and outrageous clothes that you might see on teenage pop stars. For vintage fashions, a good choice is **On the Other Hand**, a boutique that offers a fine and wide selection of second-hand clothes.

Meyer the Hatter is one of the city's most beloved shops. The family-owned store has been supplying New Orleanians of both sexes with hats for more than 100 years. Every conceivable type of hat can be found here, including Stetsons, derbies, fedoras, and berets, all of which are elegant, well crafted, and reasonably priced.

BOOKS

Independent bookstores are still going strong in New Orleans. At **Octavia Books**, located in the Uptown area, volumes are carefully chosen and sold by the book-loving staffers. The **Garden District Bookshop** has an admirable selection of non-fiction and regional titles, and it also has strong ties to writer Anne Rice, who has done several signings here. **Maple Street Bookshop**, near the Tulane University campus, is devoted to showcasing Southern literature and is a favorite of locals as well as visiting writers. In the French Quarter, **Faulkner House Books** is a charming little shop with a surprising number of books in stock. It also has many rare first editions, especially by William Faulkner, who once lived in the building. For used books, the French Quarter has **Kaboom Books**, a treasure trove of both intellectual and offbeat volumes. **Beckham's Bookshop** includes comfy reading chairs and friendly cats.

MUSIC

Music is the lifeblood of New Orleans. The greatest place to explore local music, from jazz to zydeco, is the famous **Louisiana Music Factory**, which stocks a well-cataloged range of artists. Be sure to check for free in-store performances by artists promoting their new albums. The staff members are very helpful too.

For collectors, the city has several outstanding hunting grounds. One of the best is **Jim Russell's Rare Records**, which has a great stock of rock 'n' roll 78s among its thousands of records.

A record by Oscar "Papa" Celestin, founder of the Tuxedo Brass Band

DIRECTORY

SALES TAX REIMBURSEMENT

Louisiana Tax Free Shopping Refund Center
P.O. Box 20125.
Tel 467-0723.
www.louisianataxfree.com

SHIPPING

Royal Mail Service
828 Royal St.
Map 5 D2.
Tel 522-8523.

The Wooden Box
816 S Peters St.
Map 4 C5.
Tel 568-0281.

MALLS AND SHOPPING CENTERS

Canal Place
333 Canal St. **Map** 8 C1.
Tel 522-9200.
www.theshopsat canalplace.com

Jax Brewery
600 Decatur St. **Map** 3 E5.
Tel 566-7245. **www.**jacksonbrewery.com

Lakeside Shopping Center
3301 Veterans Blvd.
Tel 835-8000. **www.**lakesideshopping.com

Riverwalk Marketplace
1 Poydras St. **Map** 8 C1.
Tel 522-1555. **www.**riverwalkmarketplace.com

ART AND ANTIQUES

Arthur Roger
432 Julia St. **Map** 4 C5.
Tel 522-1999. **www.**arthurrogergallery.com
One of two locations.

Bottom of the Barrel Antiques
1209 Decatur St.
Map 5 D1.
Tel 220-8577 or 881-6125.

Bush Antiques
2109 Magazine St.
Map 8 A3. *Tel 581-3518.*
www.bushantiques.com

Bywater Art Market
Piety & Royal sts.
Tel 944-7900. **www.**bywaterartmarket.com

Jonathan Ferrara Gallery
400 Julia St.
Map 4 C5.
Tel 522-5471.
www.jonathanferrara gallery.com

Keil's Antiques
325 Royal St.
Map 4 C2.
Tel 522-4552.
www.keilsantiques.com

LeMieux Galleries
332 Julia St.
Map 4 C5.
Tel 522-5988. **www.**lemieuxgalleries.com

Lucullus
610 Chartres St.
Map 4 C2. *Tel 528-9620.*
www.lucullusantiques.com
One of two locations.

Michalopoulos
617 Bienville St.
Map 4 C3.
Tel 558-0505. **www.**michalopoulos.com

M. S. Rau
630 Royal St.
Map 5 D2.
Tel 523-5660.
www.rauantiques.com

New Orleans School of Glassworks
727 Magazine St.
Map 4 C4. *Tel 529-7279.*
www.neworleans glassworks.org

Rodrigue Studio
721 Royal St.
Map 5 D2.
Tel 581-4244.
www.george rodrigue.com

Simon of New Orleans
1028 Jackson Ave.
Map 8 A3.
Tel 524-8201.

Stella Jones Gallery
201 St. Charles Ave.
Map 4 C3.
Tel 568-9050.
www.stellajones.com

Steve Martin Studio
624 Julia St.
Map 4 B4.
Tel 566-1390.
www.stevemartin studio.com

Stone & Press Gallery
238 Chartres St.
Map 4 C3. *Tel 561-8555.*
www.stoneandpress.com

DIRECTORY

JEWELRY

Adler's
722 Canal St. **Map** 4 B3.
Tel 523-5292.
www.adlersjewelry.com

Katy Beh Contemporary Jewelry
3701 Magazine St.
Map 7 F4. *Tel 896-9600.*
www.katybeh.com

Mignon Faget
3801 Magazine St.
Map 7 F4.
Tel 891-2005.
www.mignonfaget.com

New Orleans Silversmiths
600 Chartres St.
Map 4 C2. *Tel 522-8333.*
www.neworleans
silversmiths.com

FOOD

Aunt Sally's Praline Shop
810 Decatur St.
Map 5 D2. *Tel 524-3373.*
www.auntsallys.com

Big Fisherman
3301 Magazine St.
Map 7 F4. *Tel 897-9907.*
www.bigfisherman
seafood.com

Central Grocery
923 Decatur St.
Map 5 D2. *Tel 523-1620.*

Laura's Candies
331 Chartres St.
Map 4 C3. *Tel 525-3880.*
www.laurascandies.com

Rouse's Market
701 Royal St.
Map 5 D2. *Tel 523-1353.*
www.rouses.com

CRAFTS

French Quarter Flea Market
Decatur & St. Philip sts.
Map 5 D2.
Tel 522-2621.
www.frenchmarket.org

Idea Factory
838 Chartres St.
Map 5 D1.
Tel 524-5195.
www.ideafactory
neworleans.com

Rhino Contemporary Craft Co.
Canal Place, 3rd floor.
Map 4 C3.
Tel 523-7945.
www.rhinocrafts.com

GIFTS AND SPECIALTY STORES

Aidan Gill for Men
2026 Magazine St.
Map 8 A3.
Tel 587-9090. www.
aidangillformen.com

Bevolo Gas and Electric Lights
521 Conti St.
Map 4 C2.
Tel 522-9485.
www.bevolo.com

Bottom of the Cup Tea Room
327 Chartres St.
Map 4 C3.
Tel 524-1997.
www.bottomof
thecup.com

Cigar Factory
415 Decatur St.
Map 5 D3. *Tel 568-1003.*
www.cigarfactory
neworleans.com

Hové Parfumeur
824 Royal St.
Map 5 D1.
Tel 525-7827. www.
Hoveparfumeur.com

Metro Three
2032 Magazine St.
Map 8 A3.
Tel 558-0212.
www.metrothree.com

Rumors
537 Royal St.
Map 4 C2.
Tel 525-0292.
www.rumorsno.com

Santa's Quarters
1025 Decatur St.
Map 5 D2. *Tel 581-5820.*
www.santas
quartersno.com

Scriptura
5423 Magazine St.
Map 6 C4.
Tel 897-1555.
www.scriptura.com

Winky's
2038 Magazine St.
Map 8 A3.
Tel 568-1020.

FASHION

Fleur de Paris
523 Royal St.
Map 4 C2.
Tel 525-1899.
www.fleurdeparis.net

Funky Monkey
3127 Magazine St.
Map 7 F4. *Tel 899-5587.*

Harold Clarke Couturier
901 Iberville St.
Map 4 C2. *Tel 568-0440.*
www.haroldclarke.com

Meyer the Hatter
120 St. Charles Ave.
Map 4 C3.
Tel 525-1048. www.
meyerthehatter.com

Mimi
5500 Magazine St.
Map 6 C4. *Tel 269-6464.*
www.miminola.com

On the Other Hand
8204 Oak St. **Map** 6 A1.
Tel 861-0159.
www.ontheotherhand
consignment.com

Perlis
6070 Magazine St.
Map 6 B4. *Tel 895-8661.*
www.perlis.com
One of four locations.

Rubenstein's
102 St. Charles Ave.
Map 4 C3. *Tel 581-6666.*
www.rubensteins
neworleans.com

Style Lab
3641 Magazine St.
Map 7 E4. *Tel 304-5072.*
www.stylelabformen.com

Trashy Diva
829 Chartres St.
Map 5 D2. *Tel 581-4555.*
www.trashydiva.com
One of two locations.

Yvonne LaFleur
8131 Hampson St.
Map 6 A1. *Tel 866-9666.*
www.yvonnelafleur.com

BOOKS

Beckham's Bookshop
228 Decatur St.
Map 4 C3. *Tel 522-9875.*

Faulkner House Books
624 Pirate's Alley.
Map 5 D2. *Tel 524-2940.*
www.faulknerhouse
books.net

Garden District Bookshop
2727 Prytania St.
Map 7 F4. *Tel 895-2266.*
www.gardendistrict
bookshop.com

Kaboom Books
915 Barracks St.
Map 5 D1. *Tel 529-5780.*

Maple Street Bookshop
7523 Maple St.
Map 6 A2. *Tel 866-4916.*
www.maplestreet
bookshop.com

Octavia Books
513 Octavia St.
Map 6 C5. *Tel 899-7323.*
www.octaviabooks.com

MUSIC

Jim Russell's Rare Records
1837 Magazine St.
Map 8 B3. *Tel 522-2602.*
www.jimrussellrecords.
com

Louisiana Music Factory
210 Decatur St.
Map 4 C3. *Tel 586-1094.*
www.louisiana
musicfactory.com

What to Buy in New Orleans

Mardi Gras mask

New Orleans is the best place to discover original small boutiques that are owned by artists and designers of all sorts – jewelers, painters, potters, milliners, clothes designers, and many more – rather than large department stores. In addition to these, there are various tourist memorabilia and trinket stores, which sell T-shirts, rubber alligators, Mardi Gras beads, and other typical kitsch souvenirs. However, to experience the quintessential New Orleans, look out for the things that New Orleans does best – cuisine, cocktails, and music.

Mardi Gras poster

MARDI GRAS MEMORABILIA

Mardi Gras is New Orleans' biggest and longest party, and there are plenty of souvenirs that visitors can take home. Masks are the most alluring, and they can be found in shops and stalls throughout the city. Prices can range from as little as $20 to hundreds of dollars. Masks are often handmade by individual artists including theater costume designers. Less authentic trinkets include beads, mugs, T-shirts, and other typical souvenirs.

Flea market stands with Mardi Gras souvenirs

African Art and Crafts

The heritage of New Orleans' African cultures can be found in a number of shops. Here you can buy African art and crafts, including masks, drums, sculptures, pipes, tables, and items of personal jewelry.

African wood drum

Wood–carved African sculptures

Music

Music is the lifeblood of the city, and a musical souvenir is essential. Record stores sell recordings of great artists playing traditional and modern jazz, gospel, blues, R&B, Cajun, and zydeco.

Hand-Rolled Cigars

New Orleans is close to the Caribbean, both physically and culturally, and has a strong tradition of importing Caribbean cigars. There are several stores where cigars are still hand-rolled. Even a single cigar or a rather expensive box make a perfect gift for any cigar aficionado.

Voodoo Accoutrements

New Orleans is the one place in the United States where the voodoo religion was once openly practiced and celebrated (see p83). Supplies of the materials needed to perform voodoo healings and other rituals – candles, gris-gris to control the boss, ensure safe travel, or promote love, voodoo dolls, and more – can still be purchased at several shops in the French Quarter. These always make colorful and unusual gifts.

Voodoo candle

Gris-gris bags

Antiques

New Orleans is famous for its tradition of dealing in fine antiques. You can find 19th-century furniture and jewelry, as well as other decorative objects, for all tastes and prices.

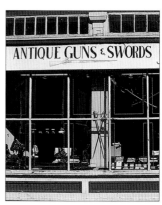

Antique shop on Royal Street

THE FLAVORS OF LOUISIANA

Louisiana is famous the world over for spicy, flavorsome cuisine *(see pp172–5)*. Most visitors want to take some of it home and duplicate those flavors in their own kitchens. In many stores, shelves are lined with hot sauces such as Tabasco, Crystal, Panola, and Cajun Chef. Strands of peppers and garlic and bottles of Cajun and Creole seasoning can be found at the French Market and numerous stores in the area. Here are some of the city's quintessential food gifts.

Roux mix for gumbos

Olive salad dressing

Beignet flour mix

An instant traditional dish

Hats

Southerners and New Orleanians in particular love hats. There are several stores selling terrific ones for both men and women (see pp189–90). They stock every available kind, from classic fedoras, derbies, and Stetsons to berets, French legion caps, and squashy barman hats.

ENTERTAINMENT IN NEW ORLEANS

In 1817, a visitor to New Orleans wrote, "There are few places where human life can be enjoyed with more pleasure." Little has changed since then, and New Orleans remains a party town to this day. Even when it is not Mardi Gras, the mood is festive, and there is always a party somewhere. Music underpins the atmosphere, from tiny neighborhood bars to late-night

Marching-band tuba player

brass band joints and the annual Jazz Fest. The rallying cry of *Laissez les bons temps rouler!* ("Let the good times roll!") is taken quite literally here. You'll also find good times in sports, including football, basketball, and horseracing, as well as casinos, stage productions, and bars, which approach an art form in the Big Easy. For New Orleans' best music venues, see pp200–1.

Street musicians playing jazz on Jackson Square

ENTERTAINMENT GUIDES

It's easy to find out what's on in New Orleans. The best guides are the monthly magazine **Offbeat**, found free in cafés, hotels, and other public places; the **Times-Picayune**'s Friday tabloid *Lagniappe*; and the weekly alternative paper **Gambit**. For gay events and entertainments, check the bi-monthly newspaper **Ambush**, distributed to gay bars and clubs in the French Quarter and the Marigny. Other sources of information are the roots music radio station **WWOZ** (90.7 FM) and classical and jazz music station **WWNO** (89.9 FM).

Alcohol plays a big role in the *bon temps* in New Orleans. Although the city has a fairly relaxed attitude toward drinking, there are still a few un-breakable rules. As in the rest of the US, the drinking age is 21, but anyone under 35 should expect to be "carded"

(asked to show a picture ID certifying one's age). Unlike most American cities, it is legal to walk around with drinks in New Orleans, but they must be in plastic cups, or "go cups." It is illegal, however, to have open alcoholic beverages in automobiles, even for passengers. Police keep a careful eye on popular gathering spots and are easy-going about tipsy folks except if there is fighting or public urination, both of which will land miscreants in jail immediately.

TICKETS

The easiest way to buy tickets for concerts, football games, theatrical productions, and other events is to call the relevant box office or **Ticketmaster** (www.ticketmaster.com). The major hotels and B&Bs usually have a concierge who can facilitate booking tickets. Student and senior-citizen discounts are available for many events.

ROCK, BLUES, AND OTHER MUSIC VENUES

Music clubs in New Orleans are almost celebrities in themselves, with their own fans, personalities, and idiosyncrasies. The **House of Blues** (see p201) and **Tipitina's** are the two leading ones by virtue of the big names they book and their unerring instinct for New Orleans authenticity. House of Blues is the largest and most expensive of the clubs; as well as enjoying top lineups, visitors here can dine at the excellent on-site restaurant.

Frenchmen Street, in the Marigny, is where the locals go for the full music experience, drifting among the various bars and clubs. The **Blue Nile** is another club with a big dance floor where Latin, alternative rock, and brass bands play. Hipsters hang out at **Dragon's Den**, where the music often goes

Jazz parade and band on the streets of the French Quarter

Live music at The Famous Door, Bourbon Street

on until daylight. Also on Frenchmen is **d.b.a.** featuring interesting musicians (often acoustic), and the crown jewel of local jazz clubs, the **Snug Harbor Jazz Bistro**.

Bars in Bourbon Street are mostly frequented by tourists, and the music played here tends to be mainstream Top 40 rock covers. There are a couple of genuine pearls on Bourbon – **The Famous Door** has live music daily, while at **Fritzel's** you can hear the best of local jazz talents – but generally speaking, to find the real New Orleans, you need to look a little farther.

At the back of the French Quarter, on Rampart Street, **Donna's Bar & Grill** is the place to see brass bands. Although not a club, the **Louisiana Music Factory** record store *(see p190)*, on Decatur, has an impressive lineup of free concerts. The shop is a great place for close encounters with blues, jazz, zydeco, and Cajun musicians who have daytime "in-stores" – live performances and autographing sessions – to promote new albums and concerts.

On Toulouse Street, **One-Eyed Jack's** is the latest incarnation of a longtime Quarter joint. The club is a bubbly mixture of alternative rock and hip-hop and Sunday-night burlesque shows. A Las Vegas-style show can be enjoyed at the **Chris Owens Club**. The iconic Owens has been performing in the Quarter for at least three decades. For clubs offering topless dancers, head to Bourbon Street.

In the Warehouse District, the **Howlin' Wolf** club is renowned for booking breaking new bands and hosting original events such as the annual Thanksgiving Turkey Bowl. The **Circle Bar** on Lee Circle is a tiny space that rocks, while **Le Bon Temps Roule**, located Uptown on Magazine Street, is a favorite spot to catch live local bands. There are several pool tables, an extensive on-tap beer selection, and better-than-average bar food.

Dance clubs are not a big New Orleans thing, but the **& Club** (say "Ampersand") in the CBD, draws large crowds of young singles, who dance into the small hours with DJs who know how to keep the party going.

For refined nightclubs that recall the elegance of earlier eras, there is **Melange**, in the Ritz-Carlton Hotel. The room itself is lovely, with numerous

romantic nooks and crannies. On weekends dapper young jazz star Jeremy Davenport and his band play to sophisticated crowds. The **Bombay Club** in the Prince Conti Hotel is another oasis of retro sophistication, with plush decor, perfect martinis, and light jazz.

Republic, a cabaret-style music lounge that harkens back to the 1940s, should appeal to those who favor hip and beautiful crowds. The venue offers everything from indie-rock concerts to fashion shows and branded theme parties with celebrity sightings. The city's major music venues will allow you to buy tickets at the door or order them by phone or online. At clubs there's usually a cover charge on weekends and for name acts. Most clubs with live music have a one- or two-drink minimum policy.

Street musician

BARS

It is possible to drink around the clock in New Orleans, which is reported to have more bars per capita than any other American city, all catering to the local passion for a good beer or a nice cocktail. As an added bonus, many bars offer free wireless Internet access to their patrons.

There are several famous bars in the French Quarter that deserve a visit. **Pat O'Brien's** is a classic bar with its own trademark drink, the

Fritzel's, Bourbon Street's traditional European jazz club

lethal rum-and-fruit Hurricane (see p174). It also has a lush courtyard with a flaming fountain and lighthearted piano music. The attractively shabby **Napoleon House** (see p59) is the kind of place where you could see aspiring novelists write their story as they nurse a drink in one of the dim corners. **Lafitte's Blacksmith Shop** (see p78), in a crumbling 18th-century building, sends waiters out to passing horse-drawn carriages to take drink orders.

New Orleans can do sleek and upscale, too, as you'll find at the **Polo Lounge** at the Windsor Court Hotel, **Whiskey Blue** at the W Hotel, and the **Swizzle Stick Bar** in Loews Hotel. In a class of its own, however, is the Hotel Monteleone's **Carousel Bar**, where the bar slowly revolves while the bartenders at the center dispense brandy Alexanders and other cocktails. The sleek **Loft 523** and **Loa at International House** are both distinctive and full of personality – and personalities!

Irish bars are a reliable source of good fun. On Decatur Street, **Kerry Irish Pub** has Guinness on tap and live music. **Molly's at the Market** is more New Orleans Irish than authentic Irish, but it is a center of Celticism, holding its own St. Patrick's Day parade every year. Uptown is **Parasol's Bar**, perhaps the most famous Irish bar of them all. It is a neighborhood hangout that turns green on St. Patrick's Day, with a huge street party that extends several blocks around the bar.

Gathering around Pat O'Brien's famous fire fountain

Serious drinkers will find **Cooter Brown's Tavern** an impressive site, with its selection of more than 400 beers. **The Bulldog**, also in the Uptown area, has a huge beer selection as well, but is better known as a college pick-up bar than for its drinks. **Bacchanal Fine Wines** in Bywater is a laid-back wine shop that holds more-or-less continual wine tastings.

Neighborhood bars are mostly friendly, welcoming places, even if you accidentally sit on a stool that is "owned" by a regular punter. **Vaughan's Lounge**, in Bywater, is a gritty spot that has live music on Thursdays and a bohemian working-class esprit de corps every night. Finally, the **F & M Patio Bar** is known for attracting big crowds after Mardi Gras balls and debutante parties, when people flock here to drink on the patio, dance, and play pool.

GAY AND LESBIAN BARS AND CLUBS

The gay community in New Orleans is large and visible. During Mardi Gras (see p40) and Southern Decadence ("the gay Mardi Gras") (see p41), the streets of the Lower French Quarter are full of wild humor and outrageous cos-tumes. The two most

popular dance clubs are the **Bourbon Pub & Parade Disco** and **Oz**, both on Bourbon Street. Nearby is **Café Lafitte in Exile**, the town's oldest gay bar, with a balcony for watching the street scene. **Good Friends** is a relaxed spot where conver-sation is easy.

The **Golden Lantern** is a historic landmark, the place where Southern Decadence first began more than 30 years ago, while **Cowpokes** is a country-and-western bar and dance club, with the unusual addition of a theater. Called The Marigny Theater, it presents works in progress and gay-themed plays in a friendly environment.

Flamboyant parade costume

THEATER, DANCE, AND CLASSICAL MUSIC

Jazz and contemporary music may dominate the arts scene in New Orleans, but there are also many gems to be found among the classical performing arts. The city has a long and affectionate history with opera. The **New Orleans Opera Association** is a small but valiant outfit bringing in recognized stars to headline its four annual productions. The company, which has staged such beloved classics as La Traviata, Faust, and Carmen, usually performs at the **Mahalia Jackson Theater of the Performing Arts** (see p80).

The brightly lit and slowly revolving Carousel Bar in the Hotel Monteleone

The **Mahalia Jackson Theater of the Performing Arts** underwent a massive renovation to reverse the damage done by the levee breaks of 2005. As a result, the building has recaptured all of the glimmer and glamor of its youth. Four more of the city's premier downtown venues were damaged by the disaster: the Municipal Auditorium, the Saenger Theatre, the State Palace Theatre, and the Orpheum (the longtime home of the local orchestra). Along with the old Joy moviehouse on Canal Street, these venues

The musicians of the Louisiana Philharmonic Orchestra

are in various stages of planning for redevelopment as part of a grand vision for a new theater district.

The **Louisiana Philharmonic Orchestra** (LPO) also has a strong traditional slant and produces highly acclaimed performances. The orchestra currently performs in the Mahalia Jackson Theater and other venues around town. The symphony also holds several outdoor concerts each year, in either Audubon or City Park.

Theater in New Orleans has become exciting with the rise of new playwrights, adventurous productions, and an experimental stage. Leading the way is **Le Chat Noir**, a cabaret that encourages young writers and often features Broadway performers in intimate shows. The **Southern Repertory Theater** is the city's leading theater company. It presents strong new works from around the country, while actively seeking out Louisiana playwrights.

There are also several nomad theater groups that perform in bars, coffeehouses, and other unconventional spaces, producing original works with New Orleans themes and reinterpreting the classics – *La Bohème* in drag, for instance.

The **New Orleans Contemporary Arts Center** *(see p97)* doesn't have a resident company but hosts numerous productions every year, many of them multimedia, avant-garde works. **Le Petit Théâtre du Vieux Carré** *(see p55)* is the city's oldest theater troupe, dating from 1916. The company leans toward musicals and comedies, usually with elaborate sets and costumes. Professional dance companies visit New Orleans several times a year under the aegis of the **New Orleans Ballet Association**. There hasn't been a New Orleans Ballet since 1991, but the organization presents important companies such as the Alvin Ailey American Dance Theater, the Miami Ballet, and the Joffrey Ballet. Several times a year, dance performances are also held at Newcomb College of Tulane University *(see pp110–11)*, a former women's college with a long history of dance innovation and study.

CASINOS

Legal gambling came to New Orleans in the 1990s, but the law allows only one full-fledged casino to exist at any one site. **Harrah's Casino** *(see p89)* is a full-service casino that is dazzling inside, with interiors that suggest a frozen Mardi Gras theme. Slot machines predominate, but there are also tables for blackjack, craps, baccarat, and poker. Harrah's has slowly ventured into live entertainment as well, with comedy and a Las Vegas-type revue. The area has two riverboat casinos – **Treasure Chest** in Kenner and **Boomtown Casino** on the West Bank.

SPORTS AND MAJOR ARENAS

New Orleans loves its sports. The vast **Louisiana Superdome** *(see p95)* is a national venue for sports, home of the annual Sugar Bowl *(see p43)*, and host to high-profile events such as the Super Bowl. The hometown teams are the **New Orleans Saints** for football and the **New Orleans Hornets** for basketball. After Katrina, the venue was closed but reopened in September 2006 after a multimillion-dollar restoration.

For baseball, the city has the Triple-A minor-league Zephyrs, a farm team of the New York Mets. They play at **Zephyr Stadium**, in suburban Jefferson Parish, a state-of-the-art facility that even has a hot tub for use if you rent the private picnic area. College baseball is a big draw, especially the Tulane, University of New Orleans, and Louisiana State University teams.

Horseracing has a long history here. The **Fair Grounds** race course *(see p126)* is one

The Superdome, one of the country's premier sports venues

of the oldest continuously operated tracks in the country. The season runs from November to March.

A major golf tournament is held at the **TPC Golf Course** on the West Bank, usually in the last week of April. The name of the event changes every few years depending on the corporate sponsorship.

TOURS

Tours, especially walking tours, are a great way to experience New Orleans. They are also the best option if you intend to visit the local cemeteries, some of which are not safe for lone visitors. The **Historic New Orleans Walking Tours** offers the best regularly scheduled tours of the French Quarter (with a cemetery component) and of the

Garden District. In the French Quarter, the volunteer **Friends of the Cabildo** also runs a good tour; the **Jean Lafitte National Historical Park** gives an excellent free daily tour of the Quarter, but there are limited spaces. Contact the **Visitors' Bureau (NOMCVB)** for information on sign-up times.

Specialty tours can be good fun. For cemetery-only tours, contact the non-profit **Save Our Cemeteries** group. The **New Orleans Jazz National Historical Park** hosts free walking tours that trace the growth of jazz. These don't have regular schedules, so check with the NOMCVB. The **New Orleans Original Cocktail Tour** explains that the cocktail was invented in New Orleans and delves into the history of French Quarter bars. The **Culinary History Tour** visits restaurants and

provides information about New Orleans food and culture.

The adventurous might enjoy a trip aboard an all-terrain airboat or a swamp tour. The **Airboat Swamp Tours** are fast and exciting; for a slower and more ecological look at swamps, try the **Pearl River Eco-Tours** or **Dr. Wagner's Honey Island Swamp Tours**. **Cajun Pride Tours** also visits swamps and plantations.

Some outfits offer combination tours with a hotel pick-up and drop-off. Be aware that bus tours around the city have limited access to the French Quarter, which bans large buses from its fragile interior streets. **Tours by Isabelle** does both city and plantation tours in small buses and vans. **New Orleans Tours Inc.** offers a wide range of tours around the city, as well as to plantations and swamps.

DIRECTORY

ENTERTAINMENT GUIDES

Ambush
www.ambushmag.com

Gambit
www.bestofneworleans.com

Offbeat
www.offbeat.com

Times-Picayune
www.nola.com

WWNO
www.wwno.org

WWOZ
www.wwoz.org

ROCK, BLUES, AND OTHER MUSIC VENUES

& Club
1100 Tulane Ave.
Map 4 B3. **Tel** 587-3737.
www.clubampersand.com

Blue Nile
532 Frenchmen St.
Map 5 E1. **Tel** 948-2583.
www.bluenilelive.com

Bombay Club
830 Conti St. **Map** 4 C2.
Tel 586-0972.
www.thebombayclub.com

Chickie Wah Wah
2828 Canal St.
Map 2 B4. **Tel** 304-4714.

Chris Owens Club
500 Bourbon St.
Map 4 C2. **Tel** 523-6400.

Circle Bar
1032 St. Charles Ave.
Map 8 B2. **Tel** 588-2616.
www.circlebarnola.com

d.b.a.
618 Frenchmen St.
Map 5 E1. **Tel** 942-3731.
www.drinkgoodstuff.com

Donna's Bar & Grill
800 N Rampart St.
Map 4 C1.
Tel 596-6914. www.donnasbarandgrill.com

Dragon's Den
435 Esplanade Ave.
Map 5 E1. **Tel** 949-1750.

The Famous Door
339 Bourbon St.
Map 4 C2. **Tel** 522-7626.

Fritzel's
733 Bourbon St.
Map 4 C2. **Tel** 561-0432.

House of Blues
225 Decatur St.
Map 4 C3. **Tel** 529-2583.
www.hob.com

Howlin' Wolf
907 S Peters St.
Map 4 C5. **Tel** 522-9653.
www.howlin-wolf.com

Le Bon Temps Roule
4801 Magazine St.
Map 7 D4. **Tel** 897-3448.

Louisiana Music Factory
210 Decatur St.
Map 4 C3. **Tel** 586-1094.
www.louisianamusicfactory.com

Melange
Ritz Carlton, 921 Canal St.
Map 4 B3. **Tel** 524-1331.
www.ritzcarlton.com

One-Eyed Jack's
615 Toulouse St.
Map 4 C2. **Tel** 569-8361.
www.oneeyedjacks.net

Republic
828 S Peters St.
Map 4 C5. **Tel** 528-8282.
www.republicnola.com

Snug Harbor Jazz Bistro
626 Frenchmen St.
Map 5 E1. **Tel** 949-0696.
www.snugjazz.com

Tipitina's
501 Napoleon Ave.
Map 7 D4. **Tel** 895-8477.
www.tipitinas.com

BARS

Bacchanal Fine Wines
600 Poland Ave.
Tel 948-9111.
www.bacchanalwine.com

The Bulldog
3236 Magazine St.
Map 7 F4. **Tel** 891-1516.
www.draftfreak.com

Carousel Bar
Hotel Monteleone,
214 Royal St. **Map** 4 C3.
Tel 523-3341. www.hotelmonteleone.com

Cooter Brown's Tavern
509 S Carrollton Ave.
Map 6 A2. **Tel** 866-9104.
www.cooterbrowns.com

F & M Patio Bar
4841 Tchoupitoulas St.
Map 7 D5. **Tel** 895-6784.

Kerry Irish Pub
331 Decatur St.
Map 4 C3. **Tel** 527-5954.

DIRECTORY

Lafitte's Blacksmith Shop
941 Bourbon St.
Map 4 D1. **Tel** 593-9761.

Loa at International House
221 Camp St. **Map** 4 C3.
Tel 553-9550.
www.ihhotel.com/loa

Loft 523
523 Gravier St. **Map** 4 C3.
Tel 200-6523.
www.loft523.com

Molly's at the Market
1107 Decatur St. **Map** 5 D2. **Tel** 525-5169. www.mollysatthemarket.net

Napoleon House
500 Chartres St.
Map 4 C2. **Tel** 524-9752.
www.napoleonhouse.com

Parasol's Bar
2533 Constance St.
Map 8 A4. **Tel** 897-5413.
www.parasols.com

Pat O'Brien's
718 St. Peter St.
Map 4 C2. **Tel** 525-4823.
www.patobriens.com

Polo Lounge
Windsor Court Hotel, 300 Gravier St. **Map** 4 C4.
Tel 523-6000. www.windsorcourthotel.com

Swizzle Stick Bar
Loews Hotel, 300 Poydras St. **Map** 4 C4.
Tel 595-3305.
www.cafeadelaide.com

Vaughan's Lounge
800 Lesseps St.
Tel 947-5562.

Whiskey Blue
W Hotel, 333 Poydras St.
Map 4 C4. **Tel** 525-9444.
www.mocbars.com

GAY AND LESBIAN BARS AND CLUBS

Bourbon Pub & Parade Disco
801 Bourbon St.
Map 4 C2. **Tel** 529-2107.
www.bourbonpub.com

Café Lafitte in Exile
901 Bourbon St.
Map 4 C1. **Tel** 522-8397.
www.lafittes.com

Cowpokes
2240 St. Claude Ave.
Tel 947-0505.
www.cowpokesno.biz

Golden Lantern
1239 Royal St. **Map** 5 D1.
Tel 529-2860.

Good Friends
740 Dauphine St.
Map 4 C2. **Tel** 566-7191.
www.goodfriendsbar.com

Oz
800 Bourbon St.
Map 4 C2. **Tel** 593-9491.
www.ozneworleans.com

THEATER, DANCE, AND CLASSICAL MUSIC

Dixon Hall
Tulane University,
6823 St. Charles Ave.
Map 8 B1.

Le Chat Noir
715 St. Charles Ave.
Map 8 B1.
Tel 581-5812. www.cabaretlechatnoir.com

Louisiana Philharmonic Orchestra
Tel 523-6530.
www.lpomusic.org

New Orleans Ballet Association
Tel 522-0996.
www.nobadance.com

New Orleans Opera Association
Tel 529-2278. www.neworleansopera.org

Southern Repertory Theater
Canal Place Mall, 3rd floor.
Map 4 C3. **Tel** 522-6545.
www.southernrep.com

CASINOS

Boomtown Casino
4132 Peters Road, Harvey.
Tel 366-7711.
www.boomtownneworleans.com

Harrah's Casino
8 Canal St. **Map** 4 C4.
Tel 533-6000. www.harrahsneworleans.com

Treasure Chest
5050 Williams Blvd,
Kenner. **Tel** 443-8000.
www.treasurechestcasino.com

SPORTS AND MAJOR ARENAS

New Orleans Hornets
Tel 525-4667.
www.hornets.com

New Orleans Saints
Tel 731-1700. www.neworleanssaints.com

TPC Golf Course
Zurich Classic Golf Tournament, 11001 Lapalco Blvd, Avondale.
Tel 436-8721.
www.tpc.com
www.pga.com

Zephyr Stadium
6000 Airline Hwy.
Tel 734-5155. www.zephyrsbaseball.com

TOURS

Airboat Swamp Tours
4262 Hwy 90.
Tel (985) 758-5531.
www.airboattours.com

Cajun Pride Tours
Tel 467-0758. www.cajunprideswamptours.com

Culinary History Tour
Tel 427-9595. www.noculinarytours.com

Dr. Wagner's Honey Island Swamp Tours
Tel 242-5877. www.honeyislandswamp.com

Friends of the Cabildo
523 St. Ann St.
Map 5 D2.
Tel 523-3939. www.friendsofthecabildo.org

Historic New Orleans Walking Tours
Tel 947-2120. www.tourneworleans.com

Jean Lafitte National Historical Park
419 Decatur St.
Map 4 C3.
Tel 589-2636.
www.nps.gov/jela

New Orleans Jazz National Historical Park
916 N Peters St.
Map 5 D2. **Tel** 589-4841.
www.nps.gov/jazz

New Orleans Original Cocktail Tour
Tel 569-1401. www.graylineneworleans.com

New Orleans Tours Inc.
Tel 592-1991.
www.notours.com

NOMCVB (New Orleans Metropolitan Convention and Visitors' Bureau)
2020 St. Charles Ave.
Tel (504) 566-5011.
www.neworleanscvb.com

Pearl River Eco-Tours
55050 US 90, Slidell.
Tel (866) 597-9267.
www.laecotour.com

Save Our Cemeteries
Tel 525-3377. www.saveourcemeteries.org

Tours by Isabelle
Tel 391-3544.
www.toursbyisabelle.com

New Orleans' Best: Music Venues

In New Orleans, where every night is Saturday
night and every Saturday night is New Year's Eve,
there's always live music playing. Look beyond
Bourbon Street and the French Quarter for the
real scene. You'll find world-class jazz, rock 'n'
roll, blues, Latin, funk, Cajun, zydeco, and that
New Orleans hybrid, brass-band funk, every night
(and some days) of the week. These clubs are
the cream of the city's club culture.

Chickie Wah Wah
*Popular in part because
it's one of the few non-
smoking venues in town,
this bar features rocka-
billy and Cajun bands,
among others.*

Maison Bourbon Jazz Club
*A favorite with visitors to the city, this
club is one of the few places on Bourbon
Street where you can hear a live Dixieland band. Good cocktails and a refined
atmosphere complete the picture.*

MID-CITY   TREMI

| 0 meters | 500 |
| 0 yards | 500 |

WAREHOUSE AND
CENTRAL BUSINESS
DISTRICTS

Maple Leaf Bar
*The quintessential off-the-
beaten-path club, hidden
in the Carrollton district.
The music starts late and
goes on for hours, with an
energized crowd that loves
to dance. The Maple Leaf Bar
is also famed for Sunday
afternoon poetry readings.*

GARDEN
DISTRICT AND
UPTOWN

Donna's Bar & Grill
*The queen of clubs
for New Orleans brass
bands. Performers blend
tubas, trumpets, trom-
bones, and drums with
rock, blues, and gospel.*

Palm Court Jazz Café
The place for a classic jazz evening led by great bands; the hostess-owner loves to lead a second line.

Snug Harbor Bistro
Not just New Orleans' premier jazz club but one of the best in the US, hosting little-known local virtuosos and big names on tour.

MARIGNY

LOWER
FRENCH
QUARTER

UPPER
FRENCH
QUARTER

Fritzel's European Jazz Pub
Fritzel's blends reverence for traditional jazz with a lively atmosphere. A favorite drop-in for visiting musicians.

Preservation Hall
The place that kept traditional jazz alive and vital. The atmosphere is musty, dusty, and old school, but the music is worth it. No food or drinks are allowed or served.

House of Blues
Technically part of a chain, but HOB is a dream rock club with several stages, bars, and hangout spots. Big names play here.

Children's Entertainment and Outdoor Activities

New Orleans is renowned as an adult playground, but there are many places in the area designed especially for the younger generation. There is an enormous variety of attractions and entertainment, from the thrill rides in City Park to a ride across the mighty Mississippi on the Canal Street ferry. The city also offers numerous outdoor activities for all ages, from deep-sea fishing, tennis, and golf, to swamp tours, birdwatching, biking, watersports, and horseback riding.

Storyland at City Park

Roller coaster ride at Storyland in City Park

Supermarket for children at the Louisiana Children's Museum

MUSEUMS FOR CHILDREN

Many museums in and around New Orleans have arts and educational programs designed specifically for young audiences. **The New Orleans Museum of Art** (NOMA) *(see p120–23)* has a museum-on-wheels program for kids, and also offers guided tours focused on children's interests. The **Louisiana Children's Museum** *(see p97)* caters to kids and parents, and is specifically designed to inspire questions through hands-on exhibits, including role-playing games.

Three museums in Kenner are the **Toy Train Museum**, the **Mardi Gras Museum**, and the adjacent **Kenner Planetarium** and they are well worth the short trip outside the city. Kenner is located to the west of the city, between New Orleans and Baton Rouge on the I-10.

ZOOS, AQUARIUMS, AND AMUSEMENT PARKS

Two major attractions for children and grown-ups alike are the **Audubon Zoo** *(see p112–13)* and the **Audubon Aquarium of the Americas** *(see p90–91)*. The zoo is home to more than 1,500 animals, many of which roam about in natural habitats. The Louisiana Swamp exhibit, the Jaguar Jungle, and the touchy-feely Embraceable Zoo are all geared toward education and understanding animals. The spectacular Audubon Aquarium of the Americas houses thousands of fish, marine mammals, and water birds. An IMAX Theater shows documentaries on ocean life, and a "Touch Pool" gives kids the opportunity to touch, feel, and see such underwater denizens as sea stars and baby sharks.

Storyland *(see p118)* in City Park has 26 "storybook" exhibits by the master Mardi Gras float creator Blaine Kern *(see p88)*. A working antique carousel with 54 beautifully carved animals, bumper cars, a miniature train, and the ubiquitous Tilt-a-Whirl complete the carnival atmosphere.

FISHING

New Orleans is a famous port. Farther south toward the Gulf, shrimp boats and the larger deep-sea boats offer a glimpse of the industries that keep Louisiana rich. Anglers can fish in Lake Pontchartrain or in City Park's lagoons, or charter a boat and try your luck at the big fish: tarpon, snapper, and marlin. **Angelle's Atchafalaya Basin Swamp Tours, Capt. Nick's Wildlife Safaris**, and **Capt. Phil Robichaux's Saltwater Guide Service** all offer fishing tours and/or charters into the swamp, coastal waterways, and marshes. Hotel shuttles, licenses, camera and film, and all equipment are provided by these companies.

Visitors at the Audubon Zoo

RIVER CRUISES

A peaceful boat ride is an alternative to the party atmosphere and noise of the city. Paddlewheelers offer short excursions up and down the Mississippi River from the French Quarter wharves. Swamp tours by flat-boat or seaplane also abound, charter boats and houseboats are readily available, and you can splash out and book a week-long cruise on the famous Delta Queen, which runs from Pittsburgh all the way to New Orleans and is operated by the **Majestic America Line**.

Lake Pontchartrain fishing area

GOLF AND TENNIS

City Park's **Bayou Oaks** is the South's largest public golf course, offering four 18-hole courses. The golf courses sustained heavy damage from flooding after Hurricane Katrina and are being rebuilt and reopened in stages, one course at a time. The driving range reopened in 2007, and the North course in June 2008. The East and West courses should be completed by 2011. The 18-hole course in **Audubon Park** *(see p111)* has undergone a $6-million redesign. It is a flat, fast course and the surroundings are beautiful. A bonus is the park's Golf Club, which serves as a bar and restaurant. The wraparound porch is the perfect place to enjoy lunch before or after your game.

There are many country golf clubs that allow guests, and some of the best and most accessible of these are **Belle Terre**, **Lakewood**, **Oak Harbor**, and the **Chateau Country Golf Club**. Golf is a year-round sport, but winter is the busiest season. If you play in summer, start early to avoid the heat and the late afternoon thunderstorms. Greens fees vary from under $20 to over $75 per person, and are highest in winter.

The **City Park Tennis Center** *(see p119)* has 21 hard courts and 13 clay courts. All are well-lit at night.

FITNESS CENTERS

Many hotels have on-site fitness centers where you can use the weights room, swim laps, relax in the sauna, or burn those extra calories on the treadmill. The **Downtown Fitness Center** welcomes guests.

DIRECTORY

MUSEUMS FOR CHILDREN

Kenner Planetarium
2020 4th St,
Rivertown, Kenner.
Tel 468-7231.
www.rivertown
kenner.com

Mardi Gras Museum
415 Williams Blvd,
Rivertown, Kenner.
Tel 468-7231.
www.rivertown
kenner.com

Toy Train Museum
519 Williams Blvd,
Rivertown, Kenner.
Tel 468-7231.
www.rivertown
kenner.com

FISHING/SWAMP TOURS

Angelle's Atchafalaya Basin Swamp Tours
Tel (337) 228-8567.

Capt. Nick's Wildlife Safaris
Tel 361-3004.

Capt. Phil Robichaux's Saltwater Guide Service
1842 Jean Lafitte Blvd,
Jean Lafitte.
Tel 689-2006.

RIVER CRUISES

Majestic America Line/Delta Queen
Robin St Wharf,
1380 Port of New Orleans
Place. **Map** 8 C3.
Tel (800) 434-1332.
www.majestic
americaline.com

GOLF AND TENNIS

Bayou Oaks
City Park, Filmore Ave.
Map 2 A1.
Tel 483-9397.
www.neworleans
citypark.com

Belle Terre
111 Fairway Dr, LaPlace.
Tel (985) 652-5000.

Chateau Country Club Golf
3600 Chateau Blvd,
Metaire. *Tel 467-1351.*
www.chateaugc.com

Lakewood
4801 Gen. DeGaulle Dr.
Tel 235-5638.

Oak Harbor
201 Oak Harbor Blvd,
Slidell. *Tel (985) 646-0110.* **www**.oak
harborgolf.com

FITNESS CENTERS

Downtown Fitness Center
333 Canal St, Suite 380.
Map 4 C3. *Tel 525-1404.*
www.downtown
fitnesscenter.com

SURVIVAL
GUIDE

PRACTICAL INFORMATION

New Orleans is known throughout the world for its lively social life and friendly atmosphere. As long as visitors take sensible precautions, they should enjoy a trouble-free stay. The Survival Guide that follows contains information that will help

NOMCVB
logo

you plan your visit. Personal Security and Health *(pp208–9)* outlines a number of recommended precautions. Banking and Currency *(pp210–11)* answers essential financial questions, while Communications *(pp212–13)* has information on the phone and postal services.

Visitor Information Center, Greenwood

FOREIGN VISITORS

Due to changing US immigration laws, visitors who are traveling from outside the US should check current entry requirements with a US embassy or consulate before leaving. All visitors must have a valid passport, and visitors from most countries must have a non-immigrant visitor's visa. Citizens of Australia, New Zealand, South Africa, the UK, and many other European countries can visit the US without a visa if they plan to stay for fewer than 90 days. All travelers under the Visa Waiver Program must pre-register with the Department of Homeland Security's Electronic System for Travel Authorization (ESTA) at https://esta.cbp.dhs.gov well in advance of their departure.

CUSTOMS ALLOWANCES

Visitors from abroad, older than 21, have the right to carry up to 100 US$ worth of cigarettes, a bottle of alcohol, and 3 lb (1.4 kg) of any kind of pipe tobacco. Fresh foods such

as cheese, plants, and all kinds of meat are prohibited, as, of course, are weapons and non-prescription drugs.

TOURIST INFORMATION

The **New Orleans Metropolitan Convention and Visitors' Bureau** (NOMCVB) is an invaluable source of information for tourists. Maps, tourist guides, and discount coupons for certain stores, restaurants, bars, and hotels are provided free of charge. It also gives help in cases of loss, theft, or accidents, offering all the pertinent information such as telephone numbers and time schedules.

OPENING HOURS

Schedules at major attractions vary, but most museums open from 10am to 5pm. Most restaurants start evening service at 5pm and continue until 10pm (11pm Friday and Saturday), or until the last guest leaves. Banks are open from 9am to 4pm. Souvenir stores in the

French Quarter are open till late, but most other places operate from 10am to 6pm. Some bars in New Orleans stay busy all day and all night, every day of the year. Live music usually starts at 10pm, and it is a tradition not to close the place until the last guest leaves.

ADMISSION CHARGES

Admission charges to museums range between $5 and $10, with up to 50 percent discounts to students (with ID cards) and senior citizens. Children under 12 do not pay in some museums. Many museums do not charge entrance fees but welcome a donation, while in others it is possible to buy membership on the spot. Most museums also have guided tours, souvenir stores, publications, independent exhibitions, and other events.

ETIQUETTE

Smoking is prohibited in many public buildings, including stores and restaurants. Check for no-smoking signs before lighting up, or smoke outside

No-smoking area in Tujagues restaurant, French Quarter

if you are unsure. The legal age for drinking alcohol is 21; however, people up to the age of 30 may be asked to show photo identification to get into bars and to buy alcohol.

Tipping is expected for most services; tip 15–20 percent of the bill in restaurants, give $1 per bag to porters, and $1 to valet parking attendants. Bartenders expect 50 cents to $1 per drink. It is permissible to consume alcoholic drinks on the street in New Orleans, but they must be in plastic containers called "go cups."

ALCOHOL AND DRIVING

Disabled parking sign

In the United States, penalties for driving under the influence of alcohol are severe. You can lose your driver's license or even spend a night in jail. If you intend to drink, ask someone else to drive your car, or take a taxi home (*see pp218–19*).

DISABLED TRAVELERS

Facilities for the physically impaired can be found all around the city; these include special parking spaces, and access and interior facilities, such as elevators or moving ramps in museums. Many historic buildings, though, do not have these facilities, nor do most restaurants and bars. Disabled visitors should enquire about mobility restrictions in advance. At the airport, facilities for the disabled are strategically placed. The Riverfront streetcar route and some buses have special ramps for wheelchairs. A number of cinemas and theaters have access ramps and may also have specially equipped bathrooms. When making a hotel reservation, be sure to ask for these services and check the width of the entrance and the rooms' doors.

ELECTRICAL APPLIANCES

Electrical current flows at 110 volts AC (alternating current), and appliances require two-prong plugs. Some non-US appliances will require both a plug converter and a 110–120-volt adaptor, compatible with the US electricity system. Most hotels have hairdryers and sockets for electrical shavers.

CONVERSION CHART

US Standard to Metric
Bear in mind that 1 US pint (0.5 liter) is a smaller measure than 1 UK pint (0.6 liter).
1 inch = 2.54 centimeters
1 foot = 30 centimeters
1 mile = 1.6 kilometers
1 ounce = 28 grams
1 pound = 454 grams
1 US quart = 0.947 liter
1 US gallon = 3.8 liters

Metric to US Standard
1 centimeter = 0.4 inch
1 meter = 3 feet 3 inches
1 kilometer = 0.6 miles
1 gram = 0.04 ounce
1 kilogram = 2.2 pounds
1 liter = 1.1 US quarts

SENIOR CITIZENS

Anyone over the age of 65 is eligible for various discounts with proof of age, including up to 50 percent off the entry fee for museums and galleries. Contact the **American Association of Retired Persons** for details. Also, try the international senior travel organization **Elderhostel**. For car rental, you may need to show your passport, and you must have a valid driver's license.

TAX FREE SHOPPING

Tax free logo

Louisiana tax-free shopping is designed to promote international tourism in Louisiana by giving a refund on sales taxes at participating merchants. It applies to those who can show a foreign passport, an international travel ticket, and who will be in the country for less than 90 days. All shops in the airport have tax-free shopping, as do several businesses throughout the city. Refunds and information can be obtained at the **Tax Free Counter**, located in the main lobby of the main terminal of the International Airport.

DIRECTORY

TOURIST INFORMATION

New Orleans Metropolitan Convention and Visitors' Bureau
2020 St. Charles Ave, LA 70130.
Tel (800) 672-6124.
www.neworleanscvb.com

New Orleans Tourism Marketing Corporation
365 Canal St, LA 70130.
Tel (504) 524-4784.
www.neworleansonline.com

STUDENT INFORMATION

STA Travel
Butler Hall
Tulane University, NO 70118.
Tel (504) 866-3850.
www.statravel.com

Travel Cuts
Tel (800) 592-2887.
www.travelcuts.com

DISABLED VISITORS' INFORMATION

Advocacy Center for the Elderly and Disabled
1010 Common St, Suite 2600,
NO 70112. *Tel (800) 960-7705.*
www.advocacyla.org

SENIOR CITIZENS

American Association of Retired Persons
601 E St NW, Washington DC,
20049. *Tel (800) 687-2277.*
www.aarp.org

Elderhostel
11 Ave de Lafayette,
Boston, MA 02111-1746.
Tel (877) 454-5768.
www.elderhostel.org

TAX FREE SHOPPING

Louisiana Tax Free Counter at the International Airport
New Orleans International Airport.
Tel (504) 467-0723.
www.louisianataxfree.com

Personal Security and Health

New Orleans is a very friendly city, and you can expect people to help you if anything goes wrong. However, as in any large city, you must take some basic precautions for safety. It is important to know how to identify and locate law enforcement officers, and also to identify the less safe areas of the city. Always check with friends and hotel staff before going out in the evening. It is also important to know how to find medical help if necessary. Although weather is generally good, New Orleans experiences some extreme weather, with high humidity in the summer and occasional damaging hurricanes.

LAW ENFORCEMENT

The New Orleans Police Department has patrols on foot, on motorcycles, on horseback and in patrol cars. All patrol the city streets, especially in the most popular areas, such as the French Quarter, the Garden District, and the Central Business District. Because New Orleans has a lively nightlife, there is a strong police presence 24 hours a day.

GUIDELINES ON SAFETY

New Orleans has made great strides in reducing crime rates, but visitors still need to be alert. Stay in a large group, if possible, when sightseeing out of doors and do not challenge a thief – no camera or amount of money is worth the risk. Police officers regularly patrol the tourist areas, but it is still wise to use common sense. Do not advertise the fact that you are a visitor: prepare the

day's itinerary in advance, and study your map before you set off. Avoid wearing expensive jewelry, and carry your camera or camcorder securely. Only carry small amounts of cash; credit cards and traveler's checks are a more secure option. Keep these close to your body in a money belt or inside pocket.

Before you leave home, take a photocopy of important documents, including your passport and visa, and keep it with you, separate from the originals. Make a note of your credit card numbers, in the event of their being stolen. Keep an eye on your belongings at all times, whether checking into or out of a hotel, standing at the airport, or sitting in a restaurant. Keep any valuables in your hotel safe, as most hotels will not guarantee their security if they are left in your room. Also be careful not to tell strangers where you are staying or to let anyone you do not know into your room.

When parking your car, avoid dark or quiet streets, and whenever

possible use well-lit public parking lots or the valet parking services of hotels and restaurants.

STAYING SAFE IN NEW ORLEANS

Since the return of the population following Hurricane Katrina, crime in New Orleans has made international headlines. However, it is important to realize that most crime is largely contained within areas historically known for territorial clashes between youths. It is unlikely that a visitor to the city

Policeman   Fireman

would wander into one of these neighborhoods since they are largely devoid of architectural or historic charm, and lack cultural attractions.

The streets of New Orleans are safe just as long as you keep certain safety measures in mind. The police run constant watches around the French Quarter. The Quarter's nightlife is characterized by high levels of alcohol consumption, and you can avoid trouble by steering clear of drunken revelers. Always use a taxi in the "back of the Quarter" area, from Rampart Street to Interstate 10. Do not travel by foot alone outside of the French Quarter at night. In general, if you feel insecure, find a taxi.

Police vehicle

Fire engine

Walgreens, one of the city's 24-hour pharmacies

LOST PROPERTY

Even though you have only a slim chance of retrieving stolen or lost property, it is important to report the loss to the police. Keep a copy of the police report if you are planning to make an insurance claim. Most credit card companies have toll-free numbers for reporting a loss, as do Thomas Cook and American Express for lost traveler's checks (see p211). If you lose your passport, contact your embassy or consulate immediately.

Airport Operations retains items that have been lost in public areas of the terminal. The office is located on the upper level of the West Lobby, and it is open 24 hours a day. You can also contact them at (504) 464-2671 or (504) 464-2672. Items that have been turned in to Lost and Found are donated to charity after 30 days. If you lose items in the airline's exclusive areas (ticket counters, gate areas, or airplanes), check with that particular airline's baggage office located on the lower level.

TRAVEL INSURANCE

Travel insurance is highly recommended. It can help in case of loss or theft of personal goods, or if travel arrangements fall through.

Visitors from abroad should obtain insurance for emergency medical or dental care, which can be expensive in the United States.

MEDICAL TREATMENT

Even if you have medical coverage you may still have to pay for any services you use, and then claim reimbursement from your insurance company. If you take medication, it is important to bring a back-up prescription with you. Pharmacies close to the French Quarter are open from 9am to 7pm every day. For longer hours there are several 24-hour pharmacies or ask your hotel for assistance. For dental emergencies, call either the New Orleans **Dental Association** or the **Medical Center of Louisiana**, which are both open 24 hours a day.

NATURAL HAZARDS

Hospital sign

Hurricanes are infrequent but devastating when they do strike. There are tried and tested emergency procedures, and if the worst should happen, follow the announcements on local television and radio. You may also check the National Hurricane Center's forecasts online at www.nhc.noaa.gov. In case of emergency, a hotline in Louisiana may also be established before a storm strikes. However, the most frequent climatic hazard to affect visitors is the sun. Use high-factor sunscreen lotions and try to wear a hat. Remember that heat can be as big a problem as sunlight; drink plenty of fluids.

There are several venomous snakes native to Louisiana, but unless you are alone in dense swamp or forest you are unlikely to encounter any. Biting and stinging insects, including mosquitoes, are a real nuisance between April and November, particularly in areas close to fresh water and swampland. Visits to parks and reserves can be uncomfortable if you do not wear a good insect repellent.

EMERGENCIES

To contact the emergency services, dial 911, free of charge, on any phone. The police patrol popular areas of town, and they have experience covering large events such as Mardi Gras (see pp28–9). If you are arrested for any reason, you have the right to remain silent and are permitted to make one phone call.

Non-US citizens should contact their embassy or consulate for legal assistance.

DIRECTORY

SECURITY AND HEALTH

Medical Center of Louisiana
Tel (800) 256-2311.

Emergencies
Tel 911.

Police (Non-Emergency)
Tel (504) 821-2222.

Fire (Non-Emergency)
Tel (504) 658-4700.

Dental Association
Tel (504) 834-6449.

PHARMACIES

RiteAid Pharmacy
3401 St. Charles Ave.
Map 7 F4.
Tel (504) 896-4575.
www.riteaid.com

Walgreens Drugstore
619 Decatur St. **Map** 4 C3.
Tel (504) 525-7263.
900 Canal St.
Map 4 B3.
Tel (504) 568-1271.
www.walgreens.com

Banking and Currency

Throughout New Orleans there are various places to access and exchange your money. Bank branches are open during the week, and there are numerous ATMs. Foreign currency can be exchanged in comparatively few places, and exchange rates tend to be poorer than at home. The best rule is to take plenty of US dollar traveler's checks, and a credit card or two.

Automated teller machine at a local branch bank

BANKING

Banks are generally open Monday to Friday from 9am to 4pm. There are some, however, that open as early as 8:30am and stay open until 5pm. Always ask if any special fees apply before you make your transaction. US dollar traveler's checks can be cashed at most banks, so long as you bring some form of identification that carries your photograph (e.g., a passport, a driver's license, or an International Student Identity Card). Foreign currency exchange is available at the main branches of large banks, many of which have separate areas or teller windows specifically for foreign exchange. Credit unions will serve only their members, so look for banks that offer service to the general public, such as Capital One and Whitney. Numerous branches of these can be found in the French Quarter, the Central Business District, and also along St. Charles Avenue.

AUTOMATED TELLER MACHINES (ATMS)

Most banks in New Orleans have automated teller machines in their lobbies or in an external wall.

There are also ATMs in various restaurants and bars around town, mainly in the French Quarter. These machines enable you to withdraw US banknotes, usually $20 bills, from your bank or credit card account at home. Be aware that a fee will be levied on your withdrawal depending on the bank; always check the bank's policy before making a withdrawal.

Before leaving home, ask your credit card company or bank which American ATM systems or banks will accept your bankcard, and check the cost of each transaction. Make sure, too, that you have (and remember) your PIN (Personal Identification Number). The largest ATM systems are Plus and Cirrus, which accept VISA, American Express, and MasterCard, as well as a number of US bank cards.

Automated teller machines give you 24-hour access to cash, but remember to take care when using them in deserted areas, especially after dark; be vigilant of people around you.

CREDIT CARDS

Credit cards are part of everyday life in New Orleans, just as they are in other parts of the country. The most widely accepted credit cards are VISA, MasterCard, American Express, Diners Club, and Discover Card.

Besides being a much safer alternative to carrying a lot of cash, credit cards also offer some useful additional benefits, such as insurance on your purchases. They are

American Express charge cards

also essential if you want to reserve a hotel room or book a rental car. Credit cards can also be useful in emergencies when cash may not be readily available.

CASHING TRAVELER'S CHECKS

Traveler's checks are by far the most convenient way to carry money, both for practicality's sake and for security (lost or stolen checks can be refunded). They may even be used as cash in many places: US dollar traveler's checks are commonly accepted in shops, restaurants, bars, and hotels. Those issued by American Express, VISA, or Thomas Cook are the most recognized. Change will be given in cash; if your checks are in large denominations, always ask if there is enough money in the cash register before you countersign, otherwise you may waste a check needlessly.

To exchange your traveler's checks into cash directly, go to a bank, an exchange bureau, or the front desk of your hotel. Remember to inquire about commission fees before starting your transaction, as these can vary greatly. All banks can exchange dollar traveler's checks, but you will get the best rates in big banks or at private exchange offices. The latter are not common, but American Express and Thomas Cook both have branches in New Orleans, as well as in a number of other cities around the state. Both companies also have toll-free numbers for reporting lost or stolen checks.

Traveler's checks in other currencies cannot be used in shops, and only some banks and hotels will exchange them. Personal checks drawn on overseas banks, such as Eurochecks, cannot be used in New Orleans.

Coins

America's coins (actual size shown) come in 1-dollar, 50-, 25-, 10-, 5-, and 1-cent pieces. The Golden Dollar, released in 2000, features the likeness of Sacagawea, a Shoshone Indian woman who assisted and guided the Lewis and Clark expedition across the northwest US. On the flip side is a Bald Eagle and 17 stars, indicating the 17 American states at the time of the exploration.

25-cent coin (a quarter)

10-cent coin (a dime)   **5-cent coin (a nickel)**   **1-cent coin (a penny)**

Bank Notes

The Golden Dollar has not replaced the dollar bill, which is still the more widely used form of this unit of currency. Paper bills were first issued in 1862 when coins were in short supply, and the Civil War needed financing. The size of the notes, the portraits, and the back designs were decided in 1929; in the 1990s the artwork for most of the bills was re-engraved.

$1 coin

DIRECTORY

Western Union
Wiring money, US.
Tel (800) 325-6000.
Wiring money, UK.
Tel 0800 833833.
www.westernunion.com

American Express
Moneygram US only.
Tel (800) 543-4080.
www.americanexpress.com

Check replacement.
Tel (800) 221-7282.
Stolen credit and charge cards.
Tel (800) 528-4800.

Thomas Cook
(and MasterCard)
Check replacement and stolen credit cards.
Tel (800) 223-9920.
www.thomascook.com

Visa
Check replacement.
Tel (800) 227-6811.
Stolen credit cards.
Tel (800) 336-8472.
www.visa.com

Diners Club
Check replacement/stolen cards.
Tel (800) 234-6377.
www.dinersclub.com

1-dollar bill ($1)

5-dollar bill ($5)

10-dollar bill ($10)

20-dollar bill ($20)

50-dollar bill ($50)

100-dollar bill ($100)

Communications

Because New Orleans is a major US city, the full range of telephone, fax, and Internet services is available. Public telephones can be found on many street corners, in shops, hotels, restaurants, and bars. Stamps are available not only at post offices but also at many drugstores and hotels, and additional postal services are available from private carrier firms.

U.S.MAIL
Postal service
logo

Local newspapers are useful for information on events around town, and national and foreign newspapers are also available.

PUBLIC TELEPHONES

Public telephones can be found all over the city, mainly in gas stations and stores. Most public telephones take coins only, but some also accept credit cards. About $8 worth of quarters is needed to make an international call. However, there is a growing number of card-operated phones, using both credit and electronic cards. Some of these take special pre-paid cards which involve dialing a toll-free number to gain access to your required number. Alternatively, you can use your credit card on some phones: dial (800) CALLATT (225-5288): at the prompt, key in your credit card number, and wait to be connected; you will be charged at normal rates. Telephone directories provide details of the going rates and are found in most public phones.

Public telephone sign

TELEPHONE CHARGES

Toll-free numbers (prefixed by 800, 866, 877, or 888) are common in the United States, and are well worth taking advantage of, though some hotels impose an access charge for these calls. You can also dial these numbers from abroad, but note that they are not toll-free.

When making a local call from a public telephone, 35 cents will buy you three minutes' time. For long-distance domestic calls the cheapest rate runs from 11pm to 8am on weekdays and weekends. Direct calls can also be made from hotel rooms, but they usually carry hefty surcharges. Unless you are using your own international telephone card, it is better to use the payphone in the lobby.

REACHING THE RIGHT NUMBER

- Direct-dial call outside the local area code within the United States and Canada: dial **1**.
- International direct-dial call: dial **011** followed by country code (UK: **44**; Australia: **61**; New Zealand: **64**) then the city or area code (omit the first 0), and the local number.
- International call via operator: dial **01**, then the country code, plus the city code (minus the first 0), and the local number.
- International directory inquiries: dial **00**.
- International operator assistance: dial **01**.
- An **800**, **866**, **877**, **or 888** prefix indicates a toll-free number.
- All directory assistance: dial **411**.
- Useful area codes: Cajun Country, **337**; Baton Rouge, **225**; southeast Louisiana (except New Orleans), **985**.

USING A COIN-OPERATED PHONE

1 Lift the receiver and wait for the dial tone.

3 Enter the number.

Coins
Make sure you have plenty of these coins available.

5 cents

10 cents

25 cents

2 Insert the correct coin or coins.

4 If you decide not to make a connection, or if the call does not get through, you can retrieve your money by pressing the coin return.

5 If the call is answered and you talk for longer than the allowed time, the operator will interrupt and ask you to deposit more coins. If you cannot complete a call, the phone returns your coins.

Directory assistance is free of charge by dialing 411 (local) or 00 (international). Operator assistance is available by dialing 0 (local) or 01 (international). All operator-assisted calls carry a surcharge. For emergency services only (fire, police, or ambulance) call 911.

International rates vary depending on which country you are contacting.

Standard US mailbox

INTERNET AND FAXES

The rise in popularity of personal computers has pushed fax machines off the list of crucial communications equipment. Faxing can usually be done at your hotel, although it is likely you will be charged for it.

For Internet access, try the **French Quarter Postal Emporium** or the **FedEx Kinko's** shops, which also offer fax, printing,

Colorful US postage stamps

and shipping services. Many hotels have business centers where guests can use a computer; if not, they should at least have dataports where you can connect your laptop. More and more places are also offering wireless Internet. Most coffee houses and bars have free Wi-Fi available for their patrons.

POSTAL SERVICES

Post offices are usually open from 9am to 5pm on weekdays, with some branches open on Saturday mornings. Drugstores and hotels sell stamps, and some department stores and transportation terminals have stamp vending machines; stamps bought from vending machines are

often a little more expensive.

Surface mail sent overseas from the US takes several weeks, so it is better to send letters via airmail, which takes five to ten working days.

All domestic mail goes first class and takes from one to five days (longer if you forget to include the zip code). You can pay extra for Priority Mail for a delivery of two to three days, or Express Mail, which offers next-day deliveries in the US, and within two to three days to many foreign countries. Be sure to use the right mailbox for the required service. Mailboxes are painted blue, while Express and Priority boxes are silver and blue.

Many Americans use private courier services, such as **UPS**, **DHL**, and **FedEx**, for both domestic and international mail; they offer next-day deliveries to most destinations.

TELEVISION AND RADIO

Most hotel televisions have cable or satellite hook-up, offering 60 channels plus the national networks (ABC, CBS, NBC, and FOX). The cable channels offer more variety: ESPN is devoted to sports, and CNN to news.

Most radio stations broadcast pop music, but if you hunt around (especially on the FM band) you can often pick up entertaining local stations. WWL (870 AM and 105.3 FM) broadcasts local news; National Public Radio WWNO (89.9 FM) broadcasts national news and classical music. The Jazz & Heritage Foundation station WWOZ (90.7 FM) is a remarkable institution, with R&B, jazz, Latin, Cajun, and zydeco programs 24 hours daily.

NEWSPAPERS

The only daily newspaper in New Orleans is *The Times-Picayune*, found in hotel lobbies and street dispensers throughout the city. *Gambit*,

a free weekly paper distributed in cafés, shops, and hotels, is a good source of more in-depth entertainment and lifestyle news. For comprehensive national and international news, look to the *New York Times or USA Today*, both of which are available from coin-operated boxes all over the CBD and French Quarter. Foreign newspapers are available at good bookstores.

Local and national newspapers

NEW ORLEANS TIME

New Orleans and Louisiana are in the Central Standard Time Zone (CST), which is six hours behind Greenwich Mean Time (GMT). If you are making an international phone call from the city, add six hours for the United Kingdom, 15 hours for Australia, and 17 hours for New Zealand.

DIRECTORY

POSTAL SERVICES

UPS
Tel (800) 742-5877.

FedEx
Tel (800) 463-3339.

DHL
Tel (800) 225-5345.

Main Post Office
701 Loyola Ave.
Tel (800) 275-8777.

INTERNET AND FAXES

FedEx Kinko's
762 and 6823 St. Charles Ave.
Tel (504) 581-2541 and (504) 862-5799.

French Quarter Postal Emporium
1000 Bourbon St.
Tel (504) 525-6651.

TRAVEL INFORMATION

Many international airlines have direct flights to New Orleans, and charter and domestic services are numerous. Growing competition between airlines has reduced prices in low seasons, making flying an even more attractive alternative to traveling by bus or train. Amtrak trains run from major cities in the United States to the center of the city. Long-distance luxury bus services offer a less

Passenger jet arriving in the city

frantic and often less expensive way to travel for those arriving from other North American cities. For visitors arriving by car or bus, there can be little to beat the spectacular views of the city when driving into New Orleans by way of the River Road. If you are planning to stay in the city center, it is not necessary to rent a car; most of the sights are within easy walking distance of one another.

Passenger jet at Armstrong International Airport

ARRIVING BY AIR

All the major US airlines, including **Continental Airlines, American Airlines, Southwest Airlines, United Airlines,** and **Delta Air Lines,** have scheduled services to New Orleans. Most also offer flights from abroad, but these usually entail a stop at a US airport en route. From Canada and Mexico, **Air Canada** and Continental Airlines have scheduled flights to New Orleans, while American Airlines, Continental, Delta, Northwest, and United Airlines operate from the UK.

AIR FARES

The cheapest round-trip fares to New Orleans are generally economy or APEX tickets on scheduled flights (which must be booked in advance). The competition between travel agencies and the numerous airlines serving New Orleans makes it well worth shopping around.

Keep an eye out for promotional fares and package tours, which offer good deals on charter flights.

Off-season fares are cheap, and you will often get a better deal if you fly in the middle of the week. During holiday periods like December, and special events like Mardi Gras *(see pp28–9)*, seats are always in big demand, and air fares can rocket to more than double their usual price.

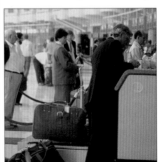
Travelers at a check-in desk, Armstrong International Airport

ARMSTRONG INTERNATIONAL AIRPORT FACILITIES

New Orleans International Airport is the ninth-largest arrival and departure airport in the United States. Visitors will find customs, sightseeing information, baggage claim, car-rental desks, and ground transportation into the city on the lower level of the airport. The top level, on the other hand, contains services for travelers departing from New Orleans, including foreign exchange offices, ticket and insurance counters, restaurants, bars, baggage handlers, and shops. The Louisiana tax-free refund offices can also be found on this level.

There are nine Telephone Display Devices (TDD) located throughout the airport. Whitney National Bank, located in the ticket lobby, is one of the main banking facilities in the airport. ATMs (automated teller machines) are located in several places; in the East Lobby near Concourse B, in the ticket lobby next to the bank, in the West Terminal, on the Lower Level near the Southwest Airlines Baggage Claim, and on the Lower Level near the Charter Baggage Claim.

There is a baggage storage-check service on the ground floor of the aiport, called

VIP Baggage Check. For security reasons, lockers are no longer available for use. There is also a Traveler's Aid booth located in the East Baggage Claim. Traveler's Aid provides assistance to travelers in distress and provides tourist information.

GETTING TO AND FROM THE AIRPORT

Armstrong International Airport is about 12 miles (19 km) from the center of the city, about a 45-minute express bus trip. Bus and taxi stands are located outside the terminal on the first level.

There are two **Airport Shuttle Services** from the airport to the Central Business District, costing $15 per trip. To get back to the airport, call from your hotel at least two hours in advance.

Jefferson Transit runs the only public bus route between downtown and the airport. The E-2 Airport Downtown Express costs $1.10 and takes about 45 minutes. The bus stops on Elks Place and Tulane Avenue. It operates seven days a week, from about 5:30am until midnight.

Taxicabs are usually plentiful, and cost about $28 to the center of the city. In the airport there are several car-rental companies, so shop around for the best rates.

GETTING TO NEW ORLEANS BY TRAIN

Trains and buses arrive and depart from Union Passenger Terminal, located at the edge of the Central Business District, a short taxi

Long-distance Greyhound bus

ride from the center of New Orleans. Three major **Amtrak** trains serve New Orleans: the *Crescent* (from New York City/Atlanta), the *City of New Orleans* (from Chicago), and the *Sunset Limited* (from Los Angeles). Noted for their comfort and luxury, all long-distance trains have a full complement of refreshment facilities and sleeping accommodations.

Passengers should reserve seats in advance on many services during peak periods. Amtrak offers special deals and packages, including 5-, 15- and 30-day passes that allow unlimited travel. These are available for only international travelers.

Visitors traveling to New Orleans by train will arrive at Amtrak's terminal in the Central Business District, near the Superdome. From here there are plenty of taxis that will take you to the main hotel areas.

GETTING TO NEW ORLEANS BY BUS

Long-distance coach services to almost all parts of the United States are operated by **Greyhound Bus Lines**. The buses are modern, clean, and safe. Some services are "express," with few stops between major destinations, while others serve a greater number of cities. If you are planning to break your journey several times along the way, or you want to tour the country on an extended trip, there are various tour packages designed to suit your

requirements. Overseas visitors should also note that passes may be less expensive if you buy them from a Greyhound agent outside the United States.

The Greyhound buses share Union Passenger Terminal (*see p221*) with the Amtrak train operations. This terminal provides full baggage, ticketing, and package express services throughout the day and into the early hours of the morning.

DIRECTORY

AIRLINES

Air Canada
Tel (888) 247-2262.
www.aircanada.com

American Airlines
Tel (800) 433-7300.
www.aa.com

Continental Airlines
Tel (800) 523-3273.
www.continental.com

Delta Air Lines
Tel (800) 221-1212.
www.delta.com

Southwest Airlines
Tel (800) 435-9792.
www.southwest.com

United Airlines
Tel (800) 864-8331.
www.united.com

TRAIN INFORMATION

Amtrak
Tel (800) 872-7245.

BUS INFORMATION

Greyhound Bus Lines
Tel (800) 231-2222.

SHUTTLE BUSES

Airport Shuttle Services
Tel (504) 522-3500.

Jefferson Transit
Tel (504) 818-1077.

Amtrak train

Getting Around New Orleans

Although most of the city's popular tourist sights in and near the French Quarter are easily accessible on foot, New Orleans also has a useful public transportation system. Bus routes cover the city, and no visitor should miss the chance to travel on the oldest streetcar in the nation. VisiTour passes allow unlimited travel on buses and streetcars for one to three days. Riverboats also provide a pleasant way to see the sights along the basin of the Mississippi River. Taxis are affordable and convenient, and are recommended for trips after dark to areas outside the French Quarter.

Bus stop sign

St. Charles Avenue streetcar on Canal Street

RTA bus, showing route number and destination

TRAVELING BY BUS

Bus stops are indicated by white and yellow signs displaying the **Regional Transit Authority (RTA)** logo. Route numbers of buses stopping there are usually listed at the bottom of the sign.

Buses stop only at designated bus stops which are located every two or three blocks, depending on the area of the city. On boarding, put the exact change or number of tokens in the fare box, or show your VisiTour pass to the driver. The pass can be bought through the RTA offices, at tourist information kiosks, and in a small number of hotels. Always ask for a transfer when you pay; this will enable you to change to another bus, if necessary.

To indicate that you want to get off, pull the cord that runs along the window, or tell the driver. The "stop requested" sign above the front window will light up. Instructions about how to open the doors are posted near the exit. Make sure you look carefully for oncoming traffic when alighting from the bus. If you are unsure where to get off, ask the driver.

Smoking, drinking, eating, and playing music are all prohibited on buses. Guide dogs for the blind are the only animals allowed on RTA vehicles. Front seats are reserved for senior citizens and disabled passengers.

STREETCARS

The Riverfront streetcar line travels a distance of 2 miles (3 km) along the Mississippi River near the Riverfront, from Esplanade Avenue, at the far side of the French Quarter, to the New Orleans Convention Center in the Central Business District. The streetcar runs about every 15 minutes from 6am to midnight during the week, and on weekends from 8am to midnight. Pay the streetcar driver when you board; you can exit from either the front of the car or the back, depending on how crowded the streetcar is. Remember to pull the cord if you want to stop at a certain street.

The first stop for the St. Charles streetcar is at the corner of Canal and Carondelet streets. The streetcar turns on to Canal Street, then back around again on St. Charles for the trip uptown. The car travels the length of St. Charles Avenue, turning on to Carrollton Avenue at the Riverbend. The line continues up Carrollton to Claiborne Avenue, where it terminates. The return trip is the reverse of the outbound trip, but St. Charles Avenue becomes one-way outbound at Lee Circle, so the final leg of the inbound trip takes Carondelet Street to get back to Canal Street.

The Canal streetcar line meets the Riverfront streetcar at Esplanade Avenue, and runs

New Orleans city bus

to City Park Avenue. There is also a spur line along North Carrollton Avenue, linking Canal Street to the NOMA at Beauregard Circle.

NEW ORLEANS TAXIS

Taxis, better known as cabs, are easily found at airports, bus and train stations, major hotels, and regular taxi stands. If you need to get somewhere on time, it is best to call a taxi company and arrange a pickup at a definite time and place. Most hotels have lines of taxis waiting outside for a fare. In general, all drivers are extremely knowledgeable and friendly, and all fares should be metered according to the distance traveled. All taxis have a light displayed on their windshield; this indicates when they are available.

Pedestrians in Jackson Square

shoes: some sidewalks and streets in New Orleans are very old and hard to navigate. Parts of Mid-City, Uptown, and the Central Business District are best avoided at night, but it is wise to be cautious at all times in all areas of New Orleans.

Taxicab

Luxury taxicab

WALKING

Because the city is made up of distinct neighborhoods, it is often simplest to take public transportation to a particular neighborhood and then to explore on foot. The French Quarter is compact, and you can stroll around it. Only outside the Quarter do you need to watch for traffic; "Walk" and "Don't walk" signs are on major streets to prevent jay-walking. Wear comfortable

Do not cross the road

You may cross the road

RIVERBOATS

Steamboats began plying the Mississippi River at the beginning of the 19th century, bringing new settlers to New Orleans from the north. Today, the riverboats, offer tours stopping at popular destinations. The **Cajun Queen** has a harbor cruise lasting an hour and a half, leaving from and returning to the Audubon Aquarium of the Americas (see pp90–91). The **Creole Queen** has two cruises; a day trip to the Chalmette Battlefield (see p88) where the Battle of New Orleans took place (see p17), and a night cruise which includes dinner accompanied by live jazz. The **John**

James Audubon, makes the trip from the Audubon Aquarium of the Americas to the Audubon Zoo (see pp112–13), taking about one hour. Finally, there is the steamboat **Natchez** (see pp64–5) which offers a two-hour tour in the morning, and a night cruise with an excellent buffet and live jazz.

DIRECTORY

RIVER BOATS

Cajun Queen
Audubon Aquarium of the Americas.
Tel (504) 529-4567.

Creole Queen
Canal St at Riverwalk.
Tel (504) 529-4567.

John James Audubon
Audubon Aquarium of the Americas / Audubon Zoo.
Tel (504) 529-4567.

Traditional paddlewheeler cruising the Mississippi River

Driving in New Orleans

Despite heavy traffic and a severe shortage of parking lots and curb-side spaces, having a car in New Orleans can be a convenience, especially if you want to visit the surrounding countryside. However, a good public transportation network *(see pp216–17)* and short distances between sights make driving in the city unnecessary. Driving in New Orleans takes patience, good driving skills, good humor, and the ability to read the road and the street signs quickly.

Streetcar and heavy traffic on Canal Street

RENTING A CAR

In New Orleans you must be at least 21 years old with a valid driver's license (US or International Driver's License) to rent a car. Rates may be high for anyone under the age of 25. All agencies require a major credit card or a large cash deposit, a reservation voucher, and insurance. In the event of a breakdown, call the car-rental company first. Members of the AAA (Automobile Association of America **www**.aaa.com) can also use their emergency number to ask for assistance.

Most car rental agencies offer a range of vehicles, from "economy" to "deluxe" models.

All rental cars are automatic, have power brakes and steering, and air-conditioning. Refill the car with gas before returning it or you will pay a large service charge and inflated gas prices.

TRAFFIC REGULATIONS

In New Orleans the traffic travels on the right side of the road. Seatbelts are compulsory for both drivers and passengers. Children under three must sit in a child seat. You can turn right on a red light unless there are signs to the contrary, but you must come to a stop first. A flashing amber light at an intersection means you must slow down,

check for oncoming traffic, and then proceed with caution. Passing (overtaking) is allowed on both sides on multi-lane roads, including Interstate highways, but it is illegal to change lanes across a double yellow or double white solid line. If a school bus stops on a two-way road to drop off or pick up children, traffic in both directions must stop until the bus moves on. On a divided highway, only traffic traveling in the same direction as the bus needs to stop. Be aware that street signs are often missing or hard to read, especially along St. Charles Avenue.

Driving under the influence (DUI) of alcohol or drugs is illegal, and is punishable by a heavy fine, loss of your license, or a jail sentence.

TRAFFIC SIGNS

Colorful signs and symbols point the way to the main tourist areas such as the French Quarter, Audubon and City Parks, and the Garden District. Street-name signs are posted on light posts or on telephone poles, as are directional and informational signs. Large red hexagonal stop signs are posted at intersections without traffic lights. Be absolutely sure to pay attention to parking restriction signs in the French Quarter; due to lack of parking spaces for residents, your car may be towed if you are even one minute over the time limit.

FUEL

Compared to European prices, gas (petrol) is relatively

TRAFFIC SIGNS

A range of different signs offer information and instructions for drivers. Speed limits may vary every few miles, depending on the conditions of the road and the amount of traffic. In more remote areas, drivers must watch out for wildlife that may stray on to the roads, especially alligators and armadillos.

Slippery road

Traffic flows in a single direction

Maximum speed in mph

Right turn restriction

Left turn allowed

Stop at intersection

inexpensive in the US. It is sold by the US gallon, equal to 3.8 liters. Gas stations are sparse downtown, so be sure to fill up the tank before driving into remote areas. Some pumps take credit cards; in self-service stations you pay after filling the tank. Many stations have a convenience store where you can buy refreshments and pay for your gas.

PARKING

Parking in New Orleans can be complicated, difficult, and costly. Parking areas and garages in hotels often post their prices at the entrance. Many of the downtown businesses have designated parking lots and offer discounted or free parking for shoppers. It is almost impossible to find a curb-side parking place in the French Quarter, and many of the streets, such as Bourbon and Royal, are often closed to traffic. The streets in the French Quarter are extremely narrow; be aware that parking on the street can result not only in a towed-away car but also one that may have received some damage from passing garbage trucks, produce or other delivery trucks, or exuberant revelers. There are parking meters all over the city, but be sure to

Insert coins

Insert card

Print receipt

Take receipt

A modern parking meter

make a note of the time limits. The city has modernized some meters, which now accept notes and credit cards. Rush hours in the city are Monday through Friday from 7 to 9am and from 4 to 6pm. Parking on any major street or thoroughfare in the city is forbidden during Mardi Gras *(pp28–9)*.

It is best not to disregard certain parking prohibitions, such as near a fire hydrant or a crosswalk, at bus stops, in handicapped, reserved, or parade route areas, and during street cleaning. Street cleaning in the French Quarter takes place every day, early in the morning. The tow-away crew in New Orleans is very active, so be aware of all "No Parking" signs. The airport has a large long- and short-term parking area if you wish to leave your car and take a taxi into the city.

No Parking and No Stopping signs

PENALTIES

If you have parked on the street and cannot find your car, first call the Claiborne Auto Pound (565-7456) to find out if it has been towed away. Be prepared to give the following information: the license plate number, the make and color of the car, and where you parked it. In order to

Pedestrianized Royal Street, at the heart of New Orleans

retrieve your car, you must first pay the fine, and have your driver's license, registration, or rental voucher available.

If your car is not at the pound, there is a chance that it has been stolen. In the latter instance, call the police department for information on how to proceed.

Traveling Outside New Orleans

The best way to see the areas around New Orleans is by car. Public transportation outside the city is scarce, so try an organized bus tour, or rent a vehicle. Take a day or two for a trip down to Avery Island or into Cajun Country; drive the Great River Road along the mighty Mississippi and visit the plantations; go exploring in the bayous. If hunting, fishing, or boating interests you, Louisiana is truly a "Sportsman's Paradise."

Amtrak train waiting to depart from New Orleans

TRAVELING BY TRAIN

The only long-distance passenger train line in the United States is Amtrak. Long-distance trains have dining and sleeping cars, and in general, reservations are needed. All trains arrive and depart from New Orleans' **Union Passenger Terminal** in the Central Business District. There are always taxis outside the Terminal, and it's just a short ride away from the French Quarter, the Garden District, and the major downtown hotels. The *Crescent* train travels every day to New Orleans from New York by way of Atlanta and intermediate points. The *City of New Orleans* train departs daily and goes to Chicago and points between. The *Sunset Limited* travels to and from the West Coast (Los Angeles) and also travels to and from Florida three times a week, with stops at intermediate points. The schedules for all of these trains may vary from season to season. Amtrak offers discounts for seniors, travelers with disabilities, students, and children. There are also a number of good-value tour packages, group rates, and promotional discounts.

REST AREA ↗

Refreshment area sign

LONG-DISTANCE BUSES

Whether you are going to other parts of the country or traveling around Louisiana, Greyhound buses *(see p215)* offer the cheapest way to get around. The buses are comfortable, clean, and modern; there are generally on-board toilets, a water cooler, and TV screens.

Bus travel to the larger cities and popular tourist destinations in Louisiana is fairly frequent. Travel to the smaller towns in Cajun Country or to off-the-beaten-path areas is not as well defined. Your best bet is to book a tour or rent a car.

Greyhound's Ameripass offers up to 60 consecutive days of unlimited travel anywhere in the US. Tickets may be less expensive if you buy them in advance, but walk-up or unrestricted fares are readily available. Ask about any discounts when you purchase your ticket. These discounts are offered to children, seniors, members of the military, students, and travelers with disabilities. Greyhound will provide assistance to disabled travelers, including priority seating and, in some cases, a personal-care assistant may travel for free. Call the ADA Assist Line for details (800-752-4841).

ROAD SIGNS

Most road signs are clear and self-explanatory. Directional signs are usually green, and tourist information signs are blue.

SPEED LIMITS

Speed limits are set by individual states. There are heavy fines for going well above the limits, which in Louisiana are as follows:
• 55–70mph (89–113km/h) on highways and Interstates.
• 20–30 mph (32–48 km/h) in residential areas.
• 15 mph (24km/h) in school zones.

Speed limits vary every few miles, so keep a close eye out for the signs. On an Interstate highway it is best to drive at or slightly above the speed limit; if you are driving more slowly, stay in the right-hand lane. The left lanes are for passing only (overtaking).

Long-distance Greyhound bus

Algiers ferry crossing the Mississippi River

DAY TRIPS AND TOURS

Each of your trips outside the metropolitan New Orleans area will take at least one full day. If you set aside two or more days, you will have just enough time to savor the great diversity of Louisiana, including the bayous, spicy food, and lively music in Lafayette, Breaux Bridge, and other Cajun Country towns. The rice and sugar plantations along the Mississippi River can also be discovered, as can the spectacular wilderness of the Atchafalaya Basin.

MISSISSIPPI RIVER FERRIES AND CRUISES

The **Canal Street Ferry** ride across the Mississippi River to Algiers Point is an experience in itself, offering excellent views between the Mississippi River and New Orleans. The passenger boarding gate is located on the upper floor of the ferry terminal at the foot of Canal Street. Passengers with cars and bicycles board on the street level of the ferry terminal.

The trip itself takes about 15 minutes. The first ferry leaves at 6am; the last departs at midnight. Remember that you may not smoke, drink alcohol, or eat food aboard the ferry. Nonetheless, the ride across the river at dawn or sunset is one of the best bargains in New Orleans (it's free), and the view of the skyline and riverfront

River cruise captain

from the other side is an experience to remember.

The **Delta Queen Steamboat Company** offers tours along the Mississippi River, from New Orleans up to Baton Rouge, Natchez, and other cities near the river. Cruises last from three to 12 days, focusing on historic sites such as plantations and old towns. There are also some cruises that travel out of the Mississippi River and into the international waters of the Gulf of Mexico; these latter are generally casino cruises, which offer dinner, cocktails, and gambling.

RULES OF THE ROAD

Vehicles are driven on the right-hand side of the road all over the United States. A right-hand turn on a red light is permitted unless a second sign prohibits doing so. Left turns are generally not allowed at intersections.

Drivers and passengers are required by law to wear seatbelts at all times, and littering is not permitted anywhere along any road, highway, or Interstate.

Swamp tour boat moored near Baton Rouge

DIRECTORY

TRAIN INFORMATION

Union Passenger Terminal
Tel (800) 872-7245.
www.amtrak.com

MISSISSIPPI RIVER FERRIES AND CRUISES

Canal Street Ferry
Foot of Canal St.
Tel (504) 376-8100.
www.dodt.state.la.us

Delta Queen Steamboat Company
Tel (800) 434-1232.
www.majesticamericaline.com

DAY TRIP TOURS

Cypress Swamp Tours
Tel (504) 581-4501.
www.westwego
swampadventures.com

Gray Line
Tel (504) 587-1401.
www.graylineneworleans.com

New Orleans Tours
Tel (504) 212-5925.
www.bigeasytours.com

Pearl River Eco Tours
Tel (866) 597-9267.
www.laecotour.com

Tours by Isabelle
Tel (504) 391-3544.
www.toursbyisabelle.com

The AAA (Automobile Association of America) offers maps, emergency roadside services, and discounts at hotels and restaurants and various tourist spots. The Association is linked with numerous automobile clubs abroad, so it is worth finding out if your home club has reciprocity with the AAA. Alternatively, many rental cars offer roadside service for an extra charge.

Be aware that many roads out in Cajun Country may be under water at certain times of the year. Watch for pedestrians, cane trucks, oil tankers, and loose cattle when driving.

STREET FINDER

The map references given with all sights and venues described in this book refer to the maps in this section. A complete index of street names and all the places of interest marked on the Street Finder can be found on the pages following the maps. The key, set out below, indicates the scales of the maps and shows what other features are marked on them, including transport terminals, hospitals, post offices, emergency services, churches, and information centers. The maps include not only the sight-seeing areas (which are color-coded), but the whole of central New Orleans and all the districts important for hotels *(see pp160–69)*, restaurants *(see pp170–85)*, shopping *(see pp186–93)*, and entertainment *(see pp194–203)*. The map on the back inside cover shows the city's public transportation routes.

| 0 kilometers | 2 |
| 0 miles | 2 |

KEY TO STREET FINDER

- ▮ Major sight
- ▮ Place of interest
- ▮ Other building
- ▭ Highway
- ▭ Railway line
- Ⓡ Train station

- 🚊 Streetcar station
- 🚌 Bus terminus
- ⛴ Ferry/boat route
- ✚ Hospital
- ℹ Tourist information
- Ⓟ Parking
- ✝ Church
- ⊠ Post office

SCALE OF MAPS 1–3 & 6–8

| 0 meters | 400 | |
| 0 yards | 400 | **1:20,400** |

SCALE OF MAPS 4–5

| 0 meters | 250 | |
| 0 yards | 250 | **1:13,400** |

8

A | **B** | **C**

1

7

2

3

4

7

5

Louisiana Superdome

Civil Courts

Custom House/ Insectarium **3**

Canal Place

Aquarium of the Americas

Harrah's Casino

New Orleans Arena

Gallier Hall

World Trade Center

SPANISH PLAZA

PERDIDO STREET
UNION STREET
GRAVIER STREET
PERDIDO ST
CARROLL STREET
PICAYUNE PLACE
NATCHEZ ST
MAGAZINE STREET
S PETERS STREET
N PETERS ST
PL DE FRANCE
FULTON STREET

POYDRAS AVENUE STREET

WAREHOUSE DISTRICT

Riverwalk Marketplace

Post Office and Federal Building

Union Station

St. Charles Avenue Streetcar

St. Patrick's Church

CONVENTION CENTER

Julia St Cruise Ship Terminal

Confederate Memorial Hall

Contemp. Arts Center

World War II Museum

Louisiana Children's Museum

Ernest N. Morial Convention Center

Louisiana Science Center

SEE PAGES 4 & 5 FOR ENLARGEMENT OF THIS AREA

Lee Circle

POEYFARRE ST

CALLIOPE STREET

GAIENNIE ST

AVENUE

BLVD

ERATO ST

CRESCENT CITY

CONNECTION

Thalia Street Wharf

ST. CHARLES AVENUE

COLISEUM SQUARE

SOPHIE WRIGHT PL

Mardi Gras World

Robin Street Wharf

Louis S McGehee School

Toby's Corner

Carroll - Crawford House

Women's Opera Guild House

Robinson House

Brevard-Wisdom-Rice House

JACKSON AVENUE

FELICITY STREET

Market Street Wharf

Musson-Bell House

Payne-Strachan House

Burke Park

TCHOUPITOULAS STREET

St. Andrew Street Wharf

Mississippi

First Avenue Wharf

Washington Avenue Wharf

Seventh Street Wharf

HUEY P. LONG AVENUE

5TH ST LAFAYETTE ST

GOVERNOR HALL AVE

RIVER ROAD

4TH ST

A | **B** | **C**

Street Finder Index

General Index

Acknowledgments

Dorling Kindersley would like to thank the many people whose help and assistance contributed to the preparation of this book.

Main Contributor
Marilyn Wood is an American travel writer who has written guidebooks to a number of cities, including New York, Toronto, Boston and London.

Additional Contributors
Ian McNulty, Sarah O'Kelley, Peter Reichard, Harriet Swift.

Additional Photography
Ian McNulty, Ian O'Leary.

Additional Picture Research
Rhiannon Furbear, Rosie Meyer, Ellen Root.

Revisions Designer
Mariana Evmolpidou.

Revisions Editor
Anna Freiberger.

Design and Editorial Assistance
Brigitte Arora, Claire Baranowski, Jyl Benson, Uma Bhattacharya, Chapel Design & Marketing Ltd., Hannah Dolan, Gadi Farfour, Fay Franklin, Jo Gardner, Vinod Harish, Mohammad Hassan, Jacky Jackson, Jasneet Kaur, Juliet Kenny, Vincent Kurien, Esther Labi, Carly Madden, Alison McGill, Ian McNulty, Sonal Modha, Mary Ormandy, Christina Park, Sangita Patel, Mani Ramaswamy, Sands Publishing Solutions, Azeem Siddiqui, Wendy Toole, Conrad Van Dyk, Dora Whitaker.

Dorling Kindersley would like to thank the following for their permission to photograph at their establishments and for their assistance with photography: New Orleans Museum of Art; St. Louis Cathedral, Cabildo, Presbytere and all other churches, museums, restaurants, hotels, shops, and other sights too numerous to thank individually.

Picture Credits
t-top; tl-top left; tlc-top left centre; tc-top centre; trc-top right centre; tr-top right; cla-centre left above; ca-centre above; cra-centre right above; cl-centre left; c-centre; cr-centre right; clb-centre left below; cb-centre below; crb-centre right below; bl-bottom left; b-bottom; bc-bottom centre; bcl-bottom centre left; br-bottom right; d-detail.

Works of art have been reproduced with permission of the following copyright holders: Portrait of a Young Girl 1935, © ADAGP, Paris and DACS, London 2006 – 122b.

The Publisher would like to thank the following individuals, companies and picture libraries for their kind permission to reproduce their photographs:

ALAMY IMAGES: EditorialFotos 173tl; Stephen Saks Photo 173c; Visions of America, LLC/ Joseph Sohm 69bc, 70cl; AUDUBON AQUARIUM OF THE AMERICAS: David Bull/Audubon Nature Institute, New Orleans 31cr; 90tr/ cra/bl/br; 91tl/cra/bl.

BIG EASY PHOTOS: Brent Daniel 47tl, 160cl, 219t; BUSH ANTIQUES: 187br.

CONTEMPORARY ARTS CENTER: 10cra; CORBIS: 137 (insert); Bettmann 36cla, 37tr/tl/crb; Richard Cummins 85t; DK Images 211cb; Philip Gould 36bl, 134cla; John Hicks, 135br; Robert Holmes 47tl, 116cla, 136–7, 135tr; 201bl; Francis G. Mayer 37bl; Underwood & Underwood 36br; COREL STOCK PHOTO LIBRARY: 22tl, 23tr/b, 207cl; 209b, 210tl, 212cr, 212clb, 214t/c/b, 220t, 215t/b.

JOHN DEMAJO: 132tr; DICKINSON COLLEGE, Carlisle, Pennsylvannia: 48cl.

FLICKR.COM: www.flickr.com/photos/ infrogmation/3345144615/ 200tr.

GETTY IMAGES: Foodpix/Melanie Acevedo 172cla.

PAUL AND LULU HILLIARD UNIVERSITY ART MUSEUM: Timothy Hursley 155t; HISTORIC NEW ORLEANS COLLECTION: Jan Brantley 15bl, 16t, 17tr/bl, 18tr/c, 19tr/clb, 32cla, 60–61 (except 61cl); HOUMAS HOUSE PLANTATION: 145br; HOTEL MONTELEONE: 196bl.

IMAX THEATRE: 91br.

LEONARDO MEDIA LTD.: 171cr; LOUSIANA OFFICE OF TOURISM: 133tl, 133br, 200tl, 206cla; LOUISIANA PHILHARMONIC ORCHESTRA: 197cl; LOUISIANA STATE MUSEUM: Greg Lambousy 74tr; LOUISIANA SUPERDOME: 95b, 197br.

MADEWOOD PLANTATION HOUSE: 142b; MCILHENNY COMPANY: 157t; Courtesy of M.S. RAU ANTIQUES: 187ca.